a341212

NOV - 2013

Acclaim for *The Wire* and *The Wire and Philosophy* . . .

"Heraclitus and Omar in the same paragraph? Who knew? 'All the pieces matter,' as Lester Freamon would say. Comes now The Wire and Philosophy, *a provocative yet fully clothed collection of essays best described as the thinking man's (and woman's) fanbook for* The Wire. *The book offers a detailed examination of the underlying significance of* The Wire*'s five seasons, its characters and themes, as seen through the funhouse mirror of the academe. Hardly your parents' philosophy text, it's a thoughtful addition to the ever-expanding canon of literature about the HBO program—a series of readable dispatches from the mountaintop, neither without a sense of humor nor of such impenetrable heft that a truss is required for a little light bedtime reading."*

— WILLIAM F. ZORZI, former Baltimore *Sun* reporter and writer for *The Wire*

*"*The Wire *combines honor, morality, sex appeal, humor, and anarchic fatalism. This terrific volume gets it right! If you find the show addictive, the chapters in* The Wire and Philosophy *will hit you like a WMD tester. Try it. I guarantee you'll be back for more."*

— GABE WARDELL, Executive Director of the Athens

D0619768

"That was one of the best shows of all time. . . . a great show." The best *Wire* character? *"It's got to be Omar, right? I mean, that guy is unbelievable, right?"*

— PRESIDENT BARACK OBAMA, live interview on
The BS Report Film Arts Institute and contributor
to Creative Loafing's Fresh Loaf blog

"The Wire certainly deserves a spot atop the Mount Olympus of television drama. I know readers will enjoy as these skilled and insightful philosophers descend from Mount Olympus to engage, discuss, analyze, and interpret the many philosophical aspects of The Wire."

— RICHARD GREENE, co-editor of *Boardwalk Empire and Philosophy*

"In David Simon's Baltimore, you might think you're gaming the system, but really the system is gaming you. Far from the Athenian agora, The Wire's tragic streets offer a setting no less rich for philosophical reflection, as this provocative book shows—a grim microcosm of a larger world where white indifference has locked in place the structural dooming of America's black inner-city underclass."

— CHARLES W. MILLS, author of *The Racial Contract* (1997)

The Wire and Philosophy

Popular Culture and Philosophy® Series Editor: George A. Reisch

VOLUME 1 *Seinfeld and Philosophy: A Book about Everything and Nothing* (2000)

VOLUME 2 *The Simpsons and Philosophy: The D'oh! of Homer* (2001)

VOLUME 3 *The Matrix and Philosophy: Welcome to the Desert of the Real* (2002)

VOLUME 4 *Buffy the Vampire Slayer and Philosophy: Fear and Trembling in Sunnydale* (2003)

VOLUME 5 *The Lord of the Rings and Philosophy: One Book to Rule Them All* (2003)

VOLUME 9 *Harry Potter and Philosophy: If Aristotle Ran Hogwarts* (2004)

VOLUME 12 *Star Wars and Philosophy: More Powerful than You Can Possibly Imagine* (2005)

VOLUME 13 *Superheroes and Philosophy: Truth, Justice, and the Socratic Way* (2005)

VOLUME 19 *Monty Python and Philosophy: Nudge Nudge, Think Think!* (2006)

VOLUME 24 *Bullshit and Philosophy: Guaranteed to Get Perfect Results Every Time* (2006)

VOLUME 25 *The Beatles and Philosophy: Nothing You Can Think that Can't Be Thunk* (2006)

VOLUME 26 *South Park and Philosophy: Bigger, Longer, and More Penetrating* (2007)

VOLUME 30 *Pink Floyd and Philosophy: Careful with that Axiom, Eugene!* (2007)

VOLUME 31 *Johnny Cash and Philosophy: The Burning Ring of Truth* (2008)

VOLUME 33 *Battlestar Galactica and Philosophy: Mission Accomplished or Mission Frakked Up?* (2008)

VOLUME 34 *iPod and Philosophy: iCon of an ePoch* (2008)

VOLUME 35 *Star Trek and Philosophy: The Wrath of Kant* (2008)

VOLUME 36 *The Legend of Zelda and Philosophy: I Link Therefore I Am* (2008)

VOLUME 37 *The Wizard of Oz and Philosophy: Wicked Wisdom of the West* (2008)

VOLUME 38 *Radiohead and Philosophy: Fitter Happier More Deductive* (2009)

VOLUME 39 *Jimmy Buffett and Philosophy: The Porpoise Driven Life* (2009) Edited by Erin McKenna and Scott L. Pratt

VOLUME 40 *Transformers and Philosophy: More than Meets the Mind* (2009) Edited by John R. Shook and Liz Stillwaggon Swan

VOLUME 41 *Stephen Colbert and Philosophy: I Am Philosophy (And So Can You!)* (2009) Edited by Aaron Allen Schiller

VOLUME 42 *Supervillains and Philosophy: Sometimes, Evil Is Its Own Reward* (2009) Edited by Ben Dyer

VOLUME 43 *The Golden Compass and Philosophy: God Bites the Dust* (2009) Edited by Richard Greene and Rachel Robison

VOLUME 44 *Led Zeppelin and Philosophy: All Will Be Revealed* (2009) Edited by Scott Calef

VOLUME 45 *World of Warcraft and Philosophy: Wrath of the Philosopher King* (2009) Edited by Luke Cuddy and John Nordlinger

Volume 46 *Mr. Monk and Philosophy: The Curious Case of the Defective Detective* (2010) Edited by D.E. Wittkower

Volume 47 *Anime and Philosophy: Wide Eyed Wonder* (2010) Edited by Josef Steiff and Tristan D. Tamplin

VOLUME 48 *The Red Sox and Philosophy: Green Monster Meditations* (2010) Edited by Michael Macomber

VOLUME 49 *Zombies, Vampires, and Philosophy: New Life for the Undead* (2010) Edited by Richard Greene and K. Silem Mohammad

VOLUME 50 *Facebook and Philosophy: What's on Your Mind?* (2010) Edited by D.E. Wittkower

VOLUME 51 *Soccer and Philosophy: Beautiful Thoughts on the Beautiful Game* (2010) Edited by Ted Richards

VOLUME 52 *Manga and Philosophy: Fullmetal Metaphysician* (2010) Edited by Josef Steiff and Adam Barkman

VOLUME 53 *Martial Arts and Philosophy: Beating and Nothingness* (2010) Edited by Graham Priest and Damon Young

VOLUME 54 *The Onion and Philosophy: Fake News Story True, Alleges Indignant Area Professor* (2010) Edited by Sharon M. Kaye

VOLUME 55 *Doctor Who and Philosophy: Bigger on the Inside* (2010) Edited by Courtland Lewis and Paula Smithka

VOLUME 56 *Dune and Philosophy: Weirding Way of the Mentat* (2011) Edited by Jeffery Nicholas

VOLUME 57 *Rush and Philosophy: Heart and Mind United* (2011) Edited by Jim Berti and Durrell Bowman

VOLUME 58 *Dexter and Philosophy: Mind over Spatter* (2011) Edited by Richard Greene, George A. Reisch, and Rachel Robison-Greene

VOLUME 59 *Halo and Philosophy: Intellect Evolved* (2011) Edited by Luke Cuddy

VOLUME 60 *SpongeBob SquarePants and Philosophy: Soaking Up Secrets Under the Sea!* (2011) Edited by Joseph J. Foy

VOLUME 61 *Sherlock Holmes and Philosophy: The Footprints of a Gigantic Mind* (2011) Edited by Josef Steiff

VOLUME 62 *Inception and Philosophy: Ideas to Die For* (2011) Edited by Thorsten Botz-Bornstein

VOLUME 63 *Philip K. Dick and Philosophy: Do Androids Have Kindred Spirits?* (2011) Edited by D.E. Wittkower

VOLUME 64 *The Rolling Stones and Philosophy: It's Just a Thought Away* (2012) Edited by Luke Dick and George A. Reisch

VOLUME 65 *Chuck Klosterman and Philosophy: The Real and the Cereal* (2012) Edited by Seth Vannatta

VOLUME 66 *Neil Gaiman and Philosophy: Gods Gone Wild!* (2012) Edited by Tracy L. Bealer, Rachel Luria, and Wayne Yuen

VOLUME 67 *Breaking Bad and Philosophy: Badder Living through Chemistry* (2012) Edited by David R. Koepsell and Robert Arp

VOLUME 68 *The Walking Dead and Philosophy: Zombie Apocalypse Now* (2012) Edited by Wayne Yuen

VOLUME 69 *Curb Your Enthusiasm and Philosophy: Awaken the Social Assassin Within* (2012) Edited by Mark Ralkowski

VOLUME 70 *Dungeons and Dragons and Philosophy: Raiding the Temple of Wisdom* (2012) Edited by Jon Cogburn and Mark Silcox

VOLUME 71 *The Catcher in the Rye and Philosophy: A Book for Bastards, Morons, and Madmen* (2012) Edited by Keith Dromm and Heather Salter

VOLUME 72 *Jeopardy! and Philosophy: What Is Knowledge in the Form of a Question?* (2012) Edited by Shaun P. Young

VOLUME 73 *The Wire and Philosophy: This America, Man* (2013) Edited by David Bzdak, Joanna Crosby, and Seth Vannatta

VOLUME 74 *Planet of the Apes and Philosophy: Great Apes Think Alike* (2013) Edited by John Huss

IN PREPARATION:

The Good Wife and Philosophy (2013) Edited by Kimberly Baltzer-Jaray and Robert Arp

Psych and Philosophy (2013) Edited by Robert Arp

Boardwalk Empire and Philosophy (2013) Edited by Richard Greene and Rachel Robison-Greene

Futurama and Philosophy (2013) Edited by Courtland Lewis and Shaun P. Young

Ender's Game and Philosophy (2013) Edited by D.E. Wittkower and Lucinda Rush

Frankenstein and Philosophy (2013) Edited by Nicolas Michaud

How I Met Your Mother and Philosophy (2014) Edited by Lorenzo von Matterhorn

Jurassic Park and Philosophy (2014) Edited by Nicolas Michaud

For full details of all Popular Culture and Philosophy® books, visit www.opencourtbooks.com.

Popular Culture and Philosophy®

The Wire and Philosophy

This America, Man

Edited by
DAVID BZDAK, JOANNA CROSBY,
and SETH VANNATTA

OPEN COURT
Chicago

Volume 73 in the series, Popular Culture and Philosophy ®, edited by George A. Reisch

To order books from Open Court, call toll-free 1-800-815-2280, or visit our website at www.opencourtbooks.com.

Open Court Publishing Company is a division of Carus Publishing Company.

Copyright © 2013 by Carus Publishing Company

First printing 2013

All rights reserved. No part of this publication may be reproduced, stored in a retrieval system, or transmitted, in any form or by any means, electronic, mechanical, photocopying, recording, or otherwise, without the prior written permission of the publisher, Open Court Publishing Company, a division of Carus Publishing Company, 70 East Lake Street, Suite 300, Chicago, Illinois 60601.

Printed and bound in the United States of America.

Although several individuals involved in the creation of *The Wire* have taken a friendly interest in this book, it is not an authorized or official publication. *The Wire and Philosophy* is an independent work of criticism, analysis, and comment and is not endorsed or approved by Home Box Office Inc.

Library of Congress Cataloging-in-Publication Data

The wire and philosophy : this America, man / edited by David Bzdak, Joanna Crosby, and Seth Vannatta.
     pages cm. — (Popular culture and philosophy ; vol. 73)
     Includes bibliographical references and index.
     ISBN 978-0-8126-9823-7 (trade paper : alk. paper) 1. Wire (Television
     program)
     I. Bzdak, David, 1968- II. Crosby, Joanna, 1966- III. Vannatta, Seth, 1973
     PN1992.77.W53W525 2013
     794.45'72—dc23

                                   2012051033

Dedicated to the memory of Robert Chew. Without Joe Stewart and his many propositions, *The Wire* wouldn't have been the show we love.

Contents

Respect for a Skill Set
  PROF JOE   ix

First Case: The Game   1

LINE 1. This Ain't Aruba, Bitch
  JOANNA CROSBY   3

LINE 2. All in the Game
  TY FAGAN   13

LINE 3. Locke'd in the Game?
  WILLIAM ALLEN   31

Second Case: The Tactics   43

LINE 4. Wee-Bey's Way
  DAVID BZDAK   45

LINE 5. When a Lie Ain't Just a Lie
  SEAN MCALEER   59

LINE 6. Came to Do Good, Stayed to Do Well
  JASON GRINNELL   71

LINE 7. Giving a Fuck when It's Not Your Turn
  JIM THOMPSON   83

LINE 8. What if Nobody Walks the Straight and
  Narrow Track?
  DON FALLIS   97

Third Case: Omar Comin'   105

LINE 9. Is Omar the Nietzschean Overman?
  W. SCOTT CLIFTON   107

LINE 10. The Best of Boys and Lads
KENN FISHER   123

LINE 11. Omar the Virtuous Thug
JONATHAN TRERISE   139

Fourth Case: The Boundaries   151

LINE 12. No Women Up in the Game
MONA ROCHA AND JAMES ROCHA   153

LINE 13. Capital *Noir*
TOMMY J. CURRY   165

LINE 14. Hard Times After Hard Time
ZACHARY HOSKINS AND NORA WIKOFF   179

Fifth Case: The Loss   191

LINE 15. *The Wire* as American Tragedy
AVRAM GURLAND-BLAKER   193

LINE 16. The Birth of Tragedy from the Spirit
of Baltimore
JOHN THOMAS BRITTINGHAM   205

LINE 17. *The Wire*, or, What to Do in Non-Evental Times
SLAVOJ ŽIŽEK   217

Sixth Case: Sentencing   237

LINE 18. Class Projects and the Project Class
SETH VANNATTA   239

LINE 19. You Gonna Get Got
KODY W. COOPER   255

LINE 20. Is Our Thing Really a Part of the Big Thing?
NATHAN ECKSTRAND   265

LINE 21. Stop Snitching, Screw the System
MYISHA CHERRY   277

Our Connect   289

Hoppers, Fiends, and Natural POH-lice   297

Index   303

Respect for a Skill Set

PROF JOE

Back in the day, when living was easy and philosophy was young, Socrates was the man with the connect. He claimed it was a divine connect, and from the way the hoppers and shorties hung around him, he had to been slingin' some good shit. Yet Socrates also tended to be an asshole, askin' troublesome questions of the brass. You might say he gave a fuck when it wasn't his turn.

In any case, Socrates started bothering the wrong people. The citizens of Athens got tired of him, as well as his boys, takin' over corners in the agora, buzzin' about like gadflies, givin' decent people a hard time. So, the leaders of a rival crew, seeing a chance to rid themselves of this troublesome so-and-so, took him to court on trumped up charges. Despite an Omarworthy defense, Socrates lost and was sentenced to death.

Now, his crew wasn't going to take this lyin' down. They bribed the jailor and arranged Socrates's escape. Socrates, though, wouldn't go! As if he knew the outta town radio stations weren't shit. He claimed he was born an Athenian and would die an Athenian. Athens served him well, he argued, and if she said he had to die, well, get on with it motherfu . . .

His crew, of course, thought he be hittin' his own stash.

Socrates valued the quality of his life more than the quantity of his life. The argument he made to his friends demanded that they, too, should be more concerned with the way they lived rather than how long. Socrates's honorable decision was odd to his crew and even more unfamiliar to us. His name rings out to this day because of the way he lived and died—he took a stand and accepted the consequences. Even when betrayed by the institutions he loved, he chose his integrity over a lesser life.

Woe to Them that Call Evil Good and Good Evil

Aristotle, who John Brittingham says is "Lester Freamon smart," thought that the purpose of the human life is flourishing. We in the US call this happiness. We're so bold we claim that we have a God-given right to pursue it.

This uniquely American myth about our path to happiness is familiar. It goes like this: God-fearing Puritans settled this land of opportunity, and their values made it great. They each had a unique role, and their duty was to hear the calling of God and fulfill it by detesting the sin of leisure and valuing hard work. The Puritans didn't hang out on the corners slingin' vials. Instead, they plowed the land and fished the shores. One of their descendants, Ben Franklin, even wrote down all their values in his famous almanac. Work, save, increase. And in the end, if they got rich, then 'at must be a sign God loves 'em.

The rest of 'em, the corner boys and fiends, to hell with 'em, be it despair, addiction, or incarceration. To hell with 'em. They skipped church, dropped out of school, and messed around with drugs. Those sinners deserve their fate.

Like Socrates, *The Wire* creator David Simon refuses to let us rest comfortably in our worldview, including the American myth just told. He doesn't provide us with warm and fuzzy feelings about the society we live in. And he doesn't wrap things up cleanly at the end of the hour or reinforce our long-held beliefs about cops and robbers, drug dealers and drug users, public servants and public defenders. Like Socrates, Simon forces us to critically confront the beliefs we hold most dear.

And like Socrates, Simon isn't selective about his targets. You a conservative who thinks tougher drug laws and expanded police powers the answer? See if those views survive *The Wire*. You a libertarian who thinks legalizing it all is a no-pain solution? Look again at Hamsterdam and listen, really listen, to the deacon. You a liberal who thinks that the right politicians with the best intentions will clean the streets and heal the young'uns? Watch Clarence Royce and Tommy Carcetti cope with their bowls of shit. You a techno-geek who thinks that the latest gadgets will make the world a better place? Check Lester Freamon and Co. work their asses off to get a wire up, and watch how fast the yos make that work obsolete.

You a capitalist, who thinks the free market is the cure? Look how the profit motive drives the dealers, dries up the docks, and makes the Baltimore *Sun* a hollow shell of a newspaper. You a socialist, who thinks government institutions will guide the invisible hand? Sheeeeit, watch how Clay Davis does things. You an optimist who thinks that the good guys usually win and the wheel of karma spins round and round? See what happens to the boys of summer. You a pessimist who thinks the world is shit and there's nothing to be done about it? Watch Bubs and Cutty claw their way up from way down in the hole.

You Wanna Quorum Up Again? Think It Over a Little?

Valuing the quality of one's life more than its length, like Socrates did, is not easy. But then, neither is sitting down to a little evening's entertainment, turning on HBO's *The Wire*. *The Wire* rebels by speaking truth to the power of the American Dream. No matter who you are or what you believe, *The Wire* will challenge you . . . like Socrates challenged the Athenians. And, also like Socrates, the show will not give you any easy answers at the end of the day. But it will make you think. Might even make you wonder what your part is in all this.

The writers in what follows, masochistic yos that they are, have taken their complicity seriously enough to face the challenge of writing about the philosophical connections and implications they found on the screen. They write a lot about tragedy, about the logic of institutions and the way they circumscribe human dignity and limit human freedom and responsibility. You'll catch them thinking about a number of big themes that run through the five seasons of *The Wire*. The First Case asks about the rules of the Game and how they relate to moral, social, and political issues. The Second Case ponders questions such as, "Are there good guys and bad guys or just different perspectives?" and "What are the various moral dimensions of lying?" In the Third Case we get jumped by Omar and wonder why so many viewers like Omar so much. Is his code a moral one, or does his code make the viewers feel comfortable because we know he won't come after us, 'cause we're not in the Game? The Fourth Case looks at the roles race, gender, power, and criminality play in the Game. The Fifth Case questions whether *The Wire*'s view of life is essentially tragic, and in the Sixth Case, we are asked to reflect on the relationship between power structures in the schools and the police force and how they impact the communities they supposedly serve.

And, of course, the biggest question of them all—Socrates's obsession—how ought we to live? Given that the world can be a terrifying, dissatisfying, ossifying, mystifying, glorifying, electrifying place, how ought we to live?

You're a fan of the show, so they're not saying nothin' new by "It's a complicated question." You won't find easy answers here, but in struggling, these folk try their best to avoid being part of the problem. Shit, they still believe in the possibility of human dignity and want more than to play amid the endless circles of the Game. They do, after all, give a fuck—even if it's not their turn.

First Case

The Game

LINE 1
This Ain't Aruba, Bitch

JOANNA CROSBY

McNULTY: Guy leaves two dozen bodies scattered all over the city, and no one gives a fuck.

MORELAND: You can go a long way in this country killing black folk. Young males, especially. Misdemeanor homicides.

McNULTY: If Marlo was killin' white women . . .

FREAMON: White children . . .

MORELAND: Tourists . . .

McNULTY: One white ex-cheerleader tourist missing in Aruba.

MORELAND: Trouble is, this ain't Aruba, bitch. ("Unconfirmed Reports")

Well, look, I've never been to Aruba, but as a resident of Baltimore, I've no doubt it ain't Aruba. No beaches, no sand, no free-flowing foo-foo drinks makin' everyone all chill and groovy.

No, Aruba it is not. Instead, Baltimore is a city of contradictions. Located on the Mid-Atlantic rust belt, once home to Bethlehem Steel's largest plants, Bal'mer now sprouts more condos than sheet metal. Technically below the Mason-Dixon line, Charm City was one of the first cities where freed Blacks could remain free. The bus stops' benches say it's The City That Reads, but thirty-eight percent of adults in the city can't. Johns Hopkins University and Medical Center is the largest employer, but the high school drop-out rate is fifty percent.

No wonder a Baltimore native coined the phrase 'misdemeanor homicide.' With the number of bodies dropped here each year, Bunk wasn't just talking about the ones in the vacants. It's not like *The Wire*'s production crew went out and spray painted 'Bodymore, Murderland' on a wall; some native son came up with that tag all on his own.

So, wassup? Well, it's mostly drug related crime, which means this group of number one males shooting at that group of number one males. Some brilliant Cracker will advise us to leave them to it until they've done the job, and, as an exit strategy for the war on drugs, it's not much worse than Hamsterdam. But really, Cracker, here, is part of the problem, not the solution.

See, on the one hand, there's this very profitable, if illicit, business with high employee turnover. Not much worry about pensions, perks or bennies, and everybody's making enough that unions will never catch on. In the 1950s, the Eye-talians from New York and Jersey (finger to the side of the nose) were more interested in partying on The Block, and left Baltimore as a mob-free zone. That left all kinds of room open for enterprising young men, a la Stringer Bell, particularly if they paired up with cold-hearted gangstas like Avon Barksdale. Capitalism abhors a vacuum.

On the other hand, the only way you get 'misdemeanor homicide' is if you have people dying in the wrong zip codes. This gets back to the theme of Season One, how the war on drugs is really a war on the underclass. This Cracker, again: We can't employ them, don't want to educate them, and would really rather they stay out of the 'good' neighborhoods.

Damn, when did the value of life miss its re-up?

Of course, 'when' is not the interesting question, it's the 'why'. According to David Simon, "The why is everything and without it, the very suggestion of human progress becomes a cosmic joke" (*The Guardian*, September 6th, 2008). 'Why' gets us into the land of philosophy—you know: navel gazing, asking silly questions like 'Why is there air?' and thinking someone outside the ivory tower should care. However, *The Wire* reminds us that we do care, and argument, if not high falutin' theory, can help us get a bit closer to the all important 'why' of the matter.

Now We Just Put Our Hand in the Next Guy's Pocket

Simon says, "Every single moment on the planet, from here on out, human beings are worth less. We are in a post-industrial age. We don't need as many of us as we once did" (Margaret Talbot in *The New Yorker*). Those whose work has disappeared have seen their role in society disappear along with the work. When manufacturing, the foundation of the American middle class, decided labor was an expendable cost and began chasing the cheapest it could find, industry and our capitalist economy told the people left behind they were expendable. Greater short-term profit has more value in our current economy than the people necessary to create the product, leaving the US with a surplus army of the unemployed. In order to justify profit over people, we have developed a narrative that strips the excess population of their humanity.

If we value life, how can anyone be expendable? The answer is, we don't really value life. Or, more specifically, we value some lives more than others.

One way to understand each season of *The Wire* is as a representation of the diminishing value of life in our post-industrial consumer-capitalist society. But how did post-industrial consumer-capitalist society become so influential?

In the 1970s, French philosopher Michel Foucault argued that the disciplinary practices adopted, normalized, and disseminated by state-sanctioned institutions produced people who could fulfill the requirements of those institutions, including education, military service, employment, marriage, medicine, religion, and the courts. In *Discipline and Punish*, Foucault gives the example of training people for a whole new class of jobs—work inside factories. Employees were required to show up at a certain time, work for a pre-determined period, and perform tasks in such a way as to maximize efficiency. In schools, students followed rigorous time schedules and learned hygienic practices on their journey to become good citizens and useful employees. Religion taught one how to confess sin or tailor a biographical narrative to particular institutional needs, a useful skill translated to medicine when explaining one's symptoms in a doctor's office or one's activities to an officer of the court.

That industrial social institutions developed cohesion and grew into self-perpetuating and interdependent systems is no surprise. Simon's argument is that post-industrial institutions have moved beyond merely using human cogs, and despite rhetoric to the opposite, require the regular sacrifice of individuals to their continued operation. The drug trade needs an army of fiends, the police force, cops chasing statistics, corner boys and hoppers. While we prattle on about the dignity and value of life, institutional practices expose the lie better than Bunk and his lie detecting copy machine.

Accepting Shit, Calling It Gold, and Saying Thank You

Simon sees each season of *The Wire* as a demonstration of life worth less:

> If the first season was about devaluing the cops who knew their beats and the corner boys slinging drugs, then the second was about devaluing the longshoremen and their labor, the third about people who wanted to make changes in the city, and the fourth was about kids who were being prepared, badly, for an economy that no longer really needs them. And the fifth? It's about the people who are supposed to be monitoring all this and sounding the alarm—the journalists. (Margaret Talbot in *The New Yorker*)

In sum, there is a war against the underclass and another against organized labor. Reform is curtailed and reformers punished, education serves to replicate the system rather than provide modes of reform, and the press is too green to investigate and too busy pandering to Wall Street and sensationalism to report what is going on. Thus, Simon says,

> It's about the very simple idea that, in this Postmodern world of ours, human beings—all of us—are worth less. We're worth less every day, . . . Whether you're a corner boy in West Baltimore, or a cop who knows his beat, or an Eastern European brought here for sex, your life is worth less. It's the triumph of capitalism over human value. (O'Rourke, "Behind *The Wire*")

At the end of Season Four, we see the seeds of the characters we've grown to love: Michael following the path of Omar; entrepreneurial Randy could have become the next Stringer Bell; Duquan turns to drugs, likely to become another Bubbles. Only Namond has a real chance at escaping the corners, not because of any bootstrapping on his part, but because Colvin threw him a life saver. Of the four, Namond seems the least deserving. He's benefited the most from The Game, even though his dad's in jail while we wish his moms was. He's weak, talks big, but is useless when it comes time to put a hurt on someone. But as *The Wire* would have it, of course that's the kid who gets the breaks.

Let Me Quit This Game Here and Go to College

'But, hey', Cracker perks up once again, 'we all make our own choices. You gotta take responsibility for yourself.' *The Wire* however is fiction, and not just any fiction. This isn't American feel-good, tie-it-up-in-44-minutes-and-put-a-happy-bow-on-it fiction. It's tragic, as in discovering you've killed your father, married your mother, popping out your own eyes kinda shit. Back to Simon:

> What we were trying to do was take the notion of Greek tragedy, of fated and doomed people, and instead of these Olympian gods, indifferent, venal, selfish, hurling lightning bolts and hitting people in the ass for no reason—instead of those guys whipping it on Oedipus or Achilles, it's the postmodern institutions . . . those are the indifferent gods. (Simon, *The New Yorker*)

Only, if it's the postmodern institutions hurling the lightning bolts, then, to paraphrase a little Public Enemy, we're all in the 'hood, up to no good, buying pain in one form or another. War on the underclass is a war on us all. Not just the brown people in the urban areas or the other side of the tracks. We are all implicated, affected, betrayed. We may not be in The Game, but the institutions are playing us, no doubt.

At this point in time, most of us take for granted that life has some inherent value, be it sacred, secular, or political. While in some ways, that value has been expanding from landed white males, to all humanity, in other ways it has shrunk by, well, about ninety-nine percent. Is human dignity a necessary falsehood upon which polity, civility, and society are made possible? If we neglect to extend dignity to every human, does civility begin to crumble? Is this really all on the backs of individuals?

Analysis from an institutional level shows us a very different picture, however. If we are to appreciate the struggle between individuals and institutions, we have to recognize institutional apathy and lethargy. Institutions have their own agendas, and while the police cars may say "To Protect and Serve," and the banners may read "Believe," institutions will serve their own needs, aggrandize and protect themselves, long before they embrace reform as more than a slogan.

Ain't Nothin' You Fear More than a Bad Headline

In the first episode of Season Three, after chasing a hopper into a common space behind row houses, Carver has a moment. Baltimore has mobilized all its resources—drug sniffing dogs, unmarked cars, dozens of cops, even the helicopter. Carver jumps up on top of Herc's sedan and makes his declaration of war: "You don't get to win, shitbird, we do!" And Carver, he's fucking heroic: on the roof of the car, all articulate an' shit. He is The Man.

And yet, what's it all for? The dogs, cars, and 'copter? A hopper with a backpack. A backpack not holding the stash, by the way. For which Carver prepped his troops before they began the bust: don't go for the runner, he warns them. After the runner bolts, we see a kid grab a lunch bag and walk off. Dealers 1, police 0.

However, the police, and by taxable extension, those of us citizens in the audience, are out a great deal more. While Carver and Co. find the kid, treat him to a little Western District hospitality, all they can really do is write him up for loitering and running from the cops. So here's Carver, our poor player, strutting across the top of a cruiser, full of sound and fury and all our resources spent for nothing. Dealers 1, police/city/taxpayers, minus how many grand?

Dealers and addicts are dehumanized, but the drugs are worth something. Police talent and effectiveness are wasted in political infighting or on ineffectual policy, leaving officers feeling alienated, disaffected, or beholden. So what is valued? It's not The Game, as any player can be sacrificed, from hopper to kingpin to police chief. It's The Show.

It's Carver on the roof of the car in his summer blockbuster moment. It's drugs on the table and bodies locked up. It's test scores, publishing awards, falling crime numbers, and rising clearance rates. It's juked stats, the graphs they produce, and the visuals captured for the paper, TV news, and these days, the Internet. Most importantly, it's the spin that tells us how to feel about the visuals, reassuring audiences that while progress may be slow, the professionals are in it for the long haul.

If the Gods Are Fucking You, You Find a Way to Fuck Them Back

Foucault shows us how institutions develop their own momentum, an ability of self-preservation and perpetuation rivaling that of any biologically driven species. Those institutions normalize modes of behavior that individuals adopt in order to survive and potentially thrive. For example, don't screw around if you want to stay married; work hard to get ahead; come to class and sit still to get a good education; keep your test scores up to be a good teacher; don't piss off (or on) the bosses to stay outta the pawn unit or off the water.

Through *The Wire*, Simon demonstrates how our post-industrial institutions have developed the ability and likelihood to betray both the individuals who comprise them and those whom they're supposed to serve. However, Simon also points us to the holes in The Show, how we can begin to look behind the curtain and see the gap between the ad and the product. "*The Wire* is dissent," he tells us. "It is perhaps the only storytelling on television that overtly suggests that our political and economic and social constructs are no longer viable, that our leadership has failed us relentlessly, and that no, we are not going to be all right" (Simon, *The New Yorker*).

You're Gonna Have to Decide Whether It's about You or about the Work

So, how are we supposed to respond to this rigged game of ours?

Simon tells us to look for dignity in private moments, not public institutions. Those indifferent gods are interested only in themselves. If the betrayal of individuals is the price of institutional self-perpetuation, so be it:

> From this point on, each life is worth a little less. The lives in West Baltimore, ravaged by job loss, drug use and the easy violence that comes with The Game; but also the lives of the rest of us, desensitized to the loss of community, of purpose and life in economically decimated neighborhoods, encouraged to consider the problem signs of immorality, lack of character, or laziness. (Simon, Berkeley Presentation 2008)

Lazy? Really? We need only look to Bubbles to see just how hard a fiend is willing to work to get to his next fix, only to be betrayed by a package that's been stepped on harder than the 'Oh' in the National Anthem at an O's game. But it's a hell of lot easier to think of the Bubbles in our own communities as bad people than extend so much as a kind word. Not only are our institutions desensitized and ready to betray us, but they are more successful the more the individuals within them, (that's you and me, darlin'), are desensitized and willing to betray one another. After all, it's just business.

Are you angry yet? "Anger is not an irrational response to this if you're a citizen" says Simon. "It's not bad to vent every now and then and let them know you no longer accept shit for gold" (Simon, Berkeley Presentation). There's only so long you can try to do more with less, stay outta the bosses' hair, and work the stats in your favor before cynicism replaces the marrow in your bones. You gotta figure out when it's your turn to give a fuck. This Simon:

> It is worthwhile to pick one or two places where you think you can assert on behalf of a better outcome and to fight with whatever means at your disposal. And you can do it thinking to yourself I'm probably not going to win. . . . 'I remember what happened to McNulty, so, ya know, it's gonna happen to me.' But Camus said, to commit to a righteous cause in the face of overwhelming odds is absurd. Then he said not to commit to a righteous cause in the face of overwhelming odds is equally absurd. But only one option offers the possibility of human dignity. (Berkeley Presentation)

Not to contradict the great journalist, he who hung out in the halls haunted by Mencken, but I don't think Camus actually said that. At least, I can't find it. Camus said some great stuff. There's not much profanity, but then, he wasn't "contractually obligated by HBO" (that's Simon's line, not mine).

In *The Rebel*, Camus *does* say, "He who despairs over an event is a coward, but he who holds hope for the human condition is a fool." This is close, I suppose, but it's a bit more Don Quixote than Bunk Moreland. The last episode of the first season of *The Newsroom*, which one might say is inspired by the fifth season of *The Wire*, is called "The Greater Fool," a phrase used two ways in the story. One is the economic theory that there will always be a greater fool who will buy a stock when it shouldn't be bought. The other, in the warm, fuzzy, hope-as-a-gateway-drug, Aaron Sorkin kind of way. Sloan Sabbith tells anchorman Will McAvoy, "The greater fool is someone with the perfect blend of self delusion and ego to think that he can succeed where others have failed. This whole country was made by greater fools." I don't really think this is what Simon has in mind.

What Simon has done is boiled down Camus's *The Myth of Sisyphus* to three sentences. You know the story, guy sentenced to a life of rolling a rock up a hill, only to have it roll down again. Here the Gods thought they'd come up with the perfect punishment: meaningless, endless labor. For Camus, Sisyphus is only truly alive on the walk back down the hill, contemplating the absurdity of his lot. We're supposed to embrace our own absurdity by "thinking Sisyphus happy." For Simon, this means being willing to take a stand: "Pick something that matters, that's bigger than yourself, that's not for your own gain and commit to it and see what happens. If nothing else, the bastards will not be able to say that they didn't know. . . . It doesn't amount to much, but it's better than being a sucker" (Berkeley Presentation). That, I believe, Simon would call the audacity of despair.

What, you expected a big car chase and an explosion? Ballet of bullets? Fireworks and romance? Slow motion and soft focus? This ain't Hollywood, my friend, not any more than it's Aruba. One could say it's Baltimore, but really? This America, man.

LINE 2
All in the Game

TY FAGAN

New dancers, new faces around the throne. But the net effect is that
the game goes on.

—DAVID SIMON, *The Wire Show Bible*

It's night in the Bronx, and someone's whistling "The Farmer
in the Dell." Omar Little, Baltimore's most feared bandit, is
taking a package off some hapless New York slinger. Cackling,
triumphant, Omar reminds the stunned corner boy of that merciless truth: *All in the game, yo . . . all in the game.* Fade out;
the first season of *The Wire* ends. But the game goes on.

Remember that little moment midway through Season Two,
when Omar helps a courthouse officer stumped by the crossword clue *Greek god of war*? "I used to love them myths," Omar
tells the bemused cop, after giving him the right answer. "Stuff
was deep. Truly" ("All Prologue").

The Wire's debt to Greek mythology is widely acknowledged,
and series creator David Simon has cited classical tragedians
like Sophocles and Aeschylus as touchstones for the show. But
The Wire has another, unacknowledged Hellenic ancestor in
Heraclitus of Ephesus, a pre-Socratic philosopher whose home
turf was Ionia, a region on the west coast of what is now
Turkey. His work survives only in fragments, vialed up in cryptic little aphorisms musing on the nature of the universe and
humanity's place within it. Heraclitus was famously cantan-
kerous—Sergeant Jay Landsman would have called him a shit-
stirrer—and his reputation for obscurity and cynicism earned
him the nickname *ho Skoteinos*, the Dark One. The world he

conceived was not so much cruel as pitilessly indifferent to the mere humans who populated it.

Consider this fragment from Heraclitus: "*Aion* is a child playing, moving game-pieces; the kingdom is a child's." The Greek word *aion* is variously rendered as *lifetime*, *time*, and even *eternity*—its meaning may embrace both human life spans and the larger cosmic time scale. The "kingdom" Heraclitus has in mind is the cosmos itself: he is comparing the world, at the level of human experience and beyond it, to a child playing a game.

This ancient metaphor is central to *The Wire*. Hardly an episode passes without some character—a dealer, a cop, a politician—referring to games or "the Game." From the show's first scene, depicting the aftermath of a dice game turned murderous, to that ubiquitous credo "all in the Game," the Game permeates everything and everyone in the series.

World as Game, Game as World

What did Heraclitus have in mind when he compared the world to a game? Most games share certain basic features. They have rules—internal norms that constrain what counts as legitimate play—and roles, which exist independently of the particular things or persons that fill them. Winning, defined by the rules of the game, is the highest good, and games often have readily quantified measures of success or failure (known, in the world of sports, as statistics). The "pieces" of a game are subject to forces larger than themselves; if they have any independent agency at all, it's tightly constrained. Finally, game-playing tends to be cyclical: when a game or match ends, players can pick up the pieces and begin anew.

The Wire's world fits Heraclitus's game fragment like one of Bunk's tailored suits. In early episodes, "the game" refers to the drug trade specifically, but the term's resonance expands as the show progresses, coming to cover every sphere of Baltimore life depicted by the show, from the schoolhouse to the newsroom to the street. Each of these games has its own strict norms and hierarchical arrangement of roles; characters who deviate from them, or try to escape them, face terrible consequences. And those roles tend to persist—think of the Barksdale organization's rigid hierarchy—even while individuals pass in and out of them. The singular importance of *winning*, best exemplified by the police's collective obsession with winning the drug war, fosters an obsession with numbers and "stats" that crowds out, or simply trumps, everything else. One of the show's cruel jokes is that the Baltimore cops are playing an unwinnable game; as Ellis Carver says, "You can't even think of calling this shit a war. . . . Wars *end*" ("The Target").

Among the early episodes of the show, D'Angelo Barksdale's chess tutorial in the low-rise courtyard stands alone for thematic heft and poignancy. Trying to school the young dealers Bodie and Wallace in terms they will find familiar, D'Angelo compares the pieces on the chessboard to various roles in the dope game: king to kingpin, rook to stash house, and so forth. By the time he comes to the pawns—generic, expendable, doomed—the allegory's dark aptness has taken hold, and the young hoppers get the picture only too well. "Pawns get capped quick," D'Angelo says. "They be out the game early." Bodie, always sharp, sees that his best hope lies in being a "smart-ass pawn" and surviving long enough to transcend his station ("The Buys").

An unspoken question lingers over this scene. If even the kingpin is only another piece on the chessboard, then who or what moves the pieces? *The Wire* spends five seasons unfolding the answer: each character's trajectory is shaped by large-scale forces that are inscrutable, capricious, and nearly impossible to resist. Heraclitus felt similar forces at work over 2,500 years ago, and he personified them with the image of a child-king playing a game. *The Wire*, by way of the same metaphor, locates them in the political and economic institutions of twenty-first-century Baltimore. And when the series concludes, it ends not with resolution but recurrence—characters take on new but familiar roles, and the Game begins anew.

Play or Get Played

Bodie's intelligence, ferocity, and loyalty to the rules of the drug game keep him alive longer than many of his boys. But at the end of the fourth season, Bodie finally meets the fate of almost all pawns. He goes out like a soldier, shot to death on a contested West Side corner. Not long before his death, and perhaps sensing the end, he rails against the Game's fundamental injustice, recalling the lesson D'Angelo once taught him:

I ain't never fucked up a count, never stole off a package, never did some shit that I wasn't told to do. I been straight up. But what come back? . . . They want me to stand with them, right? But where the fuck they at when they supposed to be standing by us? I mean, when shit goes bad and there's hell to pay, where they at? This game is rigged, man. We like them little bitches on a chessboard. ("Final Grades")

Bodie has the drug game in mind, but he could just as well be speaking of the Baltimore police department, the dying waterfront, or the school system. Characters in *The Wire* give their lives to institutions, expecting that when "shit goes bad" these institutions will reciprocate. But far more often than not, those expectations come to grief. In a rigged game, to play straight up is to invite exploitation. A pawn can't assume that following the rules makes him any less expendable.

Despite Bodie's indictment of an unnamed "them," it's difficult to identify individual participants who are responsible for rigging the Game. Rather, it is *itself* rigged—by institutional structures of incentives and norms, and sometimes by sheer bureaucratic paralysis—to condone and foster the worst impulses of human nature, treating them as "all in the Game." People who might have cooperated are encouraged to undermine each other, and cutthroat ambition is rewarded handsomely. Omar articulates the Game's core dictum with his usual pithiness: "Play or get played" ("Lessons").

Such heartlessness might seem to clash with Heraclitus's image of the world as a game played by a *child*; we rarely think of children playing with such single-minded ruthlessness. But other fragments from Heraclitus resolve this apparent tension: just as the "game" fragment asserts that the cosmic kingdom belongs to a child, elsewhere Heraclitus writes that "war is father of all and king of all," that "conflict is justice, and that all things come to pass in accordance with conflict" (*The Art and Thought of Heraclitus*, p. 67). The cosmos may be a child's game, but it's a game marked by strife and the violent struggle of opposed forces. One thinks not only of chess, that civilized clash of toy armies, but of scenes in *The Wire* where youngsters play the West Baltimore version of cops and robbers, bickering over who gets to be Omar and who has to play a hapless guardian of the stash house.

Stat Games and Stanfields

If winning the Game is the end that justifies any means, it's no surprise that *The Wire*'s institutions, from the street to the newsroom to the statehouse, are obsessed with quantifying victory: in dollars, in corners, in approval ratings, in Pulitzers, in clearance rates and arrest figures, and in test scores. What matters is the bottom line—*getting the stat*, as the cops say. This coldly capitalistic approach is especially destructive when it infects social institutions that ought to be concerned with the public good. When Roland "Prez" Pryzbylewski leaves the police department to become a schoolteacher, he thinks he's seen the last of "juking the stats," the widespread practice of massaging police data to create the appearance of effective law enforcement.

But to his shock, Prez finds that juking the stats is every bit as rampant in public education. Standardized test scores are all that anyone seems to care about, and legislative mandates like No Child Left Behind create tremendous top-down pressure to deliver "good numbers" regardless of whether students are actually learning. The kindhearted Grace Sampson, a veteran teacher fighting to do honest work in a broken system, senses Prez's dismay at having traded one rigged game for another. "Wherever you go," she tells him, "there you are" ("Know Your Place").

As the "play or get played" mentality spreads, the game-world begins to come unmoored from standards of fairness or equity. The obsession with short-term, easily-quantified victories carries a human cost almost beyond reckoning. On the street, bloody turf wars and mountains of bodies; in the police department, meaningless arrest numbers and crooked careerists; on the docks, corruption and despair; in the schools, inflated test scores and seas of uninspired children; in the newsroom, fabricated stories and a myopic fixation on profits and Pulitzers. Would-be reformers find their surrounding bureaucracies riddled with sclerotic dysfunction, cutthroat competition, or both. And as lives are lost and wasted, the institutions that make American collective life possible—law, labor, education, government, press—rot from the inside out.

The Game doesn't just foster mendacity and corruption at the level of institutions; it also dehumanizes its individual participants. The characters who "win" at their respective games—Stan Valchek, Clay Davis, Maurice Levy, Marlo Stanfield, The Greek, Bill Rawls, Scott Templeton—are the ones who show a near-total lack of concern with anything besides victory, so skillfully have they adapted to their poisonous environments. Rawls routinely and deliberately puts clearance rates and arrest stats ahead of pursuing real justice. Levy violates his legal and ethical obligations in order to keep violent criminals out of prison and line his pockets with their money. Valchek is the ultimate self-interested company toad-eater, a useful idiot whose mix of venality, political influence, and backstabbing ruthlessness is so toxically potent that he eventually becomes Police Commissioner.

Along with the mysterious figure of The Greek, Marlo Stanfield is the purest embodiment of the Game. Marlo appears almost inhumanly detached; whether his blankness is instinctive or an image cultivated by astonishing self-control is not clear. Like his rival Avon Barksdale, Marlo is merciless, disciplined, and intelligent—but he shows none of Avon's chest-thumping bravado, and this makes him an enigma. His greatest trick might be letting his rivals think, because of his soft voice and swaggerless carriage, that he's something other than what he is. Avon mistakes him for a weak-ass upstart and winds up defeated and imprisoned. Proposition Joe mistakes him for a naive youngster who needs "civilizing" and winds up shot on Marlo's order.

And while Avon thought his reign would go on forever, Marlo is grimly realistic about the fickleness of the Game. When his advisor Vinson tries to caution him against making a power grab, telling him that "prisons and graveyards" are "full of boys who wore the crown," Marlo replies, almost reflexively, "Point is, they wore it. It's my turn to wear it now" ("Homecoming"). He knows the crown isn't forever, but it's all he cares about, and for that reason he's *fit* to wear it.

Marlo can give himself to the drug game completely, because he gives no part of himself to anything else. All the obstacles he faces are external; there is nothing inside to hold him back. In the show's final episode we see that, unlike Stringer Bell before him, Marlo has no interest in leaving the drug trade behind, even when doing so is the obviously prudent move. Levy offers Marlo what he never offered Stringer—an entrée to the world of "legitimate" business—but Marlo has no use for that opportunity.

Heraclitus compared the world to a childlike, and warlike, game. It might therefore seem tempting to think of Marlo, the warrior man-child, as expressing some Heraclitean ideal of humanity. But we should remember the emptiness of Marlo's fleeting "victory" in the Game, and the fact that even he is merely a piece on the board—the inevitable product of institutions governed by game-logic. Just as the competitive and economic structure of professional sports is designed to identify and cultivate bigger, faster, and stronger athletes, the Game is rigged to produce and promote ever more effective players. Eventually, inexorably, it will produce a Marlo Stanfield.

A Man Must Have a Code

If Marlo and Bodie illustrate what the Game makes of its respective winners and losers, then what of those characters who dare to break the rules? After all, a participant in a game can flout the norms of that game up to a point, and still be considered a player. Just how much rule-breaking one can get away with depends, naturally, on how tightly the rules are enforced and how stiff the penalties are for violating them. And in every institution surveyed by *The Wire*, the organizational pressure to follow the norms of the Game is irresistibly strong.

It's easier to play along than to follow one's own conscience. Easier to juke the stats than grapple with the root causes of urban crime. Easier to pump up standardized test scores than truly reach children. Easier to back-scratch and horse-trade than undertake meaningful political reform. The characters who *do* resist the logic of The Game risk punishment, marginalization, and sometimes death. Bunny Colvin's Hamsterdam experiment means the end of his career as a police. Gus Haynes's stand against fabricated, Pulitzer-baiting journalism gets him demoted. Cedric Daniels's refusal to cook the stats for Mayor Carcetti gets him ousted as Commissioner. For the sin of speaking to the police, young Randy Wagstaff loses his home, his guardian, and what innocence he had left. Young or old, it seems that nobody breaks the rules of the Game without facing some consequences.

Omar Little stands as the show's most self-possessed rule-breaker. The perfect antithesis of Marlo (whose name, by the way, is an anagram of "Omar L"), he consistently places his own principles above the norms of the Game and achieves genuine moral progress over the course of the series. Take his reaction to the killing of William Gant, a state's witness, by the Barksdale organization. The Gant murder is a pure expression of the Game: show no mercy, brook no disloyalty, send a message. But Omar, despite his fearsome reputation for violence, draws a firm line at killing civilians. In his talks with the police (another rule violation!), he tells Bunk Moreland that he has "never put my gun on nobody who wasn't in the game." Bunk says, with not a little sarcasm in his voice, "A man must have a code" ("One Arrest").

Bunk is understandably skeptical of this seasoned killer's claim to moral principles. He can sense that Omar's code and his concern for innocent life are sincere, but he also recognizes the callous absurdity of declaring some lives sacrosanct and others expendable. This scene is echoed in the show's third season when Bunk, working a murder linked to Omar's stick-up crew, reaches out to Omar in a morally impassioned speech. Castigating him for living by a code that claims to protect civilians but utterly writes off anyone "in the game," Bunk forces Omar to recognize that even his judiciously dispensed brand of violence "ripples out" into the community with destructive results. He is asking Omar to expand his moral imagination, even though doing so would contravene the rules of the Game and put his own life in jeopardy—and Omar, after some deliberation, rises to the challenge. It's an extraordinary exchange—one of the show's finest moments—and is itself echoed by Omar's reciprocal appeal to Bunk's conscience in the fourth season.

Omar's code appears again when he takes the witness stand at Gant's trial and faces cross-examination by the unscrupulous Maurice Levy. Trying to damage Omar's credibility, Levy suddenly finds himself on the defensive.

> **Levy:** You are amoral, are you not? You are feeding off the violence and the despair of the drug trade. . . . You are a parasite who leeches off—
>
> **Omar:** Just like you, man. . . . I got the shotgun. You got the briefcase. It's all in the Game, though, right? ("All Prologue")

Levy has it wrong, of course. In his own way, Omar is deeply moral—it's the Game itself that is amoral. And Omar's rejoinder has bite, exposing the lie that Levy's drug-trade profiteering is somehow more legitimate than his own. The Omar-Levy exchange is eerily similar to a conversation between early-twentieth-century anarchist Alexander Berkman and "Lightning Al," a professional thief, in Berkman's *Prison Memoirs of an Anarchist*:

> ". . . now and then, the best of us may fall; but it don't happen very often, and it's all in the game. This whole life is a game, Mr. Berkman, and every one's got his graft."
> "Do you mean there are no honest men?" I ask, angrily.
> "Pshaw! I'm just as honest as Rockefeller or Carnegie, only they got the law with them." (p. 198)

A stickup boy always knows his own kind; Omar and Levy are playing the same game, only one of them isn't afraid to say so. Omar don't scare.

Omar's personal code also shows up in his deep emotional attachments and private loyalties, which are just as taboo in the Game as moral principles. In a pivotal Season One scene, the Barksdale crew kidnaps, tortures, and murders Omar's boyfriend and accomplice, Brandon, attempting to smoke Omar out. Brandon is burned, shot, and stabbed, his body dumped in the projects, splayed out on an abandoned van to send a message. For Avon and his soldiers, such viciousness is all in the Game, but it sets Omar on a path of retribution. When Stringer Bell deceitfully tells Omar that Brother Mouzone was responsible for the worst of Brandon's torture, Omar pays a visit to Mouzone's hotel room. Wounding him with a gut shot and ensuring himself a captive audience, Omar explains his motivations to Mouzone. The exchange is illuminating:

> **Omar:** About a year ago, a boy named Brandon got got here in Baltimore. Stuck and burned before he passed.
>
> **Mouzone:** The Game is the Game.
>
> **Omar:** Indeed. But see, that boy was beautiful. Wasn't no need for y'all to do him the way you did. ("Bad Dreams")

Brother Mouzone speaks for the Game in its blank heart-lessness: to play is to make peace with unrestrained brutality. The Game is impersonal, indifferent; it cares nothing for beauty, and so thinks nothing of destroying it. Omar accepts this point but refuses to be bound by it; his true adversary is the Game itself. Omar values things for which the Game has no use—beauty, morality, integrity, autonomy—and this gives him dignity and independence. He is a rogue piece on the board, moving on his own, for his own reasons. But such freedom has a price, and even Omar must eventually pay.

Omar's reckoning is foretold by his friend and confidant, Butchie, who, in one of the show's most overt nods to Greek mythology (so beloved by Omar himself), recalls the blind prophet Tiresias. According to mythic tradition, Tiresias's blindness to the visible world was balanced by vision of a more penetrating kind, and his clairvoyance figures in a number of Greek myths. Heraclitus would have known these stories, and it's easy to imagine the Dark One feeling some kinship with a prophet blind to the world of mere appearances but in touch with a deeper reality. And Heraclitus's very style—a collection of terse riddles, crying out for interpretation—echoes the cryptic pronouncements of seers like Tiresias.

Butchie is Omar's own private oracle. He tells Omar that "conscience do cost" ("Back Burners"), and damned if he doesn't turn out to be prophetic: when Omar skips town to avoid Marlo's wrath, Stanfield lieutenant Chris Partlow tortures and murders Butchie, counting on Omar's code to bring him back to Baltimore.

Sure enough, Omar does return, and doing so seals his fate. Before he can exact revenge for Butchie, he is shot from behind by little Kenard, a young boy at the very bottom of the Stanfield organization. Omar goes unmourned in the streets and his murder goes unnoticed in the papers; he becomes just another casualty of the Game. Omar's sudden, ignominious death shocked an awful lot of *Wire* fans (your humble author included). I think Heraclitus, like the blind seer Butchie, would have seen it coming.

Games Beyond the Game

The Game appears to doom rule-followers and rule-breakers alike. Perhaps the only sensible choice is to opt out, as Marla

Daniels advises her husband: "The game is rigged. But you cannot lose if you do not play" ("The Detail"). It certainly sounds like wise counsel. But if the world itself is a game, as Heraclitus tells us, then there can be no real escape. In another gnomic fragment, Heraclitus asks "How will one hide from that which never sets?" (p. 83). The Game, like the light of a sun that never goes down or the always-watching eye of Zeus, is ever-present and unavoidable. Seen this way, the phrase "all in the Game" becomes terribly literal: if *everything* is in the Game, then the Game must be infinite and truly inescapable. And indeed, most of the characters who try to get out of the Game suffer terribly for it.

Tragically, many characters can't even *see* an alternative to the Game. Dukie is the most wrenching example: a smart, sensitive boy, he knows he isn't fit for the street but has no other options. He's trapped, and he can feel it. This heartbreaking exchange with Cutty, to whom Dukie has come for advice, encapsulates their common predicament:

Cutty: Not everything comes down to how you carry it in the street. I mean, it do come down to that if you gonna be in the street. But that ain't the only way to be.

Dukie: Round here it is.

Cutty: Yeah. Round here it is. World is bigger than that. At least, that's what they tell me.

Dukie: Like . . . how do you get from here to the rest of the world?

Cutty: I wish I knew. ("React Quotes")

For Dukie, the idea of a world outside the Game remains only a phantasm; for Wallace, and then for D'Angelo, the possibility of escape is real but out of reach. Traumatized by the killing of Brandon and his complicity in it, Wallace tells D'Angelo, "I don't wanna play no more" ("Game Day").

When the police recruit him as a witness and move him out to stay with a relative in the countryside, it seems like Wallace just might make it out. But inevitably Wallace is pulled back, as if by magnetism, to Baltimore, the only home he knows—his place on the chessboard. And by then it's already too late; Wallace's flirtation with leaving the Game has aroused suspicion. Stringer gives the word to Bodie and Poot, and Wallace's friends gun him down in an empty West Side shithole.

Wallace's death haunts D'Angelo, as Brandon's death haunted Wallace, and it catalyzes his final break with the Barksdale organization. Born into the Game, D'Angelo comes to feel smothered by it, and in the end he only wants "what Wallace wanted, . . . to start over" ("Sentencing"). D'Angelo never gets out either, of course. He's strangled to death in a prison library, again on Stringer Bell's orders.

Stringer himself provides the most extended example of a character trying, and finally failing, to get out of the Game. Stringer is shrewd enough to play the drug game skillfully, but aware enough to see it as merely one game among many, and he is eager to leave it behind for the world of legitimate business. He tells Avon that there are "games beyond the fucking game," but he fails to see that trading one game for another is no escape at all ("Reformation").

Stringer misunderstands, in two crucial ways, the "all in the Game" proverb. First, his consuming desire to transcend the drug game leads him to break some of its most sacred rules: reaching outside the Barksdale organization to have D'Angelo killed, violating the Sunday truce in an attempt on Omar's life, and deceiving his boss and closest ally. These actions are *not* "all in the Game," despite what Stringer might have thought, and they precipitate his downfall.

Second, when Stringer tries to enter the world of legal business, he falls for exactly the kinds of deceptive practices he ought to see coming. For all his shrewdness, he cannot see how similar this new game is to the one he'd hoped to move beyond. Even in the "legitimate" business world, scamming and lying are all in the Game, and to seasoned veterans like Clay Davis and Andy Krawczyk, the naive Stringer is ripe for exploitation. Stringer is finally caught between two games, welcome in neither. He becomes, as Avon calls him, "a man without a country. Not hard enough for this right here and maybe, just maybe, not smart enough for them out there" ("Moral Midgetry").

The Game Is the Game . . . Always

In his chess lecture, D'Angelo tells Bodie and Wallace that "everybody stay who he is" ("The Buys"). That's not strictly correct. Just as the rare pawn might transcend its station on the chessboard, some characters do manage to move upward in their respective games, though this elevation typically costs them whatever principles they might have. In a more fundamental sense, though, D'Angelo's point holds true: the basic roles and structures of the Game persist even while particular individuals pass through them. Heraclitus, in his "game" fragment and elsewhere, articulates this very idea of underlying regularity persisting through recurring change. He sees the world as endlessly cyclical, governed by strife between opposed forces. One force takes a turn to dominate, then cedes its dominance to another. The particulars are in constant flux, but the underlying patterns always reassert themselves.

The Game's cyclical sameness is a running motif of *The Wire*, often underscored by its more streetwise characters. When Marlo tells Avon, "The Game is the Game," Avon replies with a knowing "Always" ("Unconfirmed Reports"). When Cutty, back on the street after a long prison term, tells Slim Charles, "Game done changed," Slim sets him straight, saying, "Game's the same. Just got more fierce" ("Hamsterdam"). Because attempts to leave the Game or break its rules are efficiently punished, and because any individual game-piece is replaceable, the Game is endlessly self-sustaining. In a document submitted to HBO early in the show's genesis, now available on the Web and known as *The Wire*'s "Show Bible," David Simon lays out a vision for how the first season will end, with a new Baltimore drug lord replacing the old one: There are "new dancers, new faces around the throne. But the net effect is that the game goes on. No matter what the government does or doesn't do, the game remains" (p. 76).

The show's final episodes make this idea of cyclical recurrence concrete, with the appearance of change masking the world's basic sameness. Familiar characters occupy new roles in their respective worlds, but those worlds are essentially unchanged. Carcetti ascends to the statehouse; Nerese Campbell takes his place as mayor and names Stan Valchek as Police Comissioner. Valchek fills the vacancy left by Daniels, forced out for refusing to be Campbell's stat-juking puppet. Before he leaves, Daniels promotes Carver to lieutenant, with Carver's rank and checkered past echoing Daniels himself. Daniels becomes a lawyer while Rhonda Pearlman moves behind the bench, filling the shoes of Judge Phelan. We last see Phelan having a familiar sort of conversation with Leander Sydnor, who appears to have succeeded McNulty and Freamon as the department's gadfly.

On the street, Bubbles has finally made good his escape from the life of a dope-chasing fiend, but Dukie appears to be headed down Bubs's old path. At the newspaper, Gus Haynes has been demoted for his insubordination, but the young and scrupulous Fletcher has taken his place. The Co-op buys out Marlo's connection with the Greek; the inflow of drugs to Baltimore continues unabated. And though Omar has been gunned down by Kenard—the very boy who once play-acted as Omar in a children's game—young Michael Lee has taken up Omar's mantle. In a scene mirroring our first encounter with Omar, we see Michael fearlessly robbing Vinson's rim shop, playing the Game for himself with a shotgun and a conscience. On the surface, much has changed—but underneath, the Game goes on.

The War on Nihilism

The most prominent complaint about *The Wire* is that it is fundamentally cynical or even nihilistic—in other words, that it depicts its characters' lives as drained of all meaning or hope. Seeing the show through the lens of Heraclitus would appear to support that claim; the Heraclitean world is bleak, and the world of *The Wire* seems just as grim. Playing the Game by the rules is no guarantee of security, and deviating from them invites harsh punishment. Simply opting out is impossible, and "victory" requires trading out any semblance of a moral conscience. And as long as the cyclically self-correcting institutions that make up the Game are insulated from fundamental change, there seems to be no end in sight, and nothing anyone does seems to matter.

If the Game is infinite and eternal, as Heraclitus would have us think, then there is nothing beyond it to hope for. To many of *The Wire*'s commentators, the show sends the message that we're "doomed." The renowned sociologist Elijah Anderson, quoted by Mark Bowden in *The Atlantic*, notes a "bottom-line cynicism" in the show's outlook (p. 54). In a *Dissent* article titled "Is *The Wire* Too Cynical?," John Atlas and

Peter Dreier claim that the show's creator David Simon "can't imagine a world where things could be different" (p. 82).

But *The Wire* is most certainly *not* a nihilistic show. On the contrary, it's a show that tries, without schmaltz or naiveté, to combat nihilism and hopelessness. It ultimately rejects—after serious consideration—the Heraclitean view of the world. Unlike Heraclitus, *The Wire* takes an essentially critical stance: its depiction of the world as a game is a way of objecting to that world, of demanding something more. And it offers hints of genuine hope through characters who see beyond the Game, who have independent convictions and the courage to act on them. Rather than resign themselves to lives made meaningless by the failing institutions they inhabit, these characters work to subvert, escape, or resist the Game; from these very acts of resistance, they fashion dignity and meaning for themselves. And while they all pay dearly for their rebellion, a lucky few are able to make real and lasting changes in themselves and their surroundings. These characters are at the heart of *The Wire*'s war on nihilism.

Bunny Colvin is an obvious example. Discouraged by the futility of the drug war and fed up with the hopelessly cyclical games that Baltimore's law enforcement and education systems have become, Colvin is determined to make a difference in his city, no matter how radical his tactics seem or what it may cost his career. From his Hamsterdam experiment and guidance of Ellis Carver, to his work with the "corner kids" at Tilghman Middle School and *de facto* adoption of Namond Brice, Colvin doesn't simply break the rules of the Game—he works deliberately to subvert and change them.

Colvin finds most of his efforts thwarted, which is no surprise; he's fighting virtually alone against entrenched and powerful forces. But there is nobility and freedom in his struggle, and there is Namond Brice to consider. When we see Namond in Season Five, he's been saved from a corner life he wasn't built for, and he appears to be on an upward trajectory. Perhaps that's Colvin's only concrete and lasting contribution—but that's surely *something*. Namond gets what was denied to D'Angelo, to Wallace, and to so many others: a chance to start over. His life has been salvaged while he's still young enough to live it, and Colvin is instrumental in giving him that second chance.

The fates of Bubbles and Cutty Wise provide further reasons to hope. By the end of the series, Bubs has logged more than a year of clean time, building a stable network of support that once again includes his long-estranged sister. He has found meaningful work, and in a crucial, heroic act of self-forgiveness, he's allowed his life's story to be told in the newspaper. By finally coming to terms with his past and the death of Sherrod, Bubbles appears ready to leave that past behind him.

And Cutty, who was himself essential to Namond's rescue, seems finally to have gotten away from the Game he gave half a lifetime to. His boxing gym has taken root in West Baltimore as a force for good, and he has turned the traits of a Barksdale soldier—his courage, loyalty, and quiet charisma—into the traits of a decent man. Neither Bubbles nor Cutty makes it out of Baltimore, of course, and both will bear scars that record the cost of their transformations, but they show that some form of escape is, after all, possible.

In an interview with television critic Alan Sepinwall, David Simon frames *The Wire*'s hard-won anti-nihilism as "an argument that even though it may be futile to rebel, it's the only alternative if you want to salvage anything that remotely resembles human dignity. I'm butchering Camus there. . . ." In fact, Simon's paraphrase is quite true to the spirit (if not the exact words) of Camus, who writes in *The Rebel* that

> a living man can be enslaved and reduced to the historic condition of an object. But if he dies in refusing to be enslaved, he reaffirms the existence of another kind of human nature which refuses to be classified as an object. (p. 208)

Perhaps, as Heraclitus says, we are mere pieces on an unfairly tilted game board, but Simon and Camus won't allow that to be the final word on the human race. Our efforts at rebellion and subversion may fail—they may be almost certain to fail—but our salvation lies in how we carry that failure.

The Wire sets out to present a clear-eyed portrait of the dying American city, that brutally Heraclitean universe where the most vulnerable human beings are seen more and more as expendable pawns: the dealers and the cops who chase them, the dock workers, the junkies, the grunt reporters, the kids and their teachers, the working poor and the out-of-work poor and the desperately poor. In the Game, they're nothing but cheap fuel for the massive, sputtering engines of late-stage American capitalism—or worse, they're simply extraneous to the system, literally worthless.

Yet to call *The Wire* nihilistic is to ignore its celebration of righteous dissent, Camus's "other kind of human nature" that won't accept the status of a mere game-piece. *The Wire* doesn't flinch from the harsh reality of the Game; rather, by giving us heroes who carry it like rebels, it challenges us to confront and transform that reality, and it shows us how to reclaim some measure of human dignity in a world rigged against it.

LINE 3
Locke'd in the Game?

WILLIAM ALLEN

The most frightening character on the *The Wire* is Marlo Stanfield. The only time we see him shoot someone, he is calm and collected. He is generally quiet and rarely do we see him angry. But the cold, calculating, and ruthless manner in which he conducts himself as leader of the Stanfield Crew makes him the last person I would like to come across in a dark alley.

Take for example a particularly chilling scene between Marlo and a grocery store security guard. At a neighborhood convenience store, Marlo blatantly steals some lollipops in front of a security guard, and the security guard confronts him outside. The security guard is frustrated—he has a crummy job, but one that supports his family. He tells Marlo that he knows who Marlo is and that he is not attempting to "step to" him or "disrespect" him, but "I am a man, and you just clipped that shit like you don't even know I'm there." Unmoved, Marlo's response is "I don't" ("Refugees").

The security guard is merely trying to get Marlo to recognize him as a fellow human being struggling to make a living, who is worthy of a modicum of respect. Based on Marlo's response, he obviously does not care about recognizing the security guard as a person due respect, nor does he empathize with the security guard's plight. The security guard is "nobody" from Marlo's perspective. The writers underscore this point by not giving the security guard a name and not showing his death, which results from the conversation.

Marlo only cares about himself and his interests; his main concern is protecting his rep and the empire he's built. He cares little about abiding by the social mores of those of us living in mainstream society, and he's arguably amoral. From his perspective, murder and other heinous acts he authorizes aren't subject to moral scrutiny, only to the cold, practical rules necessary to survive in the Game. The security guard, by confronting Marlo, falls into the category of someone challenging Marlo's power and thus the security guard has to pay for the act with his life.

In many ways Marlo embodies the (real or imagined) fears people have of African-American men from poor urban communities (if not African-American men in general.) Many people view African-American men in such communities as not having a moral conscience and refusing to abide by mainstream social values and customs. If these African-American men had a proper system of values, (like those of the Puritan work ethic offered in the introduction), then African-American communities wouldn't need something like Hamsterdam to make those spaces livable again, or so say politicians and political pundits when discussing the plight of the urban poor.

Another explanation that *The Wire* seems to promote is that such communities exist due to severe neglect by public institutions. Poor education, police enforcement, and public services in general create an environment of poverty and unemployment in which crime seems like the most reasonable means of survival. Such a position is not intended to absolve someone like Marlo of the crimes he commits, but it indicates that mere individual choice, responsibility, and "cultural values" are not enough to explain such actions.

The Game Is War, No One Is Safe

One way to understand the life of the urban poor, or underclass, of *The Wire* is that of living in an anarchic war zone. This description is particularly appropriate during times where rival gangs battle over control of corners (for example the Stanfield-Barksdale war). But even in times of "normal" street activity, the residents live under the constant threat of violence, theft, and other crimes, so that no one really lives in peace.

The drug dealers are continually on watch for the police, rival gangs, and stick-up men such as Omar. The average nondrug dealing residents, those Omar dubs 'citizens', have to be vigilant against becoming collateral damage of gang violence, being robbed by drug addicts, and drawing the ire of drug dealers (as the security guard did with Marlo).

A good example of how average residents in the community are constantly on watch is shown in their reaction to the appearance of Omar. Every time he is seen walking out of his home, (even if his intention is merely to re-up on Honey Nut Cheerios), the residents in the neighborhood warn "Omar comin'," sending those outside running into their homes in fear of violence. Their reaction is like the residents of a dusty town in an old western movie when an outlaw rolls in.

However, we're far past the days of the lawless Wild West. How is it possible that a virtual war zone can exist in the United States? Isn't everyone in our nation due the protection of "life, liberty, and the pursuit of happiness" as stated in the Declaration of Independence? As citizens, don't we have a right to certain "social goods" such as public education and law enforcement, valuable (if not necessary) things for creating a good life? In the disadvantaged communities of *The Wire* these things are minimally protected or unavailable to the point of being virtually nonexistent. Average residents such as the security guard, William Gant (the witness who testified against D'Angelo), and Nakeesha Lyles (the witness who changed her testimony against D) are not even secure in their right to life.

At first glance, *The Wire*'s characterization of the underclass as living in a war zone without state protection might prompt someone familiar with the seventeenth-century philosopher Thomas Hobbes to say: "These people are living in the state of nature!" Hobbes argues in *Leviathan* that when people do not live in a civil state bound by laws and the protection of rights, people are at war with each other; they live in what he calls a "state of nature."

Because there's no government restricting people's activities, Hobbes claims that people have complete freedom to do whatever they wish. We're naturally selfish, unsocial, competitive, and power-seeking. So, according to Hobbes, without restrictions, people in the state of nature act out of self-interest and self-preservation. It's survival of the fittest, and you best show up willing to fight.

Hobbes would clearly understand the interaction between Marlo and the security guard. Since Hobbes claims that no one in the state of nature recognizes anyone else's rights, and there is no morality, people will resort to killing, stealing, and doing whatever they deem necessary in order to survive. In this environment people are continually in fear of harm from others, thus everyone views their neighbor as a potential enemy. Hobbes claims that in this "state of war":

> Nothing can be unjust. The notions of right and wrong, justice and injustice, have there no place. Where there is no common power, there is no law; where no law, no injustice. (*Leviathan*, p. 78)

If you buy Hobbes's product, then Marlo's actions are justifiable. From such a perspective, eliminating potential threats is necessary to survive in the Game. Morality is moot. Since people can literally get away with murder, belief in the concept of justice is absurd. Even when people such as Marlo and Avon Barksdale are caught, 'justice' is not reflected in the extent of their punishment. This perspective is not the result of pure individual choice or values, but living in an environment without governance.

However, Hobbes claims that the state of nature is only possible for people who do not live in a civil state. Call Baltimore what you will, it's still a part of the United States. So although Marlo, the Corner Kids, and Bubbles all live in an isolated environment, they technically are citizens of the United States due the same rights to "life, liberty, and the pursuit of happiness" as the rest of us. How is it that they can live in a state of nature while living in a country with rights and laws?

The Game Beyond the Game

We'd have a much more difficult time describing Baltimore's west side as a state of nature, given John Locke's conception. Locke, a successor to Hobbes, argues similarly to Hobbes that in the absence of government people exist in a "state of nature." However, in Locke's state of nature people are more or less peaceful and generally understand and recognize others as due natural, inalienable rights.

Instead of finding a picture of Baltimore's oppressed communities in Hobbes's description of the state of nature, it's Locke's discussion of the state of nature where we find the Baltimore of *The Wire*. Locke addresses the fact that there can exist small groups of citizens who're oppressed in a nation where the majority of citizens enjoy the protection of rights and social goods. In such a situation, Locke claims that the oppressed group is in a state of war.

Whereas the state of war and state of nature are the same for Hobbes, Locke makes a distinction between the two. Locke recognizes that, on the one hand, even in his state of nature, small groups of people can seek to harm others. When they do, it's a state of war. However, Locke also recognizes that within an existing nation, the government or other citizens can oppress a minority group. When there is no authority one can appeal to, Locke would describe that minority group as being in a state of war with the rest of society.

So the question arises: do Marlo, Snoop, Bodie, Bubbles, Cutty, Namond's mother, and Randy's foster mother collectively count as an oppressed group of citizens in a "state of war" as Locke proposes? Technically, as citizens, they all have legal rights to life, liberty, property, and social goods. They receive public services, can call the police, and send their children to public schools. However, that doesn't guarantee that their alleys will remain clear, that the police will come in a timely manner or prove effective, nor that schools will actually teach them or their children. The problem is not the mere provision of services and rights, but the quality of services and adequate protection of rights.

In *The Wire*, the Baltimore police department is unable to eliminate drug activity. Due to the political jockeying of state officials from the police department to the mayor's office, Lt. Daniels's drug detail and other officers are compelled to "juke the stats" rather than effectively combat the drug gangs. Their weak efforts are further undermined by corrupt politicians like Clay Davis, and unscrupulous lawyers such as Maurice Levy who protect the drug lords. The most the police are able to do is harass the low-level drug dealing kids like Bodie, pushing them off their corners for an hour or two. The Barksdale and Stanfield gangs are able to sell drugs, intimidate the local community, and commit murder with virtual impunity. Even when the police are able to arrest the drug lords, the vacuum created is quickly filled. In the end, the benefit police bring to the disadvantaged neighborhoods of *The Wire* is almost nonexistent. As Public Enemy rapped, "911 is a joke."

In the public schools there are some teachers concerned with the education and well-being of their students, such as Prez. However, the teachers are overworked and forced to meet the demands of an Educational Board more concerned with bumping up state test scores than truly educating children. The effectiveness of the teachers is further limited in that the problems the students face at home and in their neighborhoods lead to poor attendance, dropping out, and behavioral problems. Possible solutions, such as Bunny Colvin's program with the corner kids, are eliminated because of lack of government support. As portrayed in *The Wire*, teachers' efforts to educate and help their students are undermined by factors inside and outside the school environment.

Institutional neglect on the part of government at all levels violates the inalienable right that people should have to substantial and equal opportunities for creating a good life, what we like to call 'the pursuit of happiness.' Thus we can say that the underclass of *The Wire* is oppressed, living in a state of war, and that Locke's account is better than Hobbes's.

The Game is Rigged . . . Play or Get Played

For those living in an environment where participants in the drug game are the best off financially, crime is a constant concern, public services are lacking, and the larger mainstream society does not seem to care about their plight. So it's not surprising that some people in the underclass of *The Wire* find themselves falling victim to the traps of street life in order to survive.

When introduced in Season Four, the Boys of Summer, Michael, Dukie, Randy, and Namond, are portrayed as "average" adolescents. In many respects they are—they go to school, they have a burgeoning interest in girls, and they like to joke around and play pranks. However, as the show delves deeper into their lives, it's evident that all of them have to deal with the effects of their negligent, even abusive, parents. Aside from their home lives, they have to navigate an environment of poverty, unemployment, violence, and drug addiction, while trying to resist the allure of the drug game. As we observe their coming of age, it's clear that the cards are stacked against their having a "normal" mainstream life. The Game is rigged against even them.

From the beginning, the Boys of Summer already understand that the police are unreliable (and some corrupt), school serves no practical purpose for survival in their world, and most adults (including their parents) have no genuine concern for them. They're essentially alone. To survive, these young people have to rely on their own wits and take advantage of the opportunities the streets provide. Such an attitude toward public institutions and their community shows that the Boys of Summer (and makers of *The Wire*) do not believe that public institutions are effective in protecting and promoting their "life, liberty, and pursuit of happiness."

In light of what the Boys of Summer have to struggle with, it's not surprising that, by the end of the series, most of the teens meet the same fates as other people in their community. Michael, in order to protect himself and his young brother, becomes a "soldier" for the Stanfield Crew, and thereafter a stick-up kid robbing drug dealers. He becomes essentially the new Omar. Dukie, left homeless when abandoned by his drug-addicted parents, becomes a drug addict himself. He's following in the footsteps of Bubbles and other drug addicts in the community. Randy is branded a "snitch" due to the police mistakenly leaking details of his coerced cooperation. As a result, his foster mother's home is firebombed, and he is sent to a group home where he is abused by the other teenagers. A once jovial kid, he's transformed into an angry teenager with an uncertain future.

By the end of the series, the only original member of the group who has the possibility of a "good life" in mainstream society is Namond, who's adopted by Bunny Colvin and moved out of the 'hood to a middle-class neighborhood. We first meet Namond as a wannabe thug, but he's the only one in the group who continues to go to school, and ends up excelling as a member of the debate team (an activity he probably would have previously mocked as for punks). The series implies that Namond's success is due to taking him out of the underclass community, allowing him to form a bond with people who're part of the mainstream, and immersing him in a community in which he can benefit from mainstream opportunities.

Morality and "the Other Way" of the Game

Blaming the outcome of Michael, Dukie, and Randy on individual choices and poor parenting is not a sufficient explanation of their fate. The perpetual cycle of poverty, unemployment, poor schooling, and poor police enforcement are responsible for the limited choices they have available in their community.

Locke argues that people living in a state of war do not have an obligation to obey the state's laws, recognize its authority, nor abide by social norms. Because the state fails to sufficiently protect the rights of the oppressed community, he would say that all acts used to secure your rights are justifiable. He provides an example of punishing a thief in a state of war. He claims that the victim of theft is justified in killing the thief, if the victim deems such a punishment fit. Even though such a punishment does not seem to fit the crime, it is justified since there is no common authority to protect rights and dictate the norms of punishment. This being the case, people are left to protect themselves based on their own judgment (however flawed their judgment might be.)

In light of Locke's argument we can see how the Avons and Marlos of the underclass come to be. In a community without proper governance, some people view criminal activity as a good way to secure life, liberty, property, and the pursuit of happiness. In the 'hood, the drug game is the best way to earn a substantial income. Even though drug dealing involves violence, risk of imprisonment, and death, without other viable opportunities available, within that context, it is a rational choice.

From such a perspective, actions that we consider immoral (and arguably are immoral) are heavily determined by the living conditions, made possible due to profound institutional neglect. Thus we can understand Marlo Stanfield better, though we can certainly condemn some of his actions. Locke would tell us that, even in a state of war, people still have inalienable rights, but we can choose to violate such rights. He thought that people who violate inalienable rights are aware of what they're doing. For example, being creatures with the capacity of reason, we know that murder is wrong.

Marlo's demeanor and rhetoric seem to be those of a person who is amoral, but he is aware that mainstream society has values that involve being civil and respecting rights. Returning to the security guard incident, Marlo ends the conversation by reminding the security guard of the reality they both live in: "You want it to be one way, but it is the other way" ("Refugees"). Initially, this may seem cryptic. However Marlo is telling the security guard that they both know the reality of their community. The drug dealers are the ones with power and the 'hood is governed by the rules of the street; but the security guard asserts (through being confrontational) that he wants it "one way." The security guard wants to live in an environment where everyone respects the law and people respect each other. Unfortunately this is not the environment they live in; it's "the other way."

Marlo's point is that such values and rights of the mainstream are not recognized in his particular community. He is aware that in the mainstream, people are due rights and such rights are protected. Keeping Locke in mind, Marlo is probably even aware that his community and all human beings are due certain rights, but since such rights are not protected, and violating them is useful, he feels no obligation to respect them.

However, apart from Marlo's beliefs or whether Marlo is amoral, his actions can be judged. Locke suggests that, apart from any one person's or group's standard of morality, what is moral depends on whether it's consistent with the natural use of reason. This concept has its problems, but I would chance to say that Marlo was very, very wrong for having the security guard killed. That act deserves a high level of moral condemnation. The security guard was no real threat to Marlo. I doubt the security guard would have bragged to people on the street about confronting Marlo, such that it would damage Marlo's rep. It was a slight transgression with no foreseeable repercussions. Marlo could have let the incident go.

Other acts by characters in the series are not as easy to judge. For example, what level of blame can we place on the average kid on the corner selling drugs? Certainly, we can say that Michael, Wallace, and Bodie are wrong for selling drugs to people with an addiction; it's the exploitation of people with an illness. However, in many cases (Michael being a prime example) we have to consider that selling drugs is the best, if not only, option to support oneself and loved ones in poor urban areas.

Without condoning the Game, it's not the fault of these kids, certainly it's less their fault than say a person without such burdens. *The Wire* reminds us that these kids should not have to live in an environment in which they feel compelled to sell drugs in the first place. If they were born into a mainstream environment with its benefits and opportunities, there is a high probability that they (and everyone in the community, even Marlo) would have made different choices. I could easily see Marlo as CEO of a corporation.

The Game Is the Game. Always?

Locke claims that the ordeal of the oppressed is only possible when the majority of citizens fail to sympathize with the plight of the oppressed and their claims, thus allowing the government to further that oppression. We can fail to sympathize with the plight of residents living in poverty-stricken areas if we don't feel that the oppressed group's condition affects our own well-being. Simply put, if the majority of citizens don't feel they're oppressed nor have concern for the oppressed, the majority sees no reason to challenge government. Locke expresses this in the following:

> For till the mischief be grown general, and the ill designs of the rulers become visible, or their attempts sensible to the greater part, the people, who are more disposed to suffer than right themselves by resistance, are not apt to stir. The examples of particular injustice or oppression of here and there an unfortunate man moves them not. (*Two Treatises*, pp. 416–18)

Without the support of the larger society, the members of the oppressed group have no power to force the government to protect their rights; their pleas fall on deaf ears. Locke concludes that the only appeal left is one to the Heavens. Talk about deaf ears. In other words, the oppressed are screwed.

The Wire and Locke suggest that as long as public officials and common citizens collectively continue to be apathetic about the plight of the underclass, succeeding generations of people will be trapped in such conditions. In the last episode of the series, we see that despite the elimination of key members of the Stanfield Gang, and changes in public officials, the cycle of poverty, violence, unemployment and drug abuse continues. There're just new faces in old roles.

The Wire suggests that a large part of the problem is that politicians primarily act for their own self-interest at the expense of the well-being of the public (the prime examples being both Mayor Royce and Mayor Carcetti who prioritize their political ambitions above serving Baltimore.) Part of the solution could lie in reforming our public institutions so that they better serve the public interest of all citizens, rather than just private interests. Keeping Locke in mind, the solution also requires that we as common citizens take a more active role in ensuring our politicians act for the benefit of all citizens. But then, we'd have to concern ourselves with the well-being of fellow citizens outside our immediate communities.

The Wire, understood from the philosophy of Locke, gives the viewer an understanding of how disadvantaged urban communities are created and why some people in such communities are compelled to make certain choices. Aside from providing entertainment, *The Wire* serves as a plea to its viewers, serving as a form of artistic protest. By providing a realistic account of Baltimore that is complex and intimate in its portrayal of characters, sympathetic to the plight of the underclass and critical of public institutions, it forces the viewer to recognize the troubles of such communities and sympathize with the people who live in them.

We can't watch *The Wire* without feeling that something's seriously wrong with our public institutions. Viewed as a piece of protest art, *The Wire* is the creators' attempt to compel the viewer to sympathize with the plight of disadvantaged communities across the nation, and engage in political action to bring about change.

Second Case

The Tactics

LINE 4
Wee-Bey's Way

David Bzdak

You askin' too much.

—Wee-Bey Brice

A lot of superlatives have been thrown at *The Wire* since its debut in 2002, but you're unlikely to hear adjectives like "uplifting" and "feel-good" among those raves—for obvious reasons. The unhappy endings on the show are too numerous to list.

Wee-Bey and Bunny

Maybe that's why a Season Four scene between Howard 'Bunny' Colvin and Roland 'Wee-Bey' Brice stands out. Bunny visits Wee-Bey, who's in prison for numerous murders, to discuss Wee-Bey's son, Namond. After reminiscing a bit about the old days on the streets of West Baltimore, Bunny makes a pitch:

> BUNNY: Your boy . . . is smart and funny, and open-hearted. And he got some flex in him. And I ain't see it at first, 'cause he was always acting out, always full up of corner talk—you know, just talking shit to hide himself. But he could go a lot of places and do a lot of things in his life, be out there in the world in a way that, you know, didn't happen for you and me. I mean, you know our kind? Shit. Man, we both know we gonna go to our grave forever knowing what block Bentalou dead-ends at, or who got their liquor license over at the Underground, or what corner Tater Man got shot on when he come out of the Musical Lounge back in '88.

WEE-BEY: Division and Gold.

BUNNY: The West side we knew . . . it's dead, man. You know, people in the game nowadays—I mean, it's a whole different breed—no code, no family, and damn sure no respect. I mean, you send Namond out on the corner now, I'm giving him maybe one, two years before he down at the morgue. And maybe, if you're lucky, up here with you.

WEE-BEY: Maybe, maybe not. That's the Game.

BUNNY: I'm talking about Namond, here, Mr. Brice. He's a lot of things, a lot of good things. I mean, before you know, he might surprise all of us given half a chance, but he ain't made for them corners, man. I mean, not like we were. That's why I come down here—because I gotta believe that you see it, being who you are and all you've been through. You know your son. It's in your hands, man.

WEE-BEY: You askin' too much.

BUNNY: Yeah, but I'm asking. ("Final Grades")

Given what we know about Wee-Bey (and David Simon), it's something of a surprise to discover that he ultimately agrees to let Bunny take Namond out of the Game. In one of the few happy endings that *The Wire* provides, we later see Namond applying his street smarts to great effect in an organized, academic debate—while Bunny and his wife beam proudly from the audience.

How did Bunny accomplish this seemingly impossible task? After all, as Wee-Bey himself stated, breaking the rules of the Game was too much for Bunny to ask. So why would a cold-blooded killer, whose allegiance to the Game was unquestioned, agree to such a request? Or, put another way, when can the rules of the Game be broken?

Answer: When it's family.

Sometimes, when it's family, nothing is too much to ask.

Valchek and Pryzbylewski

Early in the investigation of the Barksdale organization, three lower-level cops—Ellis Carver, Thomas 'Herc' Hauk, and Roland 'Prez' Pryzbylewski, decide (after a few beers) to go to the Towers and do some "police work." They unwittingly start a near-riot, during which Prez pistol-whips a young kid who ends up losing sight in one eye. Prez escapes serious punishment despite having a history of major screw-ups as a cop. Lt. Cedric Daniels, generally an honest and upright officer, provides Prez with a cover story to tell the internal investigators. In the end, Prez gets what amounts to a slap on the wrist for the incident.

Why is so much care and consideration given to a cop who probably should've been fired long ago? Well, Prez's police department rabbi is his father-in-law, Stan Valchek, a major in the Southeastern District, with political connections and pull. In other words, Prez survives as a cop, despite starting a near-riot and partially blinding a young kid, because he's family.

Sometimes, when it's family, people do things they shouldn't.

The Puzzle of Impartiality

These two examples from the show illustrate an incredibly difficult and yet important puzzle with respect to morality that I call the Puzzle of Impartiality. What is impartiality? In broad terms, it's the idea that no one individual counts for more than any other individual, morally speaking. In other words, every individual's interests should be given the same consideration. It might best be illustrated by considering counterexamples—for instance, racism and sexism. These discriminatory "isms," generally involve the view that members of one specific group—a certain race, or gender—deserve more moral consideration than members belonging to other groups. Or, in extreme cases, that only members of that special group deserve moral consideration at all. Think, for example, of the Serbs' attitude towards Croats, or Hutus towards the Tutsis in Rwanda. We recognize such attitudes as obviously wrong because they're partial—that is, they fail to give equal consideration to the interests of everyone.

Impartiality is sometimes mischaracterized as "equal treatment for all," but that's importantly wrong. After all, we don't expect an impartial judge to give the same sentence to all of those who come before her. Nor do we expect an impartial teacher to give every student the same grade. But we do generally expect such professionals to apply the same rules and processes, in the same manner, to all who come before them. So being impartial doesn't involve treating everyone exactly alike;

it's more like the ideal of providing everyone a level playing field.

When Valchek's pull saves Prez from a pink slip or prosecution, that's a violation of impartiality. Favoring someone merely because he is a family member (or friend, or colleague, or co-worker), is giving that person's interests more weight than you give the interests of others. Why should an accident of marriage (or birth, or friendship, or employment) morally privilege Prez over the boy he blinded? In fact, when judges, or police officers, or umpires, are caught treating friends and family members partially, it's considered unethical and sometimes illegal.

Impartiality is importantly connected to morality in certain contexts. Some would argue that moral progress is intimately connected with the recognition that impartiality is a virtue. Ancient humans were organized along family lines, and tended to reserve moral recognition exclusively for those who belonged "to the tribe." Early civilizations widened the circle of moral recognition, but only gradually. The Greeks bestowed moral recognition on all Greek citizens, which goes well beyond the family; but they nevertheless considered all non-Greeks to be barbarians, who could, without moral qualms, be enslaved (and the status of Greek women wasn't much better). But slowly, as time passed, the circle grew wider.

Nowadays, most cultures at least pay lip service to the idea that differences in geography, ethnicity, family, race or gender are irrelevant to questions of moral recognition. Moral progress (on this view) goes hand-in-hand with the idea that all individuals should be given equal consideration, morally speaking. And conversely, many significant moral problems we still face—such as discrimination, poverty, religious tensions, and war—would be eased if people were less partial towards their own interests and the interests of those close to them. Impartiality, then, is intimately connected with morality. As philosopher Peter Singer notes in his famous article "Famine, Affluence, and Morality": "the idea that . . . some element of impartiality or universalizability is inherent in the very notion of a moral judgment" is "now widely shared by moral philosophers."

And yet . . .

You Family, Man

If impartiality is such a moral good, and a requirement for moral progress, why does it sometimes seem so wrong? Think about Wee-Bey's decision in the scene quoted above. In one of the most poignant and redeeming moments in all five seasons of *The Wire*, Wee-Bey undoubtedly does the right thing by acting partially. That is, we admire Wee-Bey for agreeing to treat Namond differently from everyone else in the Game, because Namond is his son. Others who tried to exit were not so lucky—think of the tragedies that befell D'Angelo and Wallace.

There are other examples from the show that suggest that partiality can be an admirable trait. Think of Omar's famous "code," the one that forbids him from killing any regular "citizens," as opposed to those in the Game. It's part of Omar's great appeal that he has such a code. But it's a code that relies on partiality—the idea that some people (those outside the Game) deserve greater moral consideration than others (those playing the Game).

On the flip side, there are characters on *The Wire* who come off as pretty despicable because they fail to behave partially. For example, Namond's mother, De'Londa Brice, insists that Namond take his rightful place in the Barksdale drug organization—in no small part so that she can continue her relatively lavish lifestyle. She's verbally abusive to him when he fails, and upon hearing that Namond is at the police station, rather than bailing him out, she tells the cops to throw Namond into "baby booking," since he's going to have to experience the Juvenile Justice Center at some point. De'Londa's behavior seems especially heinous because Namond is her son. Her lack of partiality is a big reason why her character seems so morally bad.

As De'Londa's case shows, we expect parents to be partial towards their own children, and to provide them with special care and attention. The absence of such care and attention often seems like a moral failure. Think of Raylene Lee, the addict mother of Michael Lee and his younger half-brother Bug, who not only fails to provide her children with special care and attention, but brings Bug's father back into their home when he's paroled from prison, despite the fact that he has sexually abused Michael and might well do the same to Bug. The strong negative reactions this character inspires result not just from her bad behavior, but more significantly from her failure to be partial towards her own children.

So, which is it? Is impartiality a moral requirement, or not? The answer seems to be "sometimes it's required and sometimes not." But the puzzle is: how are we to decide when to be impartial, and when to make exceptions? That is, if it's okay in some contexts to demonstrate partiality, but not in others, how should we make a decision when faced with a real-life moral situation? What criteria should we use to decide?

Do Good for Your Friends and Harm Your Enemies

The Puzzle of Impartiality is not new. In Plato's *Republic*, Socrates rejects the claim that justice involves being good to your friends and harming your enemies—an obviously partial principle (that would no doubt get a lot of nods on the streets of Baltimore). Instead, Socrates endorses the view that it's always wrong to commit an injustice against another, even if that person has committed an injustice against you—something much closer to an endorsement of impartiality.

Like Socrates, advocates of the moral theory of Utilitarianism—developed systematically in the nineteenth century by Jeremy Bentham and John Stuart Mill—put great weight on the notion of impartiality. It advocates always acting so as to maximize overall happiness and minimize overall unhappiness, while giving everyone's interests equal weight. So impartiality is built right into Utilitarianism's guiding principle. Yet one of the most persistent objections to Utilitarianism is it demands too much of us as a result of that very same impartiality requirement!

Other moral theories do a better job accommodating the notion that either partiality or impartiality can be morally required. Moral theories that focus on virtues or traits of character rather than rules or principles, can argue that some virtues—such as loyalty and friendship—are partial (apply to some but not to others), while others—such as justice and sympathy—are impartial (apply equally to all). But despite this recognition, theories of Virtue Ethics still leave us with questions about when the different kinds of virtues apply.

Consider the situation that Detective Kima Greggs found herself in throughout much of Season Five. She discovered that her closest colleagues, James McNulty and Lester Freamon, detectives she respected greatly, were inventing a serial killer in order to acquire the necessary resources to put away drug kingpin Marlo Stanfield. She found herself torn between loyalty to friends, who were doing what they thought was right, and telling the truth about their illegal, and in her eyes, immoral, activities. Both loyalty and honesty are virtues, and in this case they obviously conflict. Greggs chose (impartial) honesty over (partial) loyalty, but why? How did she know that was the right thing to do in this case? The mere recognition that both honesty and loyalty are virtues is not, in itself, enough to determine that decision.

A Solution to the Puzzle

Throughout the series police officers almost always demonstrate partiality towards each other. When a police officer is harmed or killed, it is treated as a much more serious situation than if the same thing happens to a regular citizen. In Season One during a police raid on The Pit, Barksdale gang member Preston 'Bodie' Broadus punches a police officer who's trying to handcuff him. The other cops immediately start to beat the crap out of Bodie, including Greggs, who (as noted above) tends to do the right thing. At first it looks as though she's going to stop the beating. Instead, Greggs joins in, urging the other cops on in the process. The police officer who was punched was not a well-liked cop. In fact, he was terrible at his job and mostly just taking up space as he waited for retirement. But the fact that he was a police officer made the assault different from assaults on non-officers.

Later in the same season, when Greggs is shot, the top brass of the Baltimore police department show up at the hospital and a full-court press is made to find the shooters. There's no chance such a response would've occurred if the same thing had happened without a cop being shot. And again, it wasn't the brass's love for Greggs that motivated the reaction to her shooting. While Greggs was well-liked and respected by her immediate colleagues, the higher-ups didn't even know who she was (and wouldn't deign to offer their condolences to her lesbian partner, grieving at the hospital). The mere fact that she was a police officer led to the all-out effort to solve the crime.

This phenomenon—cops being partial to cops—is common and not hard to justifiy. If criminals don't fear harming police, it could lead to more police officers being harmed. And if more police are harmed, they could end up less rigorously enforcing the law. If police officers are less rigorous, that would be bad for all of us. So, perhaps this example of impartiality can be justified by reference to the greater good. If acting partially brings about more good than harm, then it's okay. Otherwise, we should behave impartially.

Then I'm a Rat

The Greater Good Principle, consistent with the moral theory of Utilitarianism (maximize happiness and minimize unhappiness), seems promising. For one thing, it can show how the practice of cops-protecting-cops can be bad, even if it's sometimes justified. In Season Five, for example, Lieutenant Carver has to decide whether or not to report Officer Colicchio, who attacked a civilian insistently honking his horn at a crime scene where police cars were blocking the road. Colicchio lost his temper and started to pull the man out of his car. He was stopped by other cops on the scene, but was unrepentant even after he learned that the civilian was a schoolteacher. Carver made the unpopular decision to report rather than cover for Colicchio, and the Greater Good principle can explain why this move was right. After all, covering for Colicchio after assaulting a respected citizen would not serve the greater good. So partiality would not be justified in this case.

Same goes for the case where Daniels covers for Prez after the near-riot at the Towers. The action left a bad taste in Daniels's mouth because it was done to cover people's asses rather than to bring about some greater good. Prez himself feels a lot of guilt, which he demonstrates when confronted with his one-eyed victim a few months later. Prez cannot bring himself to look the boy in the face. He, too, recognizes that his treatment was the result of an unjust instance of partiality.

Later in the series, Daniels and Prez find themselves in a similar situation, with Prez in trouble for a controversial shooting and Daniels still his superior officer. Prez has come a long way since that initial incident, however, and is on the road to becoming good poh-lice. Daniels behaves much as he did with respect to the first incident, trying to help Prez cover his ass before talking to internal affairs. This time, though, there is no feeling of guilt or injustice on Daniels's part, since now helping Prez means helping a good cop who's doing important work and who made a mistake that cost another officer his life. The Greater Good Principle justifies Daniels treating Prez partially at that point.

So the Greater Good Principle works as a solution to the puzzle, at least in some cases. However, there are some problems with this solution as well. First, it's very easy to rationalize partial decisions by invoking the greater good, and difficult to tell whether or not the greater good is really being served. For example, it's not hard to imagine Carver protecting Colicchio by invoking the damage it might do the police department if he didn't. And no doubt De'Londa told herself that her treatment of Namond was for the greater good of both of them, since Namond wouldn't survive on the corners unless she toughened him up.

But a more serious objection to the principle is that there are certain situations in which it does not merely seem morally acceptable of us to act partially, but morally required. Imagine, for example, if Randy Wagstaff had come home to see his apartment being fire-bombed and he had the opportunity to save either his foster mother, Miss Anna, or the next-door neighbor, a perfect stranger whom he's in a better position to rescue. Wouldn't it be wrong for him to go for the neighbor first? Or, imagine the scenario reversed, where Miss Anna comes home to a burning apartment and can save either Randy or the boy next door. Doesn't she have a positive obligation towards her foster child over anyone else? As philosopher John Cottingham wrote:

> A parent who leaves his child to burn, on the grounds that the building contains someone else whose future contribution to the general welfare promises to be greater, is not a hero; he is (rightly) an object of moral contempt, a moral leper. (p. 357)

Defending the Greater Good Principle

So does the Greater Good Principle fail? Well, a defender of that principle can point out that the kinds of objections raised against it tend to evoke strong emotions that could cloud the issue. While it's obviously true that family members and good friends have strong emotional bonds, it doesn't follow that those bonds are morally relevant. Just because parents would tend to save their own children over the children of strangers doesn't mean that's what they ought to do.

In the *Republic*, Plato suggests that children should be taken from their parents at birth and raised communally. Why? Because Plato recognized that the strong emotional bonds between parents and their children can overcome reason, leading them to do things they shouldn't, things that wouldn't be for the overall good of the Republic. Such a view recognizes the bonds of friends and family but not their moral relevance. In other words, Plato recognized that people naturally would be partial, but sought ways to prevent it in the name of the greater good.

Few modern defenders of impartiality would go so far (and, in fairness, it's not clear that Plato himself was actually advocating the communal raising of children), but the same basic point is still invoked: while we are naturally partial towards friends and family members, partiality has no moral justification unless it can be shown to serve some greater good. Peter Singer observes that while we're more likely to help a child bleeding right in front of us than we are to help children who are suffering in faraway lands, there's nothing to justify this distinction. How can geographical location confer higher moral status? Similarly, how can one's genetic "location" confer higher moral status? Both seem equally accidental and thus, morally irrelevant.

Bunk makes something like this point in response to Omar and his code of never harming "citizens." The relationship between Bunk and Omar is complex, though it's sometimes reduced to: "Bunk admires Omar, despite his criminality, because of Omar's code." This oversimplification is inaccurate, and misses much of what's interesting about the relationship. It's true that Bunk develops a grudging admiration for Omar, and probably saves his life by getting him out of prison in Season Four. But it's false that Bunk admires Omar's code. The central reason Bunk rejects the code is because of its partiality, because Omar distinguishes between "citizens" and "Game players."

When Bunk first meets him, Omar insists that: "I never put my gun on nobody who wasn't in the Game." That's when Bunk responds, "a man must have a code" ("One Arrest"). This oft-quoted line is usually taken as a sign of Bunk's approval, but a closer look shows that Bunk's tone is sarcastic rather than admiring. When Bunk and Omar meet later, Bunk makes his attitude towards Omar's code clear. Not only does he *not* admire it, he finds it repugnant. He reminds Omar that the two of them grew up in the same neighborhood, and that there were "hard cases" and "bad boys" back in the day. But then he says, practically spitting with disgust at Omar:

> As rough as that neighborhood could be, we had us a community. There was nobody, no victim, who didn't matter. And now, all we got is bodies. And predatory motherfuckers like you. And out where that girl fell, I saw kids acting like Omar. Calling you by name, glorifying your ass. It makes me sick, motherfucker, how far we done fell. ("Homecoming")

So rather than admiring Omar's code, Bunk points out the tragic consequences of dividing the world into victims who matter and victims who don't. Not only does such partiality fail to serve the greater good, it actively undermines it by destroying the community.

Bunk's speech has a strong effect on Omar, who ultimately decides to leave town after promising to give up the Game—until his friend Butchie is tortured and killed by Marlo's people. Omar returns to Baltimore, driven by intense anger because of his love for and loyalty to Butchie. His partiality, though, ultimately gets him killed.

Bunk's speech to Omar nutshells *The Wire*'s attitude about some of the main problems faced by society in general. Much of the social criticism in the show boils down to the problem of people looking out for their own. Cops look out for cops, lawyers look out for lawyers, gangs look out for their own members, politicians look out for their own party. *The Wire* demonstrates how this tribalism tends to persist beyond the point where it benefits the Greater Good. Cops protect other cops who brutalize innocent people. Lawyers protect other corrupt lawyers who put dangerous criminals back on the street. Politicians ignore constituents in need because they provide no advantage on election day.

And yet . . .

How many happy, loving relationships do we find in *The Wire*? Think of the characters who are, or become, parents: McNulty, Greggs, Bunk, Frank Sobotka, De'Londa Brice, Raylene Lee, Brianna and D'Angelo Barksdale, and Tommy Carcetti. At best, they're absentee parents, and at worst they're criminal.

Now think about how many healthy marriages, or romantic relationships, are portrayed on the show. Cedric Daniels and Rhonda Pearlman might be described in that way, and Lester Freamon and Shardene Innes. But for the most part, these types of relationships on the show are nearly as dysfunctional as the parent-child ones.

So, the lack of partiality is portrayed as a problem on the show as well. Most of the characters fail to take care of their own in a manner that is morally required of them. McNulty is a particularly interesting example. He's happiest when he's working as a patrolman, living with Beatrice Russell and her kids (and his, when he sees them), and in general laying low. Even Elana, his first wife, notices how good McNulty is at that point. In other words, McNulty flourishes when he puts himself and those close to him first. When he's looking out for his own. But when he goes back to being a detective, a job where he no doubt serves the greater good, he relapses into his old bad habits, becoming miserable to himself and those around him.

Adherence to the Greater Good Principle, then, would lead us to miss much of what's important in life, morally speaking. The idea that relationships are things that can be set down or picked up depending on "the greater good" is based on a radically mistaken view about the nature of those relationships. What kind of a friend would I be, after all, if I only looked out for you until something more important came along? What sort of parent would I be if I looked out for my children, but only so long as doing so served the greater good?

There's something too cold and calculating about this approach to personal relationships. To love someone is to care about that person for that person's sake—not as some part of a larger strategy to bring about the greater good. And someone who tells us otherwise ignores the essential role that personal relationships play in our lives. The idea, then, that we shouldn't be partial towards friends and family, doesn't survive scrutiny.

Wee-Bey's Way

We end up back where we began, then. *The Wire*, unsurprisingly, offers us no easy solutions to the Puzzle of Impartiality. It shows us a world in which we suffer both because there is too much and too little partiality.

While this chapter has only skimmed the surface of possible responses to the puzzle it could be the case that there is no solution to the puzzle, no one criterion that we can always use to decide between partiality and impartiality. There are different levels of social organization, and at some levels impartiality applies (like courtrooms), but others where it doesn't (like personal relationships). Or perhaps such things simply need to be decided on a case-by-case basis. That's a horrible thought for philosophers trying to come up with the one, true moral theory, but an unsurprising conclusion for fans of *The Wire*, a show that excels at illustrating the incredible complexities of living a good life.

It is difficult to tell whether or not this specific complexity—partiality versus impartiality—was on the minds of the makers of *The Wire*. But one of the few poignant, do-the-right-thing moments in the series comes from a stone-cold killer who does not, as a general rule, make exceptions for anyone. And the son he makes the exception for is not particularly deserving of it, especially compared to his cohorts in the Boys of Summer gang. Once he makes this decision, however, Wee-Bey never falters.

When Wee-Bey tells De'Londa his decision to let Namond get out of the Game, she's not the least bit happy for her son, and worries about being cut off from her sole remaining source of income. Ultimately, Wee-Bey has to both threaten De'Londa and reassure her about their financial situation to get her to agree to his decision:

> WEE-BEY: Remember who the fuck you talking to right here. Remember who I am. My word is still my word. In here, in Baltimore, in any place you can think of calling home, it'll be my word that finds you. A man come down here to say that my son can be anything he damn please.
>
> DE'LONDA: Except a soldier.
>
> WEE-BEY: Yeah, well look at me, up in here. Who the fuck would want to be that if they could be anything else, De'Londa? Huh?

DE'LONDA: So, you cuttin' me off, too?

WEE-BEY: You still got me. We'll get by. But you gonna let go of that boy. Bet that. ("Final Grades")

De'Londa relents in the face of Wee-Bey's ferocity, and Namond gets his happy ending.

And Wee-Bey? Wee-Bey is a character who does many morally despicable things throughout the five seasons of *The Wire*. But is there any doubt he comes off as the better parent here? The better person?

5
When a Lie Ain't Just a Lie

SEAN MCALEER

"The bigger the lie, the more they believe" says Detective William 'Bunk' Moreland in the opening of Season Five, in which the detectives turn the office photo-copier into a faux lie-detector to get a confession from a streetwise but technologically naive criminal.

The Wire is rife with liars and lying: deceptive police interrogators, cheating spouses, stat-juking bureaucrats, currency-counterfeiting dope fiends, political shakedown artists. And how couldn't it be, given the ubiquity of deception in the human condition *The Wire* so profoundly illustrates?

Consider three long-term projects of deception: Frank Sobotka's shipping arrangements with "the Greeks" at the Port of Baltimore in Season Two, Detective Jimmy McNulty's fabricating a serial killer and Scott Templeton's fabrication at the Baltimore *Sun*, both in Season Five.

Although the question of why lying and other forms of deception are wrong is interesting, we could defer to moral common sense and assume that Sobotka, McNulty, and Templeton act wrongly. Even so, I'm struck by the different degrees of wrongness their actions exhibit: Templeton's actions seem worse than McNulty's, whose are in turn worse than Sobotka's. What explains the difference? The best explanation, I think, is that the actions express different motives, intentions, and character traits, all of which are relevant to evaluating actions. This may seem obvious, but it goes against the grain of much moral philosophy.

Philosophers don't agree about much—you could substitute 'philosophers' for 'Polacks' in Sobotka's quip to his son Ziggy, "Four Polacks, six opinions" and not be far from the truth ("All Prologue"). While they agree that motives help us evaluate character, most philosophers hold that motives are irrelevant to evaluating actions.

John Stuart Mill, for example, tells us in *Utilitarianism* that "the motive has nothing to do with the morality of the action, though much with the worth of the agent" (p. 18). Immanuel Kant, whose views on what makes actions morally right are as different from Mill's as anyone's could be, would agree that motive is irrelevant to the rightness or wrongness of the action performed: the distinction between acting in accordance with duty and acting from the motive of duty is central to his *Groundwork of the Metaphysics of Morals* (the fear-inspiring title that is the closest most undergrads get to the terror felt when a solitary figure whistling "The Farmer in the Dell" appears on a darkened street corner).

Whether we know it or not, most of us join Mill and Kant in separating motive and rightness when we say that the road to Hell is paved with good intentions or that someone has done the right thing for the wrong reasons, as when Frank Sobotka tells Beatrice Russell, "I knew I was wrong. But in my head I thought I was wrong for the right reasons, you know?" ("Bad Dreams").

McNulty thinks that his good intentions justify his fabricating a serial killer, but Kima Greggs's reply—"It ain't right . . . Jimmy, you can't do this"—suggests that his good intentions can't outweigh the inherent wrongness of what he does: the ends (and the motives) don't justify the means ("Clarifications"). I'm not sure I agree with Beadie's reply to Frank, "There are different *kinds* of wrong," but at the very least there seem to be different *degrees* of wrong.

But widespread agreement is not unanimity. Michael Stocker argues that often there is an important connection between people's motives and how we evaluate their actions. For example, an action is malicious—and thereby wrong— because it is motivated by malice. And Steven Sverdlik points out that an action that is otherwise permissible is made wrong when motivated by racism.

Philosophers who are friendly to what's called virtue ethics are more likely to agree with Stocker than with Mill. Virtue ethics, which goes back to Plato and Aristotle, is the view that ethical questions are questions of character rather than duty. Where Mill focuses on consequences and Kant on the action's rational consistency, Aristotle thinks that we should focus on how and why people do what they do: an action is right if a virtuous person would perform the action in the circumstances.

It's not that motive matters for Aristotle but not for Mill and Kant, it's how motive matters: for Aristotle, motive matters for evaluating actions. I think the hows behind the actions of Sobotka, McNulty, and Templeton demonstrate that Aristotle is right.

You're More Like Me than You Know

Major Stan Valchek has finally gotten his petty, petulant, vindictive way (and all over a window for St. Casimir's). Sobotka is perp-walked into an interrogation room to face an array of charges: racketeering and wire fraud, conspiracy to import heroin, and white slavery. Do Sobotka's reasons for doing what he did matter?

The Greek urges him to "go out and spend some of the money on something you can touch. A new car, a new coat. It's why we get up in the morning, right?" ("Duck and Cover"). But Sobotka isn't motivated by new cars or coats. He wants to get the shipping canal dredged and the grain pier re-opened to save his dying union and the community it anchors. He won't use his position to give family members more hours than they have coming to them: "Seniority prevails, Zig. It's the only way to keep it halfway honest . . ." ("All Prologue"). Sobotka acts from a desire to help others and to preserve a way of life under siege by global capitalism, a way of life that he regards as valuable. If robots can move cargo more efficiently than humans, as they do at the port of Rotterdam, then there will be "Robots— piers full of robots!," with nothing left for the Sobotkas, the Tang-drinking Hares, or anyone else who makes a living on the docks ("Backwash").

While some petty pilfering is common enough, theft that threatens the long-term health of the port or Sobotka's plans to revive it, like boosting a load of digital cameras, can't be tolerated: the good of the community trumps the needs of even an out-of-luck family member. Nick needs money, but he can't see the long-term effects of his actions, that shippers will take their business elsewhere if their cargo doesn't get where it needs to go. He tries to defend his actions with the classic *tu quoque* or "you too" move: since Frank did the same sort of thing "back in the day," he's being inconsistent (among the gravest of sins in Kant's ethics) and thus is in no position to condemn Nick's theft. But Nick is neglecting how times have changed and can't see the dissimilarities. "We ain't back in the day, Nicky," Frank says. "When was the last time you saw trucks backed up for three miles outside Patapsco terminal? If it wasn't for the car-ships, we'd be starvin'" ("Hard Cases").

Frank Sobotka is no angel. He doesn't stack up well against his older brother Lou, a retired shipwright who turns down a sinecure on the Port Advisory Board because Frank has "greased" it: "Whatever I got, comes straight," he says, much to his approval-seeking younger brother's exasperation ("Duck and Cover"). Some of Frank's failings are typical, possessed by most of us to some degree, such as the weakness of will he exhibits in not sticking to his decision to break off dealings with the Greeks ("Undertow"). But others are less common and far worse, for example, abetting human trafficking and enabling the horrible deaths of more than a dozen women. While Frank did not intend the deaths of those women, his ignorance of "what was in that motherfucking can" is not innocent. Unlike Spiros, Frank does not regard the women as just another commodity to be smuggled, and he is horrified at their deaths and his complicity. But Spiros reminds him that his ignorance is intentional:

> Now you wanna know what's in the cans? Before you wanted to know nothing. Now you ask. Guns, okay? Drugs, whores, vodka, BMWs. Beluga caviar, or bombs, maybe? Bad terrorists with big nuclear bombs. I'm kidding you, Frank, it's a joke. But you don't ask . . . because you don't wanna know. ("Collateral Damage")

The tragedy of Frank Sobotka is not just that he gets his throat slit and ends up floating in the harbor, or that Ziggy won't survive a prison sentence, or that his wife, whom we never see, sleeps the day away, zonked out on Nembutal. The fullness of the tragedy is that all his good intentions and community-centered motives come to naught: the forces of "progress"—this time in the rotund form of real estate developer Andy Krawczyk, a "greed-head motherfucker," in the words of Nick Sobotka—are "tearing down the Port of Baltimore and selling it to some yuppie assholes from Washington" ("The Dickensian Aspect").

Sobotka's praiseworthy motives don't justify his actions, but they should blunt the sharp edges of moral condemnation: they make his actions less wrong. Denying any role to motive and intention in evaluating his actions doesn't merely make for a simpler moral universe, it makes for an overly simple one.

What the Fuck Did I Do?

Jimmy McNulty is no paragon of virtue: self-destructive, angry, alcoholic; an unfaithful husband, unreliable partner, disloyal subordinate, neglectful father, and all-around pain in the ass. As Sergeant Jay Landsman "eulogizes" him:

> He learned no lessons. He acknowledged no mistakes. He was as stubborn a mick as ever stumbled out of the northeast parishes to take a patrolman's shield. He brooked no authority. He did what he wanted to do and said what he wanted to say. But . . . he was natural police, yes he was. And I don't say that about many people, even when they're here on the felt; I don't give that one up unless it happens to be true. Natural police. But Christ, what an asshole . . . ("—30—")

On its face, McNulty's deception seems similar to Sobotka's: where Sobotka enables smuggling to save the union, McNulty fabricates a serial killer in order to generate the funds needed to do "real police work." Both have laudable ends furthered by wrongful means. But McNulty's project is more motivationally mixed than Sobotka's, his good intentions counter-balanced by more vices and questionable motives than Sobotka's.

McNulty is resentful that the promises that drew him out of a contented existence in the Western District have been broken: "I came back out on a promise," he tells Bunk, "and they're gonna keep that promise. Whether they know it or not" ("Not for Attribution"). This raises the philosophically interesting question of whether one can keep a promise accidentally, without intending to do so or even knowing that one is doing so. But we need not answer this question to see that McNulty's concern for promise-keeping is a rationalization; he's fueled as much by resentment, self-deception, and Jameson as by a desire to see justice done or for any moral concern with promise-keeping.

McNulty, being McNulty, concocts his plan while hung over—indeed, after a trip to the car-trunk for a snort of whisky. Bunk watches, horrified, as McNulty makes an ordinary overdose look like a homicide. Bunk attempts to talk McNulty out of his plan, but his appeals to McNulty's self-interest—"You're going to jail behind this shit, yes you are. You know what they do to police in jail? Pretty police like yourself?"—fall on deaf ears. McNulty, while enormously self-centered, is self-destructive, not self-interested ("Not for Attribution").

McNulty's plan is clever, because McNulty is clever. But we should mind Aristotle's distinction between the intellectual virtue of practical wisdom and cleverness, which is a skill but not a virtue. Practical wisdom is the capacity to deliberate well about how to live a good life. Cleverness, by contrast, lacks this moral dimension; it's the ability to figure out what actions will promote whatever end, good or not. Cleverness is required to "play the Game," or at least to play it well, and some of the gangsters in *The Wire* possess more than just cleverness: Omar has a code; Avon observes the Sunday truce. Marlo, by contrast, is all cleverness: he's relentlessly and ruthlessly efficient in his pursuit of "the crown," but he has no code.

McNulty's repeated insistence that his plan can work is a mark of cleverness: he's smart enough to convincingly fake the murders, but he's blind to the moral questions his conduct raises. Bunk hopes that Lester Freamon, the closest thing to practical wisdom *The Wire* has to offer, can talk some sense into McNulty, but Lester only adds more cleverness to the mix:

No, I mean, if you want to do it right, a straight up strangle's not enough. You're not after some vagrant. Sensationalize it. Give the killer some fucked up fantasy, something bad—real bad. It's got to grip the hearts and minds . . . No, you're onto something. I only need a few weeks to pull down Marlo Stanfield. You fly this mess right, you can give them to me. [*To Bunk:*] Who gives a damn if we fake a coupla murders that we're never gonna solve, huh? The dead men don't care. No one cares. But if it's gonna get the bosses to throw down enough coin to do police work . . . ("Not for Attribution")

The merely clever person cares only about efficiency, whether the means chosen are sufficient to realize the end. The wise person, by contrast, cares about the morality of the plan: that both the end is good and the means employed are permissible.

Being clever, while not a virtue, is not itself a vice. What makes McNulty's cleverness morally problematic is his need to be "the smartest boy in the room" ("Not for Attribution"). The FBI profile of the non-existent serial killer, which pegs him as "not a college graduate [who] feels nonetheless superior to those with advanced education" is spot-on. Lester saw it in Season Three: "A parade? A gold watch? A shining Jimmy-McNulty-day moment, when you bring in a case so sweet that everyone gets together and says: 'Oh shit, he was right all along. We should've listened to the man'" ("Slapstick").

Greggs clearly cares about both the means and the end; with Bunk, she knows that Marlo isn't worth it. And oddly enough, McNulty really agrees with Greggs. When Major William Rawls insists that McNulty get the homeless, psychotic copycat killer to confess to all the "murders," he refuses: "I did what I did. I know. And now I'm standing responsible for two fresh murders. I know what I've done here. But I'm not doing this" ("–30–"). This is not the moment at which McNulty begins to redeem himself; presumably that happened when he came clean to Beadie in a previous episode ("Clarifications"). But it signals the return of his moral vision, his ability to discern or to draw a line between right and wrong. It's instructive to contrast the self-awareness displayed by "I know what I've done here" with the signature line, "What the fuck did I do?" It's as if the question McNulty is perpetually asking, sometimes defensively, sometimes in incredulous quasi-horror, is finally answered.

One of the lessons of *The Wire* is that moral lines aren't sharp or bold or stable. It's easy to lose your way. McNulty reclaims some moral ground by what he is unwilling to do, by the line he won't cross. When Greggs reveals that she blew the whistle on them—"I didn't want to do it behind your back," she tells McNulty and Freamon, "but it had to be done."—McNulty responds, "Detective, if you think it needed doing, then I guess it did" ("–30–"). His moral clarity, even belated, is a redeeming trait.

It's in My Notes, Gus

However psychologically complicated Scott Templeton might be, morally, he's quite simple: he lies because it serves his interests. We meet him after two seemingly unimportant but deeply telling events in the newsroom of the Baltimore *Sun*. The first involves a lesson in the precise meaning of 'evacuate': buildings, not people, get evacuated (unless they're having an enema). "The details, Miss Gutierrez," says rewrite guru Jay Spry. "At the Baltimore *Sun*, God still resides in the details" ("More with Less"). The second concerns a photo of a house fire, with a burnt Barbie doll in the foreground: "No fucking way I believe in this picture," says city editor Augustus 'Gus' Haynes. "Every fire photo he brings, there's got to be a burnt doll somewhere in the debris." Both scenes express the overriding ethic of telling the story, and telling it true. No prettied-up quotes, no artfully staged photos, no inaccurate language.

Our introduction to Templeton is his complaining that Baltimore is "a shit news town" where few "stories go national." This might just be typical office griping, and his reluctance to do some unexciting grunt work, checking background for a late-breaking story, isn't especially noteworthy. But Haynes's giving credit for catching the story of Ricardo "Fat Face Rick" Hendrix's sweetheart real estate deal to the city hall reporter, rather than claiming it for himself, surely is noteworthy. Unlike Haynes, Templeton is concerned with credit: he tells Alma Gutierrez that she should've gotten more credit for her work on the story, noting that "you can't go far on contrib lines," certainly not to the *New York Times* or the *Washington Post*.

The means Templeton uses to realize that goal is to make stuff up. Unable to find a good Opening Day story from the actual fans at Camden Yards, Templeton invents a wheelchair-bound, baseball-loving teen. Haynes is uncomfortable with the story and not just because of the ham-fisted, purple prose; it's unverifiable, and that runs counter to the paper's standards. But executive editor James Whiting overrules Haynes. Miffed that Haynes asks him to get only reaction quotes on the story about Commissioner Ervin Burrell's imminent demise—a story that's been reassigned to his more experienced colleague, Roger

Twigg—we see a pouting Templeton pick up then put down the phone and just start typing. He makes up a quote from City Council President Nerese Campbell that is just too good to be true ("Not for Attribution").

Where McNulty hatches his plan while hung over, Templeton's is sourced in pique, in frustration that he's not the lead reporter on the homeless killings, a story with "legs" enough to advance his career. He calls his own cell phone and starts filling his notebook with a made-up conversation with the non-existent serial killer. Later, challenged by Haynes that he's manufactured a story of witnessing a foiled abduction of a homeless man, Templeton angrily waves his notebook, yelling, "It's in my notes, Gus. Everything that happened, everything that guy said when I got to him, every last word is in my notes" ("–30–").

The notebook, we soon learn, is empty, as Templeton hasn't yet had time to fill it with made-up quotes and events. Templeton appeals to his notes as if they're something objective, rebutting homeless combat veteran Terry Hanning's outrage that Templeton has changed important details of Hanning's story. "I know what it is to tell a story," says Hanning. "I've told plenty in my time. But there's some things that happen, you don't ever fuck with them" ("Clarifications").

Haynes, like Greggs, cares about rules and standards and ethics not for their own sakes, but because he believes that his work matters, and the rules make that work possible. "We have a standard that we follow here," Haynes tells managing editor Thomas Klebanow, justifying his "spiking" an anonymous quote in Templeton's story about a candlelight vigil for the homeless. "We have a sourcing policy here, and I know it. And I do not feel comfortable bending the rules in this instance" ("Clarifications"). Both Whiting and Klebanow are quite willing to ignore those standards when they like a story or think it will advance the paper's chances to win a Pulitzer. Like McNulty, they miss the very point of ethical codes: to rein us in when self-interest might lead us astray.

When McNulty confronts Templeton with his deception, he professes a puzzling inability to understand Templeton's motivations:

> You lying motherfucker, you're as full of shit as I am. And you've got to live with it and play it out as far as it goes, right? Trapped in the

same lie. Only difference is, I know why I did it. But fuck if I can figure out what it gets you in the end. But, hey, I'm not part of your tribe. ("–30–")

In one sense, this is preposterous: what could be easier to understand than naked self-interest, the desire for professional advancement? It's not that he literally can't understand Templeton, but he can't morally understand Templeton's shallow self-interest. Why would anyone think winning a prize is worth such dishonesty?

McNulty's coming clean, to himself and others, is a redeeming feature of his deeply flawed character, as it is for Sobotka's. It makes their deceptions less wrong than Templeton's, who lies when the truth will do and won't come clean to himself or others. "I sent him back out on the street to own his mistake, he comes back with some bullshit about stolen identities," Haynes says of Templeton's being deceived by a source. "I don't give a fuck if he gets took, everybody gets took now and again. It's about not owning up to it" ("Took").

Templeton looks shell-shocked after learning the truth from McNulty, but other than a temporarily upset stomach, he doesn't come to the kind of self-knowledge that McNulty and Sobotka did—perhaps because he doesn't get caught. He looks happy enough as he collects his Pulitzer in the closing montage, and while Haynes might be right that they might have to give it back, no fan of *The Wire* expects to see any such justice done.

When a Lie Is More than Just a Lie

When Terry Hanning tells Templeton "A lie ain't a side of the story. It's just a lie," Hanning has over-simplified ("Clarifications"). McNulty has systematically lied, but there's more to his story than that: he had reasons for lying that complicate the morality of what he did. Ditto for Sobotka. But for Templeton not so much, since there's nothing that could serve to mitigate the wrongness of his actions or complicate our moral assessment of them. There's no union or community to save, no big case to solve or justice to serve. He wants personal advancement, and he's enabled by the equally self-interested Klebanow and Whiting, who relentlessly pursue a Pulitzer Prize as their ticket to a better gig.

The characters, motives, and intentions of Sobotka, McNulty, and Templeton are powerful counter-examples to Mill's claim that motive makes no difference to an action's rightness or wrongness. Their actions are on the wrong side of the line, but they exhibit different degrees of wrongness. They act from different motives and exhibit different character traits. It's not that motive and character are always relevant, but if we're willing to countenance degrees of wrongness, to acknowledge that Templeton's actions are worse than McNulty's and Sobotka's, it's hard to see what could adequately explain that judgment but their different motives and characters.

This makes for a messier moral philosophy than Mill's sharp distinction between motive and rightness. Such a distinction may be desirable in the law, but the law is a bad model for moral philosophy. If certain areas of moral life are vague or messy or context-dependent, we distort morality if we impose on it rigid distinctions.

Call it the Haynes Principle: "I think you need a lot of context to seriously examine anything" ("Unconfirmed Reports"). If we insist that the relative goodness of McNulty's and Sobotka's motives make no difference to the morality of their actions, our moral philosophy will have the virtue of precision but the vice of inaccuracy.

6
Came to Do Good, Stayed to Do Well

JASON GRINNELL

"And when you list the cases, put a little dot next to each one. Deputy likes dots." It's the pilot episode, and Major William Rawls has already shown us a central problem that the characters in *The Wire* face. Everyone has to deal with meddling "bosses."

The bosses pressure them to worry about and fix things that aren't relevant or important, ensuring that things stay broken. There's little connection between quality police work and well-formatted bullet lists, but Rawls's comment suggests that the Deputy Ops worries more about the formatting of the paperwork than the content. The bosses are so obsessed with following the rules that they make it impossible for anyone to do good work.

Eventually, almost everyone falls in line, stops worrying about "doing good," and starts worrying about "doing well." Professional ethics and professional judgment both suffer, along with the chance of things getting better.

This isn't just something that happens in *The Wire*, it's a big part of what many of us deal with every day. We may know what our jobs demand of us and how to do them well, but we still have to submit the paperwork "proving" it. The statistics, reports, and test scores start out reasonably enough, but often end up as the definition of "doing good." Once we start thinking of arrest statistics as proof of good work, it's a short step to thinking that arrest statistics are the same thing as good work. When stats become the goal, we lose sight of professionalism, selling out ethics to the Game.

The Wire shows us what happens when people fall victim to a basic confusion about ethics, rules, and the meaning of success. Most of the characters seem to believe professional success can be reduced to easily identifiable indicators: make your stats, don't go outside the chain of command, keep your scores up, keep the count right, get the votes. If this is not the same thing as "doing good" in a moral sense, then at least it's the key to "doing well"—well enough to keep your job, impress your superiors, and get promoted. And that's what really matters.

Think about the fight over who has responsibility for investigating the dead girl in the harbor: It's not the sort of case that will be solved easily, so it will probably make whoever takes it look bad. Jay Landsman tells Jimmy McNulty: "She's their stat . . . It's all about self-preservation Jimmy. Something you never learned" ("Ebb Tide").

Plato warns us against thinking like this:

> Don't you think that cities that are badly governed behave exactly like this when they warn their citizens not to disturb the city's whole establishment on pain of death? The person who is honored and considered clever and wise in important matters by such badly governed cities is the one who serves them most pleasantly, indulges them, flatters them, anticipates their wishes, and is clever at fulfilling them. (*Republic*, line 426c)

What is Plato talking about? In *Wire* terms, he's talking about the Game. In a corrupt city (or police force, school system, or newsroom), those citizens who are rewarded are those who learn Landsman's lesson: ethics is about pleasing the bosses and self-preservation. Many characters in *The Wire* fit Plato's description, but a few have different goals, which set them at odds with their bosses.

A crucial part of professional ethics is a clear understanding of what our professional purpose really is. If we can do that, then we can ask whether we're accomplishing that goal. Aristotle develops this idea more fully in his *Nicomachean Ethics*, where he argues that ethics is about identifying the purpose or function of being human, and then trying to develop those traits (he calls them "excellences," and they include courage, honesty, and generosity).

While the notion that humans have a central purpose doesn't go over as well today, Aristotle's approach works very well for professional (and even not-so-professional) ethics. We can identify the purpose or function of a longshoreman, as Frank Sobotka shows us when he goes to work a ship and "get clean" after straying so far from his function; a police, as Cedric Daniels, Lester Freamon, and Bunk Moreland explain; and even a "corner boy," as Howard 'Bunny' Colvin has the kids in his project class explain. Only then can we speak meaningfully about the traits that make a longshoreman a good longshoreman, and a police a good police, and a corner boy a good corner boy.

If we understand our professional function correctly, we understand what counts as successful or excellent performance. Many characters in *The Wire* don't seem to have the right understanding of their professions, and so worry far more about things that are trivial or irrelevant. Because they misunderstand their functions, they misidentify what really matters and what counts as being good at their jobs.

Colvin tells us he's tired of those "came to do good, stayed to do well" types ("Home Rooms"), but the switch to "doing well" is understandable. A world in which I can think of myself as a successful police if I can just make a certain number of street arrests, a successful teacher if I can just get my student's test scores up, or a successful mayor if I can just reduce crime by some statistical percentage is easier to understand than one where qualitative assessment is taken into account.

Numbers seem reassuringly objective, and avoid the messiness of things like "professional judgment." On the other hand, pushing myself to do good—do meaningful police work, actually get my students to learn, or genuinely solve problems in my city—might mean my stats don't look as impressive, or that I make others look bad (and as Bill Rawls has taught us, they'll remember!) For many characters in *The Wire*, caught in a flawed system like the one Plato describes, it makes more sense to rip and run.

The Western District Way

"I want good, quick rips. Six, ten, twelve felony cases a month. That means no more long-ass wiretaps, no more subpoenas, no more mincing around on shit. We get on the street and come back with stats!" ("Home Rooms"). Lieutenant Marimow is demanding his detail "rip and run," which is often referred to proudly as "the Western District Way." This fast-paced street-level enforcement of the war on drugs is the dominant culture of the Baltimore Police Department. See someone dealing drugs, "jump out on him," chase him down, and arrest him, ideally as violently as possible. It's exciting, it's active, and whatever paperwork it requires is justified by the action.

The poster boy for the Western District Way is Thomas "Herc" Hauk. For Herc, being police is all about action and power. His lack of discipline and his burning desire for respect repeatedly get him in trouble. Herc prefers to curse at and abuse those he can, lie to those he can't, and protect his own self-interest whenever possible. He has little talent and even less desire to go through the process of gathering information to build a case.

Herc understands his professional function as playing the Game: make "street rips" on drug dealers. As long as he gets credit for enough arrests, he and his superiors will consider him successful. Lieutenant Dennis Mello recognizes that the "Herc" mindset is widespread, and when he sees his officers' disappointment at a new, less aggressive approach being pushed by their commander, he consoles them with: "you still get to kick the shit out of all the mopes that don't move off the corners" ("Dead Soldiers").

A rip-and-run police believes his function is to make as many street-level "rips" as possible, whether or not this has any real effect on crime. Many officers are portrayed as enjoying the beatings they administer. If you serve under bosses like Marimow, coming back with stats will placate your boss, keep you employed, and open a path to promotion. However, while coming back with stats may mean you're doing well, it doesn't mean you're doing good. Good statistical numbers are a side-effect of good police work.

This difference between those who think stats are good police work and those who see them as side effects is at the heart of many of the show's conflicts. When Detective Shakima Greggs is shot, Lieutenant Cedric Daniels even wonders aloud about the gap between his understanding of his profession and Deputy Ervin Burrell's:

BURRELL: Tomorrow, on the six o clock news, we put a lot of fucking dope on the table. A lot of it!

DANIELS: Dope on the table?

BURRELL: We need to let them know who we are. We can't for one minute let them think that this will stand. The Commissioner wants to send a message, Lieutenant. You make sure that you and your people do everything possible to see that it is heard.

DANIELS: [*muttering on his way out the door*] . . . dope on the table . .

FOERSTER: It's like the man said. We're letting them know who we are.

DANIELS: Yeah, and who the hell are we? ("The Hunt")

Daniels is upset about Greggs, but he realizes that an aggressive public response won't accomplish anything. Daniels wants to respond in a way that matters: with a thorough investigation and successful prosecution of those responsible for the shooting. He doesn't see the value of "letting them know who we are" if the charges aren't significant or won't stick. In Aristotle's terms, Burrell has misidentified the function of being a police, and so he thinks of success in terms of showing force, impressing his political bosses, and getting good publicity for the department. Daniels isn't a "come back with stats" police, and this different understanding of his profession means he sees success as making a real difference in crime and getting actual results, whether or not it makes good film for the evening news.

Juking the Stats

As Roland "Prez" Pryzbylewski knows, there's another problem with treating good stats as good work: They can be juked. "All this so we score higher on the state tests? If we're teaching the kids the test questions, what is it assessing in them?" He's told, "Nothing, it assesses us. The test scores go up, they can say the schools are improving, the test scores stay down, they can't" ("Know Your Place"). Prez recognizes this aspect of the Game. Just as at the police department, the schools play the Game of pleasing bosses and doing well, rather than doing good for the students. Meaningful teaching gives way to keeping your job.

Whatever success Prez and Howard 'Bunny' Colvin have in doing good for their students comes in spite of institutional priorities. When Prez follows orders and teaches his students canned responses to test questions, they stop listening. He's even told to keep his windows closed so his students will be drowsy and easier to control. Prez asks: "So it's about the tests?" and is told, "From now until they're done, everything's about the tests" ("Know Your Place").

Prez, like Daniels, gets hit head-on by "doing well" when another teacher informs him of his "true" function: "You don't teach math, you teach the test. North Avenue is all about the No Child Left Behind stuff getting spoon-fed." The looming standardized test "is the difference between the state taking over the schools or not." When Prez says "maybe the state should," it's clear that he has crossed a line with his bosses. He's reminded that he's on the "far side of his evaluation" and another colleague explains that the "first year isn't about the kids, it's about surviving" ("Corner Boys"). We're back to Plato's corrupt organization again, and the warning about not disturbing "the whole establishment, on pain of death."

We see the education version of the Game again when Colvin and Professor David Parenti lobby the superintendent to approve their special class. Despite the possibility of actually reaching the most difficult students in the school while simultaneously allowing their former teachers to be more effective in their classrooms, the superintendent's overriding concern is political: she demands to know if they're insinuating that the system isn't working. When assured that that is not the case, she reluctantly agrees to the program, telling the men to "make sure there is no fuss. Nothing that gets anyone upset" ("Refugees"). Eventually Colvin and Parenti are forced to use their program to "teach to the test" just like everyone else, despite the complete futility of doing so with their students. For the school superintendent there's nothing beyond the Game.

From Red to Green to Black

Bill Rawls is a master of the Game, and when a Colonel from the Maryland State Police points out that the Baltimore Police are much better suited to investigate the death of the girls in the shipping container, Rawls makes his priorities and his sense of his professional purpose clear:

I have fought and scratched and clawed for four months to get my clearance rate up above 50 percent, and right now it stands at exactly 51.6 percent. Do you happen to know what my clearance rate will be if I take thirteen whodunits? 39.4 percent. Hey, we did not get to be Colonels by being complete fucking idiots, right? ("Collateral Damage")

The homicide detectives' version of doing well is to avoid taking on any unnecessary "red" (unsolved) cases, and then to accumulate as much "green" (overtime pay) as possible before turning them "black" (solving them). Do anything else and you're guilty of "giving a fuck when it ain't your turn to give a fuck" ("The Target"). Like Rawls, the entire department worries more about its clearance rate than the fact that a murder has taken place and a killer is still free. A high clearance rate will earn them good reviews from the bosses and promotions, whereas a low clearance rate spells trouble.

There are exceptions. Bunk Moreland seems more concerned with being a real murder police than with ducking bad statistics or turning a case "black" any way possible. His self-conception and sense of purpose allow him to take only so much of the Game. He understands the importance of professional ethics, even when he sees the very different version practiced by Omar Little. When Omar comes to offer himself as witness for the murder of a juror, Bunk is surprised. Omar explains that the murderer, Bird, is out of line. He, Omar, has done many things, but he's never threatened a "citizen." Bunk summarizes Omar's explanation as "A man must have a code" ("One Arrest"). Omar's "profession" and thus his function is very different from Bunk's, and Bunk says it with sarcasm.

Bunk's intolerance for game playing is obvious in Season Three. Bunk has been ordered to stop everything he's doing and pursue a police officer's lost gun. Under great pressure to get the gun, Bunk tolerates this for a while, and eventually produces a ten-page report to appease his superiors. He defiantly tells Landsman: "Jay. I'm a murder police. I've got a double on my plate. I'm going to work it" ("Homecoming"). Bunk can't bring himself to keep hunting for one firearm among the thousands in the city simply because finding it will give the bosses a photo opportunity. Catching murderers is what a murder police does, and Bunk won't sell that out to please his superiors.

We see Bunk's commitment to doing good rather than well again when Marlo frames Omar in Season Four. Detectives Crutchfield and Holley are very happy to have eyewitness testimony, so they can easily turn the red case to black. Bunk, however, knows the witness isn't reliable, and doesn't believe Omar is responsible. Bunk's fellow detectives tell him that the witness identified Omar, and they don't care why he did so; the important thing is that the case is "solved." Bunk has good reason to believe Omar is responsible for other murders, and everyone agrees Omar is no saint, but what's bothering Bunk deeply is that "This ain't him, and that means someone else is walkin' on y'all" ("Corner Boys").

When it becomes apparent that Omar is innocent, they present their revised case file (now red again) to Landsman, who is furious, saying: "Your job is to turn red to black, not the other way." Landsman's anger notwithstanding, Bunk refuses to turn a case black simply for the sake of doing so. He's a murder police, not a come-back-with-stats police, and his purpose is to catch the actual murderer.

Lester Freamon is also committed to being a police (in fact he has earned one of the highest compliments of *The Wire*: he's "natural police"), and when he knows there are murders being committed, he's compelled to look for the bodies. When he finds one in a vacant house (one that will lead to many more), Landsman is even more angry with Lester than he was with Bunk: "Three weeks left in the year, and our unit clearance rate is under fifty percent. We do not go looking for bodies.... We do not put red up on the board voluntarily!" ("That's Got His Own"). Freamon has violated the rules of the Game as played by the homicide unit, where you only deal with those cases you must. Freamon knows this, and knows there will be trouble, but his function is to catch murderers, not to juke the stats.

The Work

So what's the alternative to playing the Game and juking stats? Daniels describes it as "the work," and for the real professionals in *The Wire*, doing the work is their professional function. Remember Daniels's speech to Carver?

Couple weeks from now, you're gonna be in some district somewhere with eleven or twelve uniforms looking to you for everything. And some of them are gonna be good police. Some of them are gonna be young and stupid. A few are gonna be pieces of shit. But all of them will take their cue from you. You show loyalty, they learn loyalty. You show them it's about the work, it'll be about the work. You show them some other kinda game, then that's the game they'll play. . . . Comes a day you're gonna have to decide whether it's about you or about the work. ("Sentencing")

Or as Plato puts it:

When children play the right games from the beginning and absorb lawfulness . . . it follows them in everything and fosters their growth, correcting anything in the city that may have gone wrong before—in other words, the very opposite of what happens when the games are lawless. (*Republic*, 425a)

Daniels and Plato agree that how we're trained and taught is crucial to how we see our function and ethics. Professionals have to be committed to doing good, rather than merely doing well, if we're going to trust them to do their jobs. They also have to be brought up in the right professional culture, so that their judgment is reliable. Focusing on doing good work in an organization devoted to doing well, though, usually gets you in trouble with the bosses who want you to come back with stats.

DANIELS: I'm not devoting my resources to cheap street arrests, Commissioner. Instead, I'm trying to bring every officer I can to bear on making quality felony cases. I could do more, but, well it's my opinion that not enough of the troops I have are sufficiently trained to properly investigate such cases.

BURRELL: Major, you just insulted your command.

DANIELS: Respectfully sir, too many of my people have spent years chasing street-level arrests. Oh, they grab bodies and make stats, but that doesn't teach you how to write a proper warrant, or testify properly as to probable cause, or use and not get used by an informant. I wish it were otherwise, but if I'm chasing felony cases I can only bring a minority of my officers to bear. ("Unto Others")

Daniels will either do meaningful police work or not be police at all. Willing to break the rules of the Game, Daniels goes outside the chain of command, admits there is a problem, and criticizes his superiors. A good Game player wouldn't do such things, but Daniels sees effective police work as his purpose and will defy superiors and risk his career to accomplish some good.

When Prez becomes a middle school math teacher, we see a character developing a grasp of his professional purpose. He's committed to teaching, not simply to being employed, and he's stunned at some of the advice he's given by the veteran teachers. It's clear that teaching isn't what he expected, and he struggles in the classroom.

When the board of education demands a ten-point increase in the scores on the standardized test for all schools, Prez works around his orders. He dutifully teaches language arts material while the area superintendent is in class observing, but as soon as she leaves, out come the dice and more lessons on probability ("Misgivings"). Prez wants to be a good math teacher—to teach math—not to merely provide canned answers in order to help juke the stats. His bosses have confused the purpose of the tests with the purpose of the profession. Adherence to the rules and the juking of stats is not the same thing as being a good teacher.

Hamsterdam and Red Ribbons

Sometimes, of course, even those characters dedicated to the work lose perspective. When Colvin becomes frustrated with what stat-based policing has done to his district, he creates Hamsterdam. He's violating a range of laws, but he thinks it is the only way to really make a difference for the majority of neighborhoods and citizens in his district.

Colvin's commitment to doing good ends up doing a great deal of harm to many. As the Deacon tells him: "No offense, but you're like the blind man and the elephant. It's a lot bigger than what you got your hand on, you just can't see it. . . . A great village of pain and you're the mayor" ("Moral Midgetry"). Although sincere in his desire to be a good police, Colvin sees his professional purpose too narrowly, and is perhaps too willing to sacrifice some for the sake of others. He gets caught up in a different set of numbers—the number of citizens he can help—and losing sight of other crucial elements of being a police: protecting all citizens, and defending the rule of law.

McNulty, too, gets carried away with his zeal to fight crime. His professional judgment is flawed by his single-minded commitment to stopping Marlo, just as he was earlier obsessed with stopping Stringer Bell. Perhaps to an even greater degree than Colvin, McNulty has lost sight of the big picture, and he lacks any humility or respect for the rule of law. McNulty has gone so far in his rejection of stat-based policing that it has undermined his professional judgment. Aristotle tells us that ethics is about striving for excellence in our roles, and that McNulty should strive to do what a good police would do. McNulty's mistake is that he has turned that on its head, and is so sure of himself that he thinks being a good police is doing whatever McNulty would do.

The character ethics approach that asks us to think about our functions can create dilemmas when we play multiple roles and those roles come into conflict. Bunk gets caught in exactly this situation. The ethics of being a good police means he should report (or even arrest) McNulty over the homeless "murders." On the other hand, Bunk thinks one component of friendship is keeping a friend's secrets (McNulty has kept plenty for him, after all). Bunk places his personal ethics above his professional ethics in this case. Greggs is caught in the same bind, but she prioritizes her role as a police above her role as McNulty's friend, and goes to Daniels.

Unless we're prepared to worry only about "doing well," ethical reasoning is complicated and messy. We need good professional and practical judgment to know what's worth pursuing and how best to pursue it, and that good judgment requires that we are well trained in a setting that encourages good ethical reasoning. That's easier said than accomplished.

Same as It Ever Was

The Wire shows us a troubling paradox of society. To be effective, professionals need good mentors to train them and the freedom to do their jobs as they see fit. We have to trust them to be, well, professionals. Ideally, we trust that they know what they are doing, how to do it well, and are dedicated to accomplishing the goals of their professions. That freedom means we rely a great deal on their professional ethics and judgment to guide their conduct.

The downside is we're reluctant to trust them to do the right thing in part because we're not confident we know what the right thing is. Thus, it makes sense to use rules, numbers, and data to describe doing a job properly. In *The Wire*, however, those things designed as tools to help evaluate professionalism can easily take the place of professionalism.

It's all too easy to confuse being good at following the rules and making stats with being good at, and doing good in, our professions. Our attempt to qualify what professionalism means undermines our ability to rely on professional ethics to guide our action.

The characters in *The Wire* who refuse to identify their professional excellence with their reports often do a great deal of good. But trusting the professional judgment of real, flawed, human beings can have its downside. Colvin, McNulty, and Freamon lose their way and make quite a mess. *The Wire* presents us with a fairly stark choice: Attempt to define a profession in terms of stats, rules, and numbers and eliminate true professional excellence, or allow excellence a chance to flourish and accept the possible downside.

While they may not be traditional "good guys," many of the characters who elicit our respect and admiration in *The Wire* are those who have a richer conception of professionalism and professional ethics. They remain committed to doing good, not merely doing well. They play the Game when necessary, but they are about more than the Game, and resist selling out to it completely.[1]

---

[1] I would like to thank John Draeger, John Burnight, and Danielle Morris for their many thoughtful suggestions, helpful comments, and support (and, in the case of Burnight, for recommending I check out *The Wire* in the first place).

LINE 7
Giving a Fuck when It's Not Your Turn

JIM THOMPSON

As Lieutenant Cedric Daniels's newly constituted detail moves into its dank basement quarters, several officers volunteer to help Thomas "Herc" Hauk push a desk through a door. In the comic scene that follows, they struggle manfully—without realizing that the teams on either side of the door are pushing in opposite directions ("Old Cases"). This scene is one of many in *The Wire* that offer funny but telling commentary on modern bureaucracy.

Wrestling the desk is a brilliant metaphor. The word bureaucracy is itself derived from the French word for desk (*bureau*) and the Greek word for rule (*kratos*). Bureaucracy is rule by desks, the papers that sit on the desks, the formal rules and regulations that require the papers, and the people who sit behind the desks that contain them. In *The Wire*, we see police officers at their desks as often as on the street. To their great frustration, they struggle with countless forms and files to keep up with a staggering number of rules, regulations, and demands for documentation. This bureaucracy, as much as anyone's individual depravity, often is the greatest obstacle to justice.

The Chain of Command

We might think bureaucracy a vice peculiar to government and that if we could be free from its heavy hand, we could be free from bureaucracy. Not so. *The Wire* deftly illustrates a thesis by German philosopher and sociologist Max Weber, that the growth of formal institutions and bureaucracy is a hallmark of modern life itself. Bureaucracy reigns not just in government but in any large institution or organization, be it in business, education, journalism, or crime. Avon Barksdale and Stringer Bell aren't successful just because they're tougher than everyone else but also because they run a smart and well-disciplined organization.

Avon and Stringer preside over a hierarchy with set offices and strict rules. When Avon's nephew D'Angelo, in high spirits after his release from detention, is eager to chat about how the Barksdale organization has managed to get him acquitted, an angry Roland 'Wee-Bey' Brice pulls his SUV to the side of the road.

> **WEE-BEY:** Let's walk. What's the rule?
>
> **D'ANGELO:** I know the rule.
>
> **WEE-BEY:** Say it!
>
> **D'ANGELO:** Don't talk in the car. Or on the phone, or anyplace that ain't ours, and don't say shit to anybody who ain't us. But it was just you, yo. It was your fucking truck. [*Wee-Bey glares at him.*] Don't talk in the car. ("The Target")

Other rules of the Barksdale organization are equally strict: No messing with the count, no using the product, no insubordination. Rule-breakers are disciplined, sidelined, or, like the hapless Orlando, shot. When Avon and Stringer suspect that the police are on to them, they "tighten up" by putting stricter rules on themselves.

As with the police, we see Avon and Stringer in their offices more often than on the street. The piles of cash constantly being sorted and counted communicate their success, but also that a successful criminal is as much manager and accountant as thug. In an effort to get his subordinates to think less like gangsters and more like businessmen, Stringer even institutes *Robert's Rules of Order*.

Shit Rolls Downhill

The story is so absorbing that we may overlook *The Wire*'s nuanced portrait of life in modern institutions. Its many comic scenes are matched by others that are purely tragic. Even the humor bites, because *The Wire* reveals an unfair world where people don't get what they deserve. Random events, carefully managed images, political cunning, and patronage often matter more than merit or substance. For all its humor, *The Wire* challenges us to confront soberly how we should live in this world.

Life and work in a modern bureaucracy can be difficult whatever our place in the chain of command. Superiors depend on their subordinates to work hard and make them look good, and subordinates depend on their superiors to reward their efforts. Hence Major William Rawls's fury at Detective Jimmy McNulty for embarrassing him in front of his superior, Deputy Commissioner of Operations Ervin Burrell, by speaking to Judge Daniel Phelan about the Barksdale gang without his knowledge. Avon Barksdale is likewise frustrated with his nephew D'Angelo for not keeping his head in the game and forcing the organization to take extra time, money, and risk to acquit him of a murder he didn't need to commit.

> **AVON:** The first thing you do, you get all emotional. You pull your gun out. You do some dumb shit. And now we gotta work around.
>
> **D'ANGELO:** I know.
>
> **AVON:** Yo, you ain't saying one mother-fucking thing I want to hear.
>
> **D'ANGELO:** You right. You right. I mean, I've gotta start thinking more. You be sayin' that all the time and you right. ("The Target")

The organization is only as good as those who work in it, but organizations don't necessarily reward good work. Because superiors and subordinates are exposed to each other's successes and failures, political cunning and personal loyalty can matter more than actual merit.

It helps to have a patron. Avon doesn't tolerate D'Angelo's sloppiness simply out of familial affection but because he trusts family. He counts on D'Angelo's loyalty to his family. Robert Jackall observes (in *Moral Mazes*) that something like the hierarchy of medieval feudalism re-emerges in modern bureaucracy, but without feudalism's stability. We can move up or down in a modern bureaucratic organization at any time, based on whim or chance. Or the structure of the organization can change suddenly. For the ambitious, angling for promotion and staving off demotion are constant parts of the Game.

The system isn't fair. Jackall observes that, in the hierarchy of modern bureaucracy, credit flows up and responsibility flows down. People lower down in the hierarchy have to accept whatever is given to them from above. In a comic scene that masterfully distills a major theme, Herc puts it simply: "It's the chain of command, baby. The shit always rolls downhill" ("The Target").

In another vignette, D'Angelo teaches Malik 'Poot' Carr and Wallace the ways of the world, after Wallace says the genius who invented the Chicken McNugget must be a millionaire.

> **D'ANGELO:** Please. The man who invented them things is just some sad ass down in the basement of McDonalds, thinking up some shit to make some money for the real players.
>
> **POOT:** Nah, man, that ain't right.
>
> **D'ANGELO:** Fuck right. It ain't about right. It's about money. Now do you think Ronald McDonald is going to go down in that basement and say, "Hey Mister Nugget, you the bomb. We sellin' chicken faster than you can tear the bone out, so I'm going to write my clowny-ass name on this fat-ass check for you?" The n— who invented those things is still workin' in the basement for regular wage, thinkin' of some shit to make the fries taste better, or some shit like that. Believe.
>
> **WALLACE:** Still had the idea, though. ("The Detail")

Those at the bottom of the hierarchy receive credit for their work only if their superiors deign to give it to them. D'Angelo reinforces the point when he teaches Wallace and Preston 'Bodie' Broadus to play chess. Wallace asks, "How do you get to be the king?" D'Angelo responds, "It ain't like that. . . . The king stay the king." As for those at the bottom, "The pawns get capped quick. They be out of the game early" ("The Buys").

It's the Message

If they don't want to be sacrificed like pawns, astute players must be concerned about their place in the hierarchy. Success isn't just about doing good work. It's also about communicating loyalty and strength.

On the street, the message can be simple and brutal. A well-placed corpse, like the body of William Gant after he testified against D'Angelo Barksdale, the body of Omar's partner Brandon after they raided a Barksdale stash house, the bodies of 'Junebug', his wife, and his bodyguard after he insulted Marlo Stanfield, sends a message to not snitch, steal, or speak against those in power.

In the police department, an exquisitely cruel demotion, like Lester Freamon to the pawnshop unit, Jimmy McNulty to the boat, and Cedric Daniels to evidence control, sends the message not to cross your superior. D'Angelo Barksdale is himself demoted for his mistake from the high-rise tower at 221 West Fremont to the low-rise 'Pit'. He's spared a worse fate only because he's family. When D'Angelo balks at beating an addict for passing counterfeit bills, Stringer Bell reminds him:

STRINGER: It's all in the Game.

D'ANGELO: I'm saying it was only a couple dollars. . . .

STRINGER: It ain't the money.

D'ANGELO: We fucked him up so bad. . . .

STRINGER: Yeah. It's the message, D'. You can't show no weakness.
   ("The Target")

Officer Shakima Greggs is shot during an ill-advised "buy-bust" operation that was pressured on Daniels by his boss, Burrell, who was pressured by his boss, Commissioner of Police Warren Frazier, who was pressured by his boss, Mayor Clarence Royce. In response to the shooting, Frazier demands that his subordinates make high profile arrests and put "dope on the table" ("The Hunt"). His aim is to send a message to the public and to his political patrons. For Frazier, Burrell and other political actors, the move is entirely rational.

Frazier proudly declares at the ensuing press conference that his department has sent a powerful message to the drug dealers. But Daniels and those in his unit close to the streets know that the symbolic raids are premature. In fact, they have exposed their unit's careful surveillance of the Barksdale organization and are likely to allow those responsible for the shooting to escape justice. Though politically useful for those in charge, the raids betray the department's mission to protect the city and quell the violence.

This complex case is one of many examples in *The Wire* of how bureaucracies go wrong. Here it's due to aloof and cynical players, like Frazier and Burrell, who have lost touch with the substance of the institutions they lead. But even without cynicism or ill will, the incentives put before people in large bureaucratic institutions are often unintentionally perverse. As Detectives William 'Bunk' Moreland and Jimmy McNulty repeatedly remind each other, it doesn't pay to give a fuck when it ain't your turn to give a fuck.

The art of self-preservation, of deflecting responsibility for errors and claiming credit for successes, is as important to their careers as doing real police work. Decisions that make sense for one person or group, or even for the organization as a whole, like "dope on the table," may run counter to the institution's mission. Ultimately, some institutions take on a life of their own and cease to pursue their stated goals at all.

The Game Remains the Same

For Rawls, Baltimore's murders are reduced to index cards and clearance rates. When a young woman is found floating face-down in Baltimore Harbor, followed by thirteen more in a shipping container on the docks, a fight breaks out among the authorities over proper jurisdiction. No one wants the paperwork or the responsibility. Newly promoted Colonel Rawls puts it most precisely: if the Baltimore Police Department has to investigate the murders, it will lower his clearance rate for the year from 51.6 percent to 39.4 percent ("Collateral Damage").

'The Greek' and his fellow traffickers also grieve in numerical terms. For them, each woman represented a potential revenue stream of $250,000–$500,000 per year. McNulty's response is more ambiguous. He feels the human tragedy of the fourteen young women, but he also welcomes the opportunity to prove his prowess as a detective and exact revenge on Rawls by forcing him to take the case.

Paradoxically, the very attempt to get beyond appearances to scientific, quantitatively accurate data can distort both our perception and our incentives. The process of applying standard, formal, routine measures to social interactions may drain them of their substance and their humanity. The women found at the dock and in the harbor aren't the only ones reduced to their role in a system. By creating formal offices, standard procedures, and quantifiable measurements, modern bureaucracies make the people who inhabit them interchangeable, and thus disposable. We become "human resources" for organizations and institutions that have taken on a life of their own. Against our will, they no longer serve us. We serve them.

The Wire poignantly shows how difficult it is to break free from the circumstances and institutions that entrap us. We're encouraged to admire rather than pity those who fight against the odds, and wonder how we would fare in similar circumstances. When we see D'Angelo, Wallace, Bodie, and Poot hang out in the Pit, we admire their ability to negotiate a harsh world with resilience. They're decent young men put into an indecent system, with a remarkable ability to fashion a meaningful life with some semblance of community, even as they have been abandoned by society at large and, in some cases, their own families. Constrained by their fate, they aren't determined by it, attempting to take charge of their lives. We ache for Randy Wagstaff and Duquan 'Dukie' Weems, who fail because they are failed by the adults and institutions who are supposed to protect them.

The Wire's commentary on the absurdity of modern bureaucracy has the pathos of ancient tragedy. At the end of five seasons, many of the characters who we have come to care about are dead, but the institutions and forms of life in West Baltimore remain the same. Warren Frazier and Ervin Burrell are retired, but the new police commissioner, Stan Valchek, is another political hack. Avon Barksdale and Marlo Stanfield are out of the Game, but their deputies have taken their places. Bubbles overcomes addiction, but Dukie succumbs. Omar Little is dead, but Michael Lee fills the void. The Game persists.

Giving a Fuck

The Wire's unflinching, unflattering portrait of our world evokes cynicism, despair, and outrage. The appropriate response isn't jaded complacency but disciplined resistance to the injustice of it all. Our world shouldn't be like this and doesn't have to be.

Omar Little is among the most admirable players of the Game. Smart, strong, and fearless, he follows a strict moral code, robbing only drug dealers and never putting his gun on a "citizen" or "taxpayer." Omar is one of the few characters to best cynical attorney Maurice Levy, during a cross-examination in Marquis 'Bird' Hilton's murder trial.

> LEVY: You are amoral, are you not? You are feeding off the violence and the despair of the drug trade. You're stealing from those who are themselves stealing the lifeblood from our city. You are a parasite who leeches off the culture of drugs.
>
> OMAR: Just like you, man.
>
> LEVY: Excuse me, what?
>
> OMAR: I got the shotgun. You got the briefcase. It's all in the Game, though, right? ("All Prologue")

At least Omar is honest about who he is. Unlike Levy, he accepts risk and responsibility for what he does. But when Omar tries to tell Bunk Moreland that the police don't really care about the death of a member of his crew, Bunk explodes.

> OMAR: Shit, the way y'all look on things, ain't no victim to even speak on.
>
> BUNK: Bullshit, boy. No victim? I just came from Tosha's people, remember? All this death, you don't think that ripples out? You don't even know what the fuck I'm talking about. I was a few years ahead of you at Edmondson. But I know you remember the neighborhood. How it was. We had some bad boys for real. . . . Them hard cases would come up to me and say, "Go home, school boy, you don't belong here." Didn't realize at the time what they were doing for me. As rough as the neighborhood could be, we had us a community. . . . Makes me sick, motherfucker, how far we done fell. ("Homecoming")

For Bunk, life and death are not a game.

Although McNulty vainly wants to be the best cop in Baltimore, in his better moments he also knows that the Game is more than a game. The crime and suffering are real, often inflicted on those who least deserve it. As with Bunk, Jimmy's destructive drinking and womanizing seem to be a response to the futility of his job. He carries around a picture of one of the women found at the docks for months, partly in an attempt to locate her family, but mostly as a reminder of her humanity. When the morgue finally releases her body as a Jane Doe, McNulty complains, "It ain't right, Doc." The medical examiner responds, "What the fuck ever is?" ("All Prologue"). McNulty tears up the picture during a drinking session with Bunk. His relationship with Beadie Russell improves only when he sets aside his obsession with work.

Like Moreland and McNulty, the admirable characters in *The Wire* hold themselves, their colleagues, and the institutions where they live and work to a higher standard. These characters realize that rules and principles matter. For all their potential absurdity, forms and regulations can also guard human integrity and hold institutions to account.

Editor Augustus "Gus" Haynes recalls an era when the Baltimore *Sun* had an attribution policy so strict that it wouldn't print a quotation without the speaker's middle initial. The policy might seem like a bureaucratic absurdity, conceived by a boss removed from the reality of a reporter's job, but the policy had a serious point. It honored accuracy and truth as the goals of journalism. Vice always starts small, as Haynes notes when he confronts his boss, managing editor Thomas Klebanow, about reporter Scott Templeton:

HAYNES: We cannot run this shit.

KLEBANOW: Are you suggesting that Scott made any of this up?

HAYNES: You ever notice the guys who do that—the Blairs, the Glasses, the Kelleys—they always start with somethin' small. You know, just a little quote that they clean up, and then it's a whole anecdote, and pretty soon they're saying some amazing shit. They're the lucky ones who just happen to be standing on the right street corner in Tel Aviv when the pizza joint blows up and the human head rolls down the street with the eyes still blinking. ("–30–")

Klebanow, however, is more interested in circulation, advertising, and the potential for a Pulitzer Prize than reporting the truth. The story runs.

. . . When It Ain't Your Turn

Haynes is demoted for his effort to uncover the truth, while Templeton wins a Pulitzer for his lie. *The Wire* is clear that we can't expect justice for those who stand up for what is right. Often, their only reward is to maintain their integrity and self-respect. As Butchie observes to Omar, "Conscience do cost" ("Back Burners").

Many characters in *The Wire* face defining moments when they must weigh that cost. Some must decide how to live with themselves if they cross an ethical line or fail to stand up for what's right. Others struggle to redeem themselves from errors already committed. Some must do both at once. Former gang member 'Cutty' Wise reaches that moment when he finds he can no longer pull the trigger even on a drug dealer who has cheated him. As he tells Avon Barksdale, "Whatever it is in you that let's you flow like you flow and do that thing? It ain't in me no more. . . . The Game ain't in me no more. None of it" ("Homecoming").

Likewise, when Brianna Barksdale asks D'Angelo if he is ready to step up and fill Avon's shoes, he replies, "Ma, you know I ain't. I ain't ready, and I ain't never going to be ready for this Game" ("Sentencing"). At her urging, he agrees to take a twenty-year sentence for his family, but he wants nothing more to do with them.

On the police force, the moment comes in different ways for Cedric Daniels, Ellis Carver, and Jimmy McNulty. Daniels faces an ongoing conflict between his ambition and his integrity. He learns to love his job, but must constantly risk his career to put real police work ahead of political games. At a crucial juncture for his career and his marriage, he has to decide whether or not to accept responsibility for investigating the fourteen dead women found at the harbor. He tells his wife, "I love the job, Marla." Dismayed, she responds, "The job doesn't love you" ("Backwash"). In the end, Daniels gives up the ultimate professional prize of being Commissioner of Police, and his hopes of reforming the department, because his professional integrity won't let him juke the stats.

DANIELS: I'll swallow a lie when I have to. I've swallowed a few big ones lately. But the stat games, that lie, it's what ruined this department. Shining up shit and calling it gold, so majors become colonels and mayors become governors, pretending to do police work while one generation fucking trains the next how not to do the job, and then. . . . Well, this is the lie I can't live with. . . .

MARLA: The tree that doesn't bend, breaks, Cedric.

DANIELS: Bend too far and you're already broken. ("–30–")

All the Pieces Matter

As Daniels warns Carver before his upcoming promotion, "There comes a day you're going to have to decide whether it's about you or it's about the work" ("Sentencing"). Daniels knows that Carver has "earned" his promotion to the rank of sergeant in part by providing Burrell information about Daniels's unit behind his back. He also knows that Carver and his partner Herc have been less than scrupulous about the professional standards of police work. Gradually, however, Carver learns the lesson. In a poignant moment Herc attempts to persuade him against writing up hot-headed officer Anthony Colicchio, who refuses to apologize for dragging a teacher out of his car. Herc pleads with his friend:

HAUK: He fucked up. He knows this. He's proud. He doesn't want to beg. . . . Come on Carv, you cannot do one of your own guys . . .

CARVER: I never told you, Herc. Never said a fucking word. But when I gave you that kid to debrief last year, on what's-his-face, you were supposed to get him to Bunk Moreland. You remember that?

HAUK: Yeah. I fucked up. So what?

CARVER: So it mattered.

HAUK: So what the fuck does this have to do with Colicchio?

CARVER: It all matters. I know we thought that it didn't, but it does. ("Transitions")

Having seen the consequences of what might seem like a small mistake, Carver no longer sees the rules and regulations as stupid, bureaucratic obstacles. When Greggs faces a similar choice about whether or not to report McNulty, Carver tells her that the decision to report Colicchio felt like shit, but he had no choice.

Even the wayward McNulty comes to see that it all matters. From the start, he is impatient with the bureaucracy. He's harsh even on his allies if they compromise with the system in order to get things done. Even more than Daniels, he repeatedly risks his career to put the substance of his work first. Hence the ongoing joke between McNulty and Bunk, "There you go again, giving a fuck when it ain't your turn to give a fuck" ("The Target").

To Bunk's disgust, however, McNulty crosses a line when he fabricates evidence of a serial killer to increase the money flowing into the homicide unit. At first, McNulty enjoys being able to dole out resources to colleagues who need them. But the decision comes back to haunt him. To his surprise, he quickly finds himself forced to make the same sort of compromises that he has long despised in his superiors. After negotiating with Detective Crutchfield on how much support he can provide, McNulty begins to explain how to fudge the paperwork.

> **CRUTCHFIELD:** It's cool. I know the drill.
>
> **McNULTY:** You do?
>
> **CRUTCHFIELD:** You're doing good here, boss.
>
> **McNULTY:** What did you just call me? ("Took")

Worse, McNulty sees time and effort squandered on searching for the fictitious killer, and he learns that the parents of one of his "victims" are traumatized by the false report of sexual mutilation.

Keeping Down the Devil

In the end, McNulty's transgression costs him his career. He's lucky to escape prison, while his target Marlo Stanfield walks free. But his greatest punishment seems to be his own remorse and self-loathing. In a moment of truth, he angrily admits the lie to reporter Scott Templeton, who has also contributed to it, and profited from it. Astonished, Templeton protests, "You're not serious. . . ." McNulty confesses, "No. I'm a fucking joke, and so are you" ("–30–").

Like Daniels and Carver, McNulty ultimately discovers a line he won't cross. In a move that baffles and infuriates his old nemesis, William Rawls, now acting commissioner, McNulty refuses to pin the fake murders on a deranged copycat:

> **RAWLS:** If he's NCR, what the fuck is the difference if he cops to two or six? Either way, they tie his arms and feed him green Jello.
>
> **McNULTY:** Sir, he did the last two.
>
> **RAWLS:** Motherfucker. You are a cunt hair away from indictment and you see fit to argue with me?
>
> **McNULTY:** I did what I did. I know. And now I'm standing responsible for two fresh murders. I know what I've done here, but I'm not doing this. ("–30–")

If *The Wire* is a bitter, absurdist critique of modern institutional bureaucracy, a tragic lament for the pointless suffering it creates, an angry rage against the injustice of it all, it is also a testament to moments of self-knowledge and resistance such as these. The only escape from the iron cage of futility and absurdity in modern institutional life, the only way to keep the devil down in the hole, is for people to stand up, even when it ain't their turn. To remember our common humanity and hold each other to account. To remember that all the pieces matter.[1]

[1] I'm grateful to my wife and colleague Dr. Julie Marie Meadows for extensive collaboration on this chapter.

LINE 8
What if Nobody Walks the Straight and Narrow Track?

DON FALLIS

FREDERICKS: If Marnell say I had the gun, he lying.

LANDSMAN: The machine tells the tale, son.

BUNK: We ready, professor? We'll start with an easy one. Is your name in fact DeShawn Fredericks?

FREDERICKS: Yeah.

NORRIS: True.

BUNK: And do you reside in fact on the 1200 block of Woodyear Street in West Baltimore?

FREDERICKS: Yeah.

NORRIS: True.

BUNK: And did you and Marnell shoot your boy Pookie down on Cary Street just like Marnell said you did?

FREDERICKS: Naw. No.

NORRIS: Lie. You lying motherfucker.

BUNK: Tch, tch, tch.

LANDSMAN: Machine is never wrong, son.

FREDERICKS: Fuck, man! Nigger can't never keep his damn mouth shut. I should've busted a cap in Pookie ass my own self. ("More with Less")

Baltimore's West Side (at least as depicted in *The Wire*) is full of liars. Pretty much everyone is willing to lie if they think it

97

will be advantageous. The perps lie to the cops, the cops lie to perps, and each lies to their own.

When D'Angelo Barksdale asks his uncle how the spiked heroin got into the prison, Avon Barksdale says, "Look, man, I ain't had nothing to do with it" ("Hard Cases"). Russell "Stringer" Bell tells Omar Little that it was Brother Mouzone who tortured Brandon before killing him. While Marquis "Bird" Hilton did kill William Gant, Omar lies on the witness stand about witnessing the event. Bird is right on all counts when he leaps up and shouts at Omar, "You're a lying cocksucker, man" ("All Prologue").

And you don't have to be in West Baltimore to lie. Detective Jimmy McNulty tells his colleagues that he is chasing a serial killer of homeless people. Detectives Hauk and Carver lie to Lieutenant Daniels about their informant, Fuzzy Dunlop. This treatment is no more than Daniels deserves as he had previously instructed them on how to lie to Internal Affairs after their disastrous late-night visit to the high-rises.

It's not like cops and drug dealers have cornered the market. Witnesses often perjure themselves in *The Wire*, as when the dockworkers (hailing from east of downtown) lie to the grand jury, despite Detective Ray Cole's warning that "you lie to us, you hurt our feelings, you lie to them it's perjury" ("Undertow"). Even downtown lawyers lie, as when Maurice Levy claims that he is only representing Preston "Bodie" Broadus because "my firm is making it a priority to identify a number of city youths who are in crisis, and to undertake efforts to reorder their lives" ("The Wire").

Scott Templeton lies to readers and editors of the Baltimore *Sun*. After failing to get a good interview for opening day at the ballpark, he makes up a story about a handicapped orphan skipping school to attend the game. In fact, he then has to tell several other lies to cover up that lie, falling victim to Friedrich Nietzsche's warning in *Human, All Too Human*, "He who tells a lie seldom realizes what a heavy burden he has assumed; for, in order to maintain a lie, he has to invent twenty more" (p. 40).

Having fooled young Fredericks into confessing, Detective "Bunk" Moreland quips to his fellow detectives, "the bigger the lie, the more they believe" ("More with Less," Season Five). And thus, *The Wire*'s writers implicate all of us in the universe of lies.

Kant on the Streets of West Baltimore

The existence of the world of unbridled deception depicted in *The Wire* conflicts with Immanuel Kant's claim that universal lying is an impossibility. Now, it is certainly possible for some people to lie. As Kant was well aware, most of us do it a little, and some of us do it a lot. But Kant thought that such lying is only possible because it happens relatively infrequently. We are able to lie because most of the time people tell the truth.

In his *Foundations of the Metaphysics of Morals*, Kant asks us to imagine what would happen if everyone lied whenever it was to their advantage to mislead. In that case, no one would believe what anyone else said. If nobody was going to believe you, there would be no point in lying. So, Kant concludes that 'Lie whenever it is to your advantage to mislead' is a rule that "would necessarily destroy itself as soon as it was made a universal law" (p. 19).

This seems like a pretty plausible argument that it is not possible for *everyone* to follow this rule. And yet a whole lot of successful lying goes on in *The Wire*. Almost all of the characters in *The Wire* lie whenever it is to their advantage to mislead. If Kant's right, why hasn't their practice of lying self-destructed?

Princeton philosopher David Lewis goes even further in his *Philosophical Papers*, arguing that for communication to be possible at all, we have to tell the truth at least half the time. Lewis concludes that it is not possible for there to be "a population of inveterate liars who are untruthful more often than not" (p. 182). But *The Wire* certainly seems to be a counterexample to that claim.

Now, at this point, you might be wondering why philosophers are so interested in whether or not it is possible for everybody to lie whenever it is to their advantage to mislead. It turns out that Kant thinks that it's wrong for us to do something if we can't rationally intend that everyone do the same thing in similar circumstances. And we can't rationally intend something that's impossible. So, Kant thinks that lying is wrong if universal lying is impossible.

However, imagine that Felicia "Snoop" Pearson, shows up at your door looking for your kid brother. You could reasonably assume that Snoop is planning to kill your brother because, say, there's a rumor going around that he's been talking to the police. If everyone always lied to Snoop in such circumstances, then Kant might be right and it would be futile for you to lie to her now (since she won't believe anything anyone says in such circumstances). However, not everyone does lie to Snoop in such circumstances. So, it might be possible for you to save your brother's life by lying to Snoop about where he is. Why would it be wrong to do so? Unlike a Kantian, a utilitarian (that is, someone who thinks that we should do whatever will bring about the most happiness) would certainly recommend lying to save the kid's life. But before we start worrying too much about this, is Kant right that universal lying is impossible?

Trying to Negotiate a Truce

While *The Wire* seems to be a counter-example to Kant's claim that universal lying is impossible, maybe there is some respect in which, much like the interests of the members of the New Day Co-Op, the views of David Simon and Kant actually coincide. In other words, maybe this conflict between *The Wire* and Kant can be resolved.

Even Kant would have to concede that, if everyone lied whenever it was to their advantage to mislead, people could still go around spouting falsehoods. Kant's claim is only that there would be no point in their doing so. In other words, he argues that universal lying is impossible for a bunch of rational beings. But maybe the characters in *The Wire* are just irrational, believing what other people say even when there's good reason not to. Or maybe they're irrational in that they tell lies even when there's no chance anybody will believe what they say. However, that can't be what's going on. While the characters in *The Wire* are complex people who can be counted on to do some bad things, they're all pretty savvy (with exceptions like Snot Boogie proving the rule).

Another way we might resolve the conflict is to remember that *The Wire* is just a fiction and impossible things happen in fiction. That might have been a reasonable thing to say if I had offered up *Game of Thrones* as a counter-example to Kant's claim. However, David Simon is clearly striving to capture reality in a way that George R.R. Martin is not. So, is the world depicted in *The Wire* a real possibility? In other words, is Kant wrong about the impossibility of universal lying?

Nothing but the Truth

Oxford philosopher Derek Parfit argues in *On What Matters* that Kant's wrong. According to Parfit, even if everyone lied whenever it's beneficial, there'd still be situations where it would be of greatest benefit to tell the truth. If people sometimes tell the truth, we can't be sure that they're lying on any given occasion. People would retain the ability to deceive. Thus, there would still be a point to their lying to us.

Consider Reginald "Bubbles" Cousins. He certainly lies when it's to his advantage. In fact, he even teaches Johnny Weeks how to deceive more effectively. However, after Shakima Greggs is shot while working undercover, the cops pick up Bubbles because they think that he might be involved. But he says truthfully, "Look, I didn't do shit here" ("The Hunt"). So, Bubbles can lie successfully because people have to allow for the possibility that he may be telling the truth.

But while Parfit shows it's possible for us to lie if it would benefit us, he has to assume that we are often better off telling the truth, that we usually have no motivation to lie. This may be a fairly safe assumption even in *The Wire*. After all, Omar has a lot of opportunities to say, "True dat" and "No doubt."

But what if we are talking about a situation where people always have a motivation to mislead? Then nobody should believe what anybody says on the off chance that they might be speaking the truth this time. So, it looks like Kant is at least right that lying is futile in such situations. However, characters in *The Wire* sometimes find themselves in exactly this sort of situation. And contrary to what Kant predicts, they lie and deceive. Let's consider the drug dealer.

Putting Out Shit and Calling It Pandemic

STRINGER: What are the options when you've got an inferior product in an aggressive marketplace?

PROFESSOR LUCAS: Well, if you have a large share of the market you buy up the competition.

STRINGER: And if you don't?

PROFESSOR LUCAS: Reduce price and increase market share.

STRINGER: That assumes low overhead.

PROFESSOR LUCAS: Of course. Otherwise you operate at a loss. And worse, as your prices drop, your product eventually loses consumer credibility. You know, the new CEO of WorldCom was faced with this very problem. The company was linked to one of the largest fraud cases in history. So he proposed . . .

STRINGER: To change the name.

PROFESSOR LUCAS: Exactly. ("Undertow")

While the primary business portrayed in *The Wire* is the distribution of illegal narcotics, Stringer Bell's experience in his community college economics classroom demonstrates to him that the practices that work in the world of the legitimate marketplace also work in his. Yellow tops become blue tops become red tops. Death grip becomes pandemic becomes dark horse.

Drug dealers like Stringer always have a motivation to mislead their customers (and they succeed in doing it). In order to create more product (and more profit), drug dealers typically cut their heroin with some percentage of baking soda. In fact, in the second season of *The Wire*, the Barksdale organization has lost its connect. They're getting product from Atlanta, but it's already "been walked on. Each one weaker than the other" ("Undertow"). In other words, the purity of the heroin is much less than what is typically found on the street. Thus, Stringer is *highly motivated* to deceive his customers about the quality of his product.

On the face of it, cutting heroin with baking soda certainly seems like a deceptive practice. But the dealers might argue that they are not really lying to their customers because everyone knows street heroin is not pure but is cut with baking soda, milk powder, or some other white powder. In fact, the dealers might claim that they are actually doing the user a favor as, according to *Encyclopædia Britannica*, "the unwitting injection of relatively pure heroin is a major cause of heroin overdose."

As Bubbles learns the hard way, however, some drug dealers are selling *pure* baking soda. Using a fishing line from a roof top during one of his capers, Bubbles steals a drug dealer's stash out of an old tire. But when Johnny shoots up, it becomes clear that the vials contain only baking soda. (Hard work gone to hell.) That drug dealer was definitely trying to deceive his customers.

During the second season, most of the dealers on the West Side are selling mainly baking soda because Stringer is "cutting shit with shit right now, trying to cheat" ("Undertow"). String talks to his business class prof, and uses a little rebranding to further deceive the hard-working fiends. When he explains this to his crew, we find that they also understand basic marketing principles; no surprise there, as they have been marketed to their entire lives.

Addiction means the benefit of getting high (or the cost of failing to get high) is, well, high. Thus, fiends are willing to buy from drug dealers even if there is a chance that they won't get much heroin. If there's not much chance that they'll get any heroin, fiends will be highly motivated to identify the drug dealers who are really selling heroin. But the demand for heroin is so high that a lot of dealers can get away with selling a lot of baking soda.

In order for this situation to develop, there did have to be a time in the past when most drug dealers sold heroin. The business would not have gotten off the ground in the first place if everybody was just selling baking soda. But once the drug dealing business has gotten started, there can be quite a bit of baking soda on the market.

In fact, this is where Lewis makes his mistake. In order for "I'm innocent" to mean what it means, there did have to be a time in the past when people, at least for the most part, only said it when they really were innocent. If people only ever said, "I'm innocent," when they were guilty, the phrase would not mean what it now does. It would mean "I'm guilty." But once it has the meaning that it actually has, a whole lot of guilty people can lie by saying, "I'm innocent."

But there's a limit to how much baking soda you can sell, calling it heroin. At least a few drug dealers have to tell the truth and sell real heroin. Suppose that all drug dealers on the West Side were to always sell pure baking soda. At that point, even the most desperate fiends would stop buying it. As Prop Joe told Stringer, you'd have, "half the West Side coming over the Fallsway twice a day because Eastside dope be kicking the shit outta Westside dope." This is why Stringer's deception ultimately falls apart. Eventually, "every dope fiend in the city knows that Avon been putting out piss, calling it shit" ("Backwash").

Kant himself foresaw the possibility that universal lying might occur in the short term. For instance, he writes that "it would be futile to make a pretense of my intention in regard to future actions to those who would not believe this pretense or—if they overhastily did so—who would pay me back in my own coin" (p. 19). Kant is just claiming that universal lying cannot persist.

Wrapping Up the Case

I could lie to you and claim that everybody in *The Wire* lies whenever it is to their advantage to mislead. But to be honest, there are at least a few exceptions. Even though telling the truth gets him killed, Gant identifies D'Angelo as the person that shot "Pooh" Blanchard. Also, despite Bunk encouraging her to lie so that it will be easier to get a conviction, Greggs refuses to claim that she can positively identify Roland "Wee-Bey" Brice as one of the people who shot her. As she laments, "Sometimes things just got to play hard" ("Sentencing"). Thus, West Baltimore (at least as depicted in *The Wire*) can't serve as a counter-example to Kant's claim that universal lying is an impossibility. But if we imagine a world very much like West Baltimore where everybody does lie whenever it is to their advantage to mislead (and where everybody always has a motivation to mislead), then it looks like Kant is right that lying is futile. It is just not possible for nobody to walk the straight and narrow track.[1]

[1] I would like to thank David Bzdak, Tony Doyle, Terry Horgan, James Mahon, Kay Mathiesen, Alan Mattlage, Bill Taylor, and Seth Vannatta for helpful suggestions on this chapter.

Third Case

Omar Comin'

LINE 9
Is Omar the Nietzschean Overman?

SCOTT CLIFTON

The marketplace of drugs. The low-rises. The pit. "Got your yellow tops!" Thin drug addicts stumble their way to young black men, who take their wrinkled tens and twenties. A signal sent to the runners—boys waiting fifty feet away who run over, small vials in hand. The cops staked out atop a nearby building, hoping to get a photo of a kingpin on a random visit to the frontlines, are on break and not watching.

Enter a man in a trench coat, carrying a sawed-off shotgun. Whistling "The Farmer in the Dell," flanked by two accomplices, he approaches the stash house, an abandoned apartment where the large reserve of drugs is kept. The trio enters the house. He orders the five or six inside to get their hands up. He aims the shotgun at one. "Hey, yo, where it at?" he asks. The man refuses to say. He blasts him in the kneecap. The injured man's screams convince one of the others to tell him where the stash is. The trenchcoat-wearing figure walks out, having robbed drugs dealers of their drugs. Behold Omar Little.

The marketplace of ideas. The three-thousand-year-old history of moral philosophy, the study of right and wrong. The warbling of disagreement, cackle of dialogue. "Good is what God says it is." "Good is what the Law says it is." "No, good is what realizes the ends of humanity." "Good is what reason determines to be right." "Good is what maximizes happiness, evil what maximizes unhappiness." Enter a man in a topcoat, carrying a walking stick. He winces against the light, his cheeks blush. He pushes his way into the crowd, into the middle of the market, but gets shoved back, toward the edges of the mass. From here he sees clearly, and proceeds to speak clearly. "You all say that this is good and that evil, but not one of you has noticed that the scales are underweight. I ask you: what good is this value system of good and evil?" Behold Friedrich Nietzsche.

Playing the Game for Themselves

Omar and Nietzsche are figures on the margin, playing the game for themselves. Still, they are both potentially *explosive*. "I am dynamite," wrote Nietzsche, claiming to have great power, even while he received little recognition while he lived (*Ecce Homo*, "Why I Am a Destiny," p. 1). Omar too has great power—and seeing just how much power Omar has is a gift the creators of *The Wire* give to us, the viewers.

These two figures, Omar and Nietzsche, are made for one another.

Nietzsche is best known for his statement "God is dead," often misunderstood as a simple expression of atheism. It's not just this, however . . . it's a diagnosis. Looking at the nineteenth-century Europe in which he lived, Nietzsche judged that even as people *professed* to believe in God, their actions showed that they really didn't. God is dead because people have stopped believing in him, though without realizing that they have. Nietzsche observed the onset of a sickness in the civilized world.

The moral system of good and evil—primarily Christian morality—and probably the entire value system of which it is a part, *depend* on belief in God. Take away this belief and you take away morality and values, leaving only nihilism, the idea that there is no moral reality at all. Walking the straight and narrow track won't help, if Jesus cannot save your soul, and the only devil to keep "way down in the hole" is your own imperfect nature.

Casual readers of Nietzsche think he ends with nihilism, but he actually begins here. Society is sick. How can it be made well again? How can we *avoid* nihilism, if we have fundamentally rejected the idea of God? Answering these questions is one of Nietzsche's overarching goals. One answer he offers is that we must learn to see what is contingent and changeable for what it is, and consequently break free of the prejudices and dogmatism society drums into us from birth. Once we do that, we will no longer be engaged in *denying* life, a perspective as common in our day as it was in Nietzsche's, but in *affirming* life. Recovering from life-denial and such deep pessimism about human nature is part of recovering from the illness of nihilism. The model he gives us of how to achieve these transformations is what Nietzsche calls the "overman" (sometimes translated as "superman").

Since the overman will be an answer to nihilism, and not a continuation of it, this figure will espouse a moral code, and one quite distinct from the Christian morality. This is why when Omar—a man who kills, steals, and lies—says "A man gotta have a code," our interest is piqued ("Unto Others").

What is this code? Omar, depicted throughout as undergoing a kind of transformation of his own, stands apart from the rest of the world of *The Wire,* because he openly admits to the constraints of morality. What are these constraints? More importantly, what are they for him? And is his moral code what Nietzsche envisions morality to be for the future? In short, is Omar an example of the Nietzschean overman?

Woe to Them that Call Evil Good and Good Evil

The Wire is pervaded by moral questions and issues. We see dilemmas between consequentialist and duty-based moral reasoning:

- **Should Herc lie about where he got his information about Marlo?**
- **Is McNulty right to lie about the existence of a serial killer if it results in the police department's getting more resources?**
- **Is there something fundamentally wrong about the creation of Hamsterdam?**

We see individuals working on improving their own moral characters:

- **Cutty (trying to get himself right)**
- **Prez (trying to find his purpose in life)**
- **Bubbles (trying to kick his drug habit)**

We see discussions of whether there are moral absolutes:

- **Bodie criticizing Marlo's ruthlessness as a violation of the criminal's code**
- **Omar's criticizing Stringer and Avon for breaking the "Sunday truce"**
- **Kima's reporting of McNulty and Lester to Daniels for their manufacturing of the "Red Ribbon Killer" case**

Morality is often presupposed, however. It's assumed that there is good and evil, and the debates, if there are any, are really just over which actions are good and which evil. Note the irony in the card accompanying the flowers sent to Butchie's funeral. It reads, "Butchie, Woe to them that call evil good and good evil. Your true and loyal friend, Proposition Joe" ("Transitions").

Butchie's death, a crucial event in Omar's life, belongs in our investigation here. But before we get into that, we need some specifics about Nietzsche's vision of the overman. The overman will certainly not call what is evil good and what is good evil. Instead, he will question the very basis of this distinction between good and evil.

When Nietzsche wrote, he didn't think the overman had yet come to be. He, and his literary mouthpiece, Zarathustra, were preparers of the way, bridges from man to the overman. It's not clear whether Nietzsche thinks of the overman as the actual next evolutionary step or an unattainable exemplar. Nietzsche is an intentionally shifty writer; it's tough to nail down precisely what he means. He characteristically contradicts himself. He uses some of his terms in idiosyncratic ways. He admits that he likes to wear masks in order not to be easily understood, and even to be misunderstood, by inappropriate readers. This explains why the Nazis were able to misread him and co-opt his writings for their own purposes.

Nietzsche speaks directly of the overman in only one of his published works, the poeticized *Thus Spoke Zarathustra*. There is a thread, however, beginning in the so-called Free Spirit trilogy—*Human, All Too Human, Daybreak,* and *The Gay Science*—and extending through *Beyond Good and Evil* and *On the Genealogy of Morality*, that can help us find the contours of the overman. Upon reconstituting the portrait of the overman, we can then determine whether Omar fits the bill.

Nietzsche sees humanity as an assortment of psychological *types*. Humans are nothing more than animals. They are perhaps more complex than other animals, but no less predictable and observable. Humans can be studied and explained naturalistically. We don't need transcendent metaphysics or religion to explain human action. Moreover, we can reject the notions of souls, selves, and higher worlds.

Nietzsche distinguishes two broad types of people: higher types and lower types. The lower types display reasoning and behavior little different from that of herd animals—indeed, Nietzsche often refers to this population simply as "the herd." The higher types, however, are those humans closest to the overman. The overman too is a type, even if unrealized thus far. He will share some characteristics with, and be an example of, other types, nevertheless. Let's look at four of these types: the free spirit, the non-dogmatic, the noble, and the value creator and ask whether Omar fits any or all of them.

In the Wind, So to Speak

The overman will be a *free spirit*. What does Nietzsche mean by "free spirit"? It's not what we might call "free-thinkers" or "bohemians." To see what the free spirit is, we should ask what the free spirit is free *of*.

The free spirit is free of convention and tradition. He will not consent to anything simply because "this is how it's been done." He will think "differently from what, on the basis of his origin, environment, his class and profession, or on the basis of the dominant views of the age, would have been expected of him" (*Human, All Too Human,* section 225). The "fettered spirit," on the other hand, will do things because of habit or tradition (*Human, All Too Human,* section 226).

Consider some of the street-level characters in *The Wire*. Why do they enter and stay in the drug business? Avon, for example, has been in the Game for most of his life. His father was a well-known and hardened criminal figure of Baltimore. His sister, Brianna, is involved in the drug trade. His nephew, D'Angelo, is one of his lieutenants early on. The family business is crime. Avon is in the Game because this is what was expected of him. Reputation too is a key element of Avon's chosen way of life. This explains why Stringer, who consummates several investments that make Avon and himself wealthy enough to leave the Game, isn't able to lure Avon away. "This ain't about your business class," he tells Stringer. "The street is the street . . . always" ("Port in a Storm"). He likes the warlike nature of owning corners, and it's clear that he's been taught to like it by those who raised him. He's doing what is "expected of him."

Contrast Avon's being in the drug business with Marlo's. We get very little background information about Marlo, but we can ultimately see that he's in the Game not because it's what is expected of him, but because he chooses this life. When he learns that he must retire, after he receives the stet (an inactivation of the charges against him, which would disappear after a year), he pretends that he's ready to do this. He sells his connect to the Greek and is prepared to invest his money. Yet, as he rubs elbows with movers and shakers at a party, he eventually ducks out, finding his way to a corner where he provokes one of the dealers into a fight. He gets knifed in the altercation—a cut on his forearm—and as he touches and tastes the blood, smiling, we can see the thrill being in the Game gives him. This is why he lives.

Most people are fettered spirits. Marlo is only relatively freer than Avon, but not a free spirit. Fettered spirits will take up positions or roles based on what their parents and friends do, while the free spirit will be a "contradiction to his today" (*Beyond Good and Evil,* section 212). He will seem out of place, distant, and he will feel this distance—experiencing what Nietzsche calls "pathos of distance"—and embrace it. Thus, he will be free of the almost universal need to belong.

The free spirit will observe the world from a height, as if he is not really a part of it. More than anything, he will not be invested in what happens to him. This is why Marlo isn't a free spirit. The free spirit will learn to love fate and necessity— *amor fati*—and eventually come to assent to every single thing that happens in his life—good and bad. Even more than assenting, he will eventually *affirm* life to such an extent that if he had the power, he would will that every event in his life should occur—and re-occur—eternally.

The free spirit will be in, but not of, the world. This will ensure that he won't remain "stuck" to any particular person, a country, pity or compassion, science, or even one's own detachment or virtues. This freedom is almost absolute—freedom from excessive attachment to other persons, events, and even oneself.

Is Omar a Free Spirit?

When Omar leaves Baltimore in order to let things cool down with Avon, McNulty tells him at the bus station, "Go easy, Omar. . . . Stay free" ("The Cost"). McNulty is probably referring to Omar's freedom from arrest, but we can also ask whether he is free in Nietzsche's sense. He's certainly freer than most of the other characters on the show. For example, we're struck by his apparent rootlessness. When asked under oath where he lives, he responds, "No place in particular." When he is further pressed as to whether this means that he is homeless, he says, "In the wind, so to speak" ("All Prologue"). We never see any permanent abode for Omar, only temporary hideouts. Even his apartment in Puerto Rico, after he has gone into retirement, is more like a resting place, good for the time being, but not permanent.

He displays no strong attachment to money or material goods. Having amassed a tidy sum as a result of robbing dealers for years, he could live more comfortably. Wealth is only secondary, however, to the imposition of his own will on the players of the street.

Sometimes we see just how much power he wields. For instance, on a Honey Nut Cheerios run, clad only in silken pajamas, he pauses on the way back and leans against a building to smoke a Newport. From out of nowhere a bag falls beside him with a thud. Those hiding inside the building know that Omar is outside and assume he is about to come in, shotgun blazing, and so they have dropped their stash in the hopes that he won't.

When he gets back, he throws the bag on the kitchen table and tells Renaldo, his partner, that he doesn't even want the loot. "It ain't what you taking," he says, "it's who you taking it from, you feel me?" Renaldo shakes his head. Omar thinks a moment, then says, "How you expect to run with wolves come night when you spend the day sporting with puppies" ("Home Rooms")?

Omar does have sexual attachments, but these can be rela-tively superficial. He has three boyfriends within the time period of the show: Brandon, Dante, and Renaldo. It can't be denied, however, that he is more than sexually attached to Brandon.

For example, when he views Brandon's body in the morgue, after Brandon had been tortured and killed, his scream fills the halls. The depth of feeling in that scream is unmistakable—he loved Brandon. His attachment was deeper than mere sexual attraction. He spends a lot of time avenging Brandon's death—not just Brandon's being killed, but *how* he was killed. At the same time, he also seems to have learned a lesson about attach-ment, for later he has no problem in dropping Dante after learning that Dante had given him up to Brother Mouzone. And he seems interested in little more than Renaldo's physical beauty.

Omar seems to be in a process of transformation, an evolu-tion from being someone "stuck to" certain things in life to being a free spirit. As such processes go, however, it consists of progression and regression, advance and backslide. When one of his partners in crime, Tosha, dies, he's clearly upset. But there's a moment, when he presses a lit cigarette into his palm, when he seems to say, "No more. I can't feel like this anymore." From that point on, accomplices are accomplices only.

Omar's detachment is stretched to its limit when Butchie is murdered by Chris and Snoop. When Omar hears about it, his eyes well up. He loved Butchie, the blind father-figure. Ultimately, his love for Butchie seals Omar's fate. Omar ends up being fettered, but only after a period in which he was a free spirit. Had he lived, he would have likely freed himself again.

And You Him, Ain't You? . . . Danger

The overman will be *non-dogmatic*. What does this term mean? More than just a free spirit, the non-dogmatic individual will be something "higher, greater, and thoroughly different that does not want to be misunderstood and mistaken for something else" (*Beyond Good and Evil,* section 44). The overman will not hold a dogmatism about *truth*—that is, he will not embrace the "will to truth."

Nietzsche asks why value truth over progress: *"why not rather* untruth? and uncertainty? even ignorance?" (*Beyond Good and Evil,* section 1). An obvious answer to these questions is that you are often worse off having been deceived. But doesn't untruth sometimes benefit, too? When you stand for an *unconditional* pursuit of truth, you're standing on *faith* that truth is better than untruth. This faith the overman will reject.

Consider Greggs's going to Deputy Commissioner Daniels about McNulty and Freamon. One possible explanation of her decision is that, all things considered, she believes that deception weakens the police department and that more criminals will be caught and convicted if police officers like McNulty are run off the force. If this were her reasoning, then she would be a Rule-Utilitarian, having judged that better consequences result from adhering to truth.

A better explanation of her decision is that she adopts an absolutist position about truth. When McNulty initially tells her about what he has done, she says, "You can't do this" ("Clarifications"). Later, after she further expresses resistance, he reminds her that his scheme has resulted in Marlo's arrest. There's no doubt about what she thinks of that rationale: "Fuck Marlo," she says. "Fuck you" ("Late Editions").

Marlo ends up walking. McNulty and Freamon end up leaving the police force, since they would never again be able to do real police work. The streets of Baltimore are less safe as a result of Gregg's decision. She knows this, even as she does what she does. And McNulty recognizes why she did what she did. "Detective," he says at his and Freamon's "wake," "if you think it needed doing, I guess it did" ("–30–").

Kima's so committed to preserving the truth that she knowingly sets into motion a process that ends in Marlo's freedom. The overman rejects this absolutist position. He will be what Nietzsche calls an "attempter," a person who exercises a kind of skepticism that "despises and nevertheless seizes," "undermines and takes possession," "does not believe but does not lose itself in the process," "gives the spirit dangerous freedom, but . . . is severe on the heart" (section 209). This skepticism gives the free spirit its freedom. What is important is not truth, taken in isolation, but species-enhancement and individual-preservation. Truth is important only insofar as it helps us achieve these.

Is Omar Non-Dogmatic about Truth?

Omar, Brandon, and Bailey are planning to rob an Eastside gang of its drugs. Omar explains that as he comes down the street, the dealers will run to the alley, where Brandon and Bailey will be waiting. "Rats always run to holes in times of danger," he says. Brandon smiles. "And you him, ain't you? . . . Danger." Omar replies, "Naw, man, I'm just a nigga with a plan, that's all." "And a shotgun," adds Bailey ("The Pager").

Omar is danger because he uses truth as a tool, and doesn't value it unconditionally. For example, he has no qualms about lying under oath in the William Gant murder trial about seeing Bird pull the trigger. In this instance not telling the truth achieves more, especially since Omar knows that Bird committed the killing. In the same trial Omar exploits the reluctance of others to face the uncomfortable truth. When Levy, the attorney, says that Omar is immoral, and is "feeding off the violence and despair of the drug trade," "stealing from those who themselves are stealing the lifeblood of our city" and is "a parasite who leeches off the drug culture," Omar responds by saying, "Just like you man. . . . I got the shotgun. You got the briefcase. It's all in the Game though, right?" ("All Prologue").

Omar also capitalizes on the will to truth found in others. After he has been set up by Marlo for the death of a "taxpayer," he asks Bunk for help. Bunk says that even if he has been set up for this job, there are plenty more that he did do for which he should be punished. But Omar sees through this posturing: "You think on this. . . . Now if Omar didn't kill that delivery lady, somebody else did. But you giving 'em a free walk right now, ain't you" ("Unto Others")?

Omar generally rejects the unconditional pursuit of truth. Every once in a while, however, we see him backslide, rejecting moments of advantage because of a lingering embrace of truth for truth's sake. This is seen most clearly in his relationship to Brother Mouzone. Stringer has led Omar to believe that Brother Mouzone was responsible for the torture and death of Brandon, so Omar tracks the Brother down at a motel and shoots him in the gut. As Omar stands above him, ready to finish him off, he reminds Brother Mouzone of the person whose death he is avenging. The Brother responds, "You got some wrong information." Omar says, "Man, you lying to live." "I am at peace with my god," the Brother says. "Do what you will" ("Bad Dreams").

Omar realizes that the Brother has no motivation to lie. It's clear that he had nothing to do with Brandon's death. At this point Omar the killer would have no apparent reason to let Brother Mouzone live, unless his *only* reason to kill him was his belief that the Brother had killed Brandon. Once he discovers the truth, he lets the Brother live, even calling for an ambulance.

Why then would a non-dogmatist about truth make such a decision? It would have been much easier for Omar to have finished the job. Surely Omar realizes that when Brother Mouzone recovers, he will be seeking some kind of repayment for the injury. Is this an instance of Omar's relapsing, becoming a fettered spirit—fettered by a dogmatism about truth?

It's hard to say, but here is one reason to think that Omar is still displaying a non-dogmatism about truth. Brother Mouzone will likely seek vengeance from someone. It might be Omar, it might also be whoever gave Omar the "wrong information"—that is, the person who set the Brother up. It's possible that Omar is forward-looking enough to see the day when the two of them will be allied under one cause.

We can see that Omar isn't always so ready to let people go, however. He finds Savino outside a club, knowing that he's one of Marlo's muscle, and suspecting that he was present at Butchie's death. Savino says that he wasn't there. Omar replies, "So you innocent, huh?" Savino nods. "Let me ask you something though. Being that you muscle for Marlo, what you was gonna do if you was there, huh? Riddle me that." Savino gives no response. Omar pauses, and seems to be considering letting Savino go, as he had with Brother Mouzone. After a moment, though, he says, "You know what, yo?" and shoots Savino in the head ("Took").

This is in stark contrast to how he handled Brother Mouzone and suggests that he is a non-dogmatist after all.

You Come at the King . . . You Best Not Miss!

The overman will be *noble*. What does this term mean? As I noted earlier Nietzsche believes in a hierarchy of psychological types. There will be strong individuals, leaders, warriors. There will also be weak individuals, followers, peasants. Nietzsche provides an historical narrative in *On the Genealogy of Morality* in which we begin with what nature has created: the strong class—the nobility, possessing wealth and control, because of the traits bestowed upon it by nature, among them health, strength, and assertiveness—and the peasant class—serving the nobility, because of the traits bestowed upon it by nature, among them weakness and servility. At some point in history, Nietzsche claims, the peasants rebel, and the world is changed so that the peasant traits are valued. The Christian values of forbearance and service displace the noble virtues. Nonetheless, we see individuals today who possess the noble traits. What are they?

The noble individual has reverence for himself and an instinct for rank. Egalitarianism, both social and political, is a foreign concept to him. He recognizes that the world is constructed of the hierarchy of types; some individuals have more worth than others. The noble man will be active, rather than reactive. He will act upon instinct, rather than waiting on others to act and then responding.

The Wire is full of reactive types—those that don't engage until they have been engaged by others. For example, the first season revolves around the order given by Judge Phelan to form the detail to investigate Avon Barksdale and the subsequent tepid responses to the order. McNulty spends most of his time railing at the inertia of the people around him.

The noble individual will be more than active—he will be strong, having "great health," described as a spirit "strengthened by wars and victories, for whom conquering, adventure, danger, pain have become even a need." The noble embraces the "will to power," described as "seeking above all to *discharge* your strength" (*Beyond Good and Evil*, section 13).

The noble "would need acclimatization to sharp high air, to wintry journeys, to ice and mountain ranges in every sense." For this, he will need "a kind of sublime malice," "an ultimate most self-assured mischievousness of knowledge" (*On the Genealogy of Morality,* II, section 24). The noble looks at himself and declares himself to be good—*a good specimen,* of the human animal. He doesn't have to look to the judgment of others to estimate his own value. The noble knows he is noble and doesn't shrink from the fact.

Is Omar a Noble?

In retaliation for Omar's taking his drugs from the stash house, Avon has his minions search Omar's apartment, torch his van, and put a bounty on Omar's head. At each turn Omar is watching them, from a distance. One night, Wee-Bey and Stinkum move in to take out a rival corner dealer, Scar. Wee-Bey goes down the road on foot and then moves back up toward the corner. Stinkum comes from above. As Stinkum nears the corner, Omar emerges from the shadows, says "Hey now!" and comes out blasting. Stinkum lies dead. Wee-Bey shoots at Omar from down the street and Omar returns fire. Wee-Bey takes one in the leg, and scurries for cover behind a parked car. After a few moments, he hears the familiar whistled tune. Then, "Bey, listen here. . . . You come at the king, you best not miss" ("Lessons").

It's in Omar's nature to act, and not just react. Wee-Bey and Stinkum believe that they are hunting, but they are the hunted. Omar could have spent a period of time hiding and then returned after things had cooled down. But he chooses to engage, even when he isn't being directly engaged by others.

At any given time he could give up the hunt, but he comes back time and again. When he leaves town, after realizing that he is outmatched in numbers, he still can't help himself, taking up the hunt in the Bronx. He is addicted to overcoming others—"conquering, adventure, danger, pain" are a need for Omar. Firmly embracing the will to power, he possesses the great health, he evinces "sublime malice."

From the very fact that he's described as "on the hunt," it's clear how distant Omar is from the rest of the individuals of the street. He stands apart, he is acclimatized to the "sharp high air," feeling and embracing the pathos of distance. He is a warrior, an imposer, using the streets as his battleground, his hunting-ground, while not becoming part and parcel of the land. He's a warrior, but a ruler too. When he and Renaldo rob Old Face Andre, who runs the corner store, of the re-up package, Omar remarks, "Yo, you see the look on his mug? . . . That's the reason we get up every morning" ("Home Rooms").

Is Omar a noble? Oh, indeed.

A Man Gotta Have a Code

Finally, the overman will be a *value-creator*. What does this term mean? As I mentioned earlier, the noble is contrasted with the peasant. The historical narrative Nietzsche gives us is intended to show that in spite of our perception of morality of good and evil as universal, absolute, and timeless, our moral system is actually contingent and historically determined. Moreover, the way this system was created and developed gives us reason to reject the system outright.

Thousands of years ago, Nietzsche claims, the nobles ruled. They ruled because of their natural strengths, which allowed them to oppress the lower types—the peasants. Because the nobles had the "great health" referred to earlier, the peasants—weak, servile, deferential—were unable to free themselves. But they desperately wanted to turn the tables on the nobles. They looked at the nobles, saw such great power, and experienced a deep *resentment* toward their rulers, so deep that it controlled their every waking moment. There had to be a way to usurp the nobles' power, but it had to be done indirectly.

The peasants realized that as things stood, their traits were deemed bad, while those of the nobles were deemed good. This was in part because the nobles ruled, but it was also a *reason* the nobles ruled. If there was some way to change the societal perception of the traits of the nobles and the peasants—if there was a way to make their traits desirable and the nobles' undesirable—they would be able to take power for themselves. Thus, they undertook a rebellion.

This rebellion, according to Nietzsche, was effected by a wholesale *overturning* of the existing value system. What the peasants did was more than just switching tags—placing the label of "good" on their own traits and "bad" on those of the nobles. Such a move wouldn't have been very effective, since the nobles were obviously still in power even during the rebellion. What was necessary was a *replacement* of the old value system. What began as a good-bad value system, focused on successful maneuvering in the world and achievement of desired ends, was replaced by a *moral* system of good and evil. Material wealth in this life, on the new value system, wouldn't imply eternal wealth in the afterlife.

What did guarantee eternal happiness after death, in the light of the peasant rebellion? Possession of the peasants' traits, of course—the very weakness, meekness, and servility responsible for their being oppressed in this life. The peasants looked at the nobles and their distinctive traits, and designated these traits, and anyone who possessed them, as evil. Then they designated the opposites of these traits as good—but now *morally* good. Anyone exhibiting weakness and distaste for power would receive the rewards of the afterlife, and anyone not exhibiting them—that is, the nobles—wouldn't. In this way the peasants were able to *change the world* simply by changing the predominant value system and, subsequently, determining their own place within the new system.

While Nietzsche has very little love in his heart for the peasants, he does respect them for this one thing: their being value-creators. This is also something the overman should possess, though the overman won't create new values because of resentment or weakness. He will do so because it's in his nature, as the strong and independent figure that he is.

Thus, the overman will be a free spirit, non-dogmatic about truth, noble, *and* a value-creator. Since we've seen evidence that Omar satisfies the first three descriptors, this fourth will tell the tale of Omar as the overman.

Omar the Lion

Is Omar a value-creator? We've seen that Omar is undergoing a transformation as he makes his way through the streets of Baltimore, taking on more and more powerful enemies. His code doesn't change, however, so we might think that he created a value-system prior to the beginning of the narrative. As we mull over this possibility let's consider a parable that appears in Nietzsche's book *Thus Spoke Zarathustra*.

Called "On the Three Metamorphoses," it describes three transformations. In the first metamorphosis the spirit morphs into a camel. It becomes a beast of burden, cheerfully taking upon itself the heaviest and most difficult of loads. It speeds into the desert, away from friends and everything it's always known. This is the breaking of the fetters, the freeing of the spirit.

In the second metamorphosis the camel becomes a lion. It conquers its own freedom and becomes master of the desert. The lion must slay the dragon of the "Thou Shalt," the Christian morality of good and evil. After this metamorphosis, the lion stands tall as the free spirit, the non-dogmatist, the noble. Omar roams the streets of Baltimore as the lion, once a camel, now a king. Wounded, yet still mighty, he's struck down not by another lion, or even another predator, but a member of the herd, too small and inconsequential for the lion even to see.

But there follows a third metamorphosis in the parable. The lion becomes a child, "innocence and forgetting, a new beginning, a game, a self-propelled wheel, a first movement, a sacred 'Yes'." The child begins anew because the "first movement" is the creation of new values. This child represents the overman—the new man. The underweight scales Nietzsche announces in the marketplace of ideas are now set right.

Does Omar set the scales right? His code is distinguished from the moralities of other people by his calling different things good and different things evil. The code still preserves the polar opposites of "good" and "evil," however. It's different only in what Omar places on each side of the scale—he accepts the scale nonetheless.

Omar is a noble, no doubt, prepared to become brutal and violent when necessary, but he doesn't need to continually re-establish his own superiority. He knows he is good. We find him in Puerto Rico, after having robbed the New Day Co-Op of their drugs (and having sold their drugs back to them!), handing out candy to the local children. This would have been a nice lasting image to have of him, had he not been forced to come back to the streets.

Omar is a lion, but remains a lion, never undergoing the third metamorphosis, never becoming a value-creator, thus never becoming the overman. At no point does he question the prevailing value system. In that respect he is not that different from the other characters of *The Wire,* or the rest of us for that matter. Far from being the overman, Omar is noble, but human, all too human.

LINE 10
The Best of Boys and Lads

KENN FISHER

They are the best of boys and lads, because they are the most manly in their nature . . . they are bold and brave and masculine, and they tend to cherish what is like themselves. Do you want me to prove it? Look, these are the only kind of boys who grow up to be real men in politics . . . they naturally pay no attention to marriage or to making babies. . . . They, however, are quite satisfied to live their lives with one another unmarried.

— PLATO, *Symposium*, line 192a

In the first season of *The Wire*, Avon Barksdale finds out that Omar Little, a rogue member of West Baltimore's criminal culture who has been robbing him, is gay. This infuriates Avon so much that he doubles the bounty on Omar's head, calls him a faggot and a cocksucker, and then triples the bounty should he get a chance to "holler" at Omar before he kills him. It wasn't enough that this man got the bold idea that it was okay to steal from Avon, but he then had the audacity to be queer on top of that!

What Avon didn't understand, and what ultimately gave Omar his power over his enemies, was the very fact that he was gay. Not only did being gay give Omar qualities that made him better able to go to war with Avon, but the mere fact that he was gay, and still had the nerve to confront Avon in the homophobic setting of the streets of West Baltimore, made him more fearless than Avon could ever be.

This is one in a series of complex ways that *The Wire* studies sexual diversity. At a time when homosexuality is a prominently debated social issue in America, *The Wire* chose to take a stand on the subject, showing that homosexuality is a tool of empowerment and that homosexuals are, in fact, the most excellent in their respective fields. The program features two gay main characters: both Omar Little and Kima Greggs, representing opposing sides in the war on drugs, excel within their fields more than any of their heterosexual counterparts.

Moreover, the series explores other issues related to homosexuality and philosophy. Specifically, *The Wire* explores the relationship between the homosexuals' public and private lives—and how that relates to their interaction with those around them, it investigates a thematic connection between Omar and perhaps philosophy's most famous homosexual, Socrates, and it examines which aspects deserve focus when examining homosexuals and homosexuality.

It's Pronounced 'Goo'd Poh-lees', with the Emphasis on the 'Oh'

Like all good philosophers, we must first define our terms. The writers of *The Wire* make it pretty easy to define police officers who excel at their job: Throughout the series, the terms "good police" or "natural police" come up often. There is a very clear line in Baltimore's police department as to who is "good police" and who is not. The term is used for the first time in the second episode of the series, "The Detail," when Lieutenant Daniels describes being sent a "good police" who would get it in his head to do "good police work." He then describes the antonym of "good police" as someone who doesn't dig in, and doesn't do anything "fancy."

We start to figure out throughout Season One exactly what it means to be "good police." This is someone who goes above and beyond the bare minimum of what a Baltimore police officer is required to do. Good police are those who "give a fuck when it's not their turn to give a fuck." It's someone who knows that drugs and money on the table doesn't mean a good case has been made, and that it takes time and patience to affect the community.

At the same time, the term refers to honesty and integrity pertaining to the job. Someone who doesn't falsify evidence to ensure conviction of a perp that they know to be guilty is called "real police." Throughout the series, we watch as Carver becomes "good police." In Season One, he's no better than Herc when it comes to his attitude towards criminals, or in stealing money that is evidence from a crime scene. However, his arc shows him develop as an officer (specifically through the guidance of Daniels and Bunny Colvin) and by the end of the series, he is a model police. The series expresses this by showing Carver turn on Colicchio, a violent and unrepentant fellow officer. Carver learns when to risk his friends at work in order to uphold his own integrity. Greggs later asks Carver about this decision as a means to decide whether or not to make a similar decision in her own career.

On the street, the definition of excellence is quite different: The drug leaders of west Baltimore throughout the series (Avon and Stringer, followed by Marlo) have two things in common. The first is that they hold power, they hold their corners, and are able to rise because of a combination of strength, courage, and intelligence. The second is that they (at least Avon and Marlo) hold their *honor* higher than anything. Avon and Marlo both became obsessed with Omar when he was able to steal from them without being caught. In Avon's case, it distracted him throughout Season One, indirectly adding to his plate as he dealt with other issues that eventually led to his arrest. In Marlo's case, the greatest insult that he felt throughout the series was finding out that Omar was calling out his name on the streets, and that he didn't have a chance to retaliate. One of Stringer's only non-economically calculated moves throughout the series was to try to order a hit on Clay Davis when the politician had tarnished his pride. All three risked their lives, and everything that they had earned, just to have their names ring out as fierce on the street.

So, what is this honor? It's being the best, being feared, and not just surviving, (which is itself an achievement), but rising amongst the ranks. Honor is holding your corner against not only the police, but the rival gangs who also want the corner. It's to stand tall, when you're defending your corner, or when you are about to be shot dead by your own friends. It's being cautious, strategic, and patient, as you maneuver yourself like a chess piece on the game board of West Baltimore, using opportunities and wit to advance yourself in the Game.

The Best of the Best

Kima Greggs is presented to us as the most excellent police. From her first scene, she is shown as one of the more competent officers, and she is the only main character in the police storyline who maintains her status as being excellent. In the pilot, Lieutenant Daniels describes her as the best officer working under him. She's often seen as the only one in the room who is doing work, and she plays a leadership role to the more inexperienced officers surrounding her. A large part of the Special Crimes Unit's case on the Barksdale crew in the first season relied on the information given by Bubbles, who was Kima's CI (she says herself that police are only as good as their CIs). She's calm when Prez shoots the wall, supportive of Jimmy when he is less than politic, and loyal to Daniels when she deals with the brass. To finish the first season, an injured Kima refuses to implicate Wee-Bey in her attempted murder, despite pressure from Bunk, even though everyone involved, (including her), knew that he was one of the people who shot her down. She honestly did not see him shoot at her, and refused to lie to catch a perp. When Bunk relates this to McNulty later, he labels her "real police."

There are many characters that are portrayed as being "good police," or a variation thereof (Pryzbylewski is good police in the office only; Carver matures into a "good police" as the series progresses; Daniels is "good police" on-screen, but an unnamed scandal looms over him from events prior to the series); however, Greggs is the only "good police" character who maintains the stature that the term implies throughout the series. In the last season of the series, McNulty and Freamon— two standards for "good" or "natural police"—are both pushed too far when restrictions in resources force them to create an elaborate lie in order to illegally wiretap Marlo. Bunk, who's extremely critical of these actions, nevertheless fails to actually stop his friends from what they are doing, and in fact, becomes silently complicit when he literally leaves the room as Jimmy is tampering with evidence.

Kima takes the step that Bunk is unable to take, and informs her superiors about McNulty's acts. The decision to do so was not easy for her, because like everyone else who had known what was going on, she was aware that these actions would ultimately bring down a serial murderer. But Kima was the only one who was able to get over this moral dilemma, all in the interest of justice and professional ethics.

Omar is a whole different kind of animal, whose cultural appeal is impossible to deny. While campaigning for his presidential bid in 2008, Barack Obama called Omar his favorite character and *The Wire* his favorite show. Is there any question why? Omar is the guy who robs people who terrify the rest of us. But it's more than that. He is clever, and precise. He has a moral code that he lives by that we all appreciate and understand: he doesn't touch civilians. And he's queer—an undeniable reason why his character is so incomparable and endearing. The character has often been described as a modern-day Robin Hood—but Robin Hood had allies, and only the one enemy. Omar is Robin Hood being chased equally by the government and the Merry Men.

Our introduction to Omar is of a man waiting patiently, observing the habits of the crew that he's about to hit. In his second scene, he sees that there are undercover cops watching the same crew. They don't notice him, and of course the crew is oblivious to both. It takes David Simon only two scenes to establish Omar's skills to the viewer. When he robs the crew, he is fast, effective, and to the point. The boys pay him, so Omar doesn't need to kill anyone.

Omar seems to be the one man who can't die (I know what you're thinking: he does die. I'll concede that he *can* in fact die, but that is beside the point—he is unable to die in the sense that when he is specifically trying not to die—he cannot be killed.) He holds his head up high and stands against anyone who stands in his way. Then, as if to kick them while they're down, Omar steals from them as they are trying to retaliate. In fact, he's so good at what he does, he doesn't even have to actively hold up people. In the Season Four episode, "Home Rooms," after a trip to the store for cereal, Omar stands in front of a drug house to have a cigarette, and a bag full of drugs and money is thrown out at him.

Omar's challenge to the drug lords that he fights against is in itself what makes him at least their equal (and certainly raises him to a higher level than everyone else on the streets). What makes him rise above the likes of Avon, Stringer, and Marlo is that he always beats them. They are never able to stop him from robbing them. Even when they put a very high price on his head, they are not able to kill him. He embarrasses these men at their own game, and has the audacity to live after doing so. What's more: all of this adds to Omar's name on the street and ultimately his reputation that raises him to a semi-mythological figure. Upon every failure to eliminate Omar, he grows stronger.

Both Kima and Omar live by a code that at times contradicts the general rules of their environment, and that code ultimately makes them the best at their jobs. If Omar didn't have his rule against attacking civilians, Bunk wouldn't have known that he could not have been guilty of the murder he was arrested for in Season Four. What's more, regardless of Omar's guilt in that murder, Omar's code is why Bunk went out of his way to get him out of jail for that faulty charge. This clearly saved his life, and gave him the chance to commit his masterpiece robbery of Marlo and the entire Co-Op later that season. Furthermore, Omar broke a pivotal "street" rule in the second season by witnessing against Bird. Doing this helped Omar get revenge against the Barksdale empire for torturing Brandon, and began his relationship with the police and district attorneys that would lead to him being treated better in the aforementioned arrest in Season Four.

Greggs's code is what brings her to inform her superiors about McNulty's and Freamon's actions in Season Five. When she finds out about the actions, she thinks about it, and even asks Carver for his advice, as he had written up someone in his division earlier that season. Once her colleagues find out that she had betrayed them, they are anything but upset with her. They understand that she actually did the right thing and that she had to live by her code, because she was better police.

Why Being Homosexual Makes You More Excellent

In the Season One episode, "The Buys," McNulty finds out that Greggs is a lesbian. The conversation goes:

> **McNulty:** Should have known. . . . I worked with one other female police officer that was worth a damn, only one.

GREGGS: A lesbian?

MCNULTY: Yeah.

This is not to say that homosexuality brings an inherent superiority in the quality of the work that you perform, but rather that being homosexual provides circumstances which make it easier for a person to achieve excellence, much in the way that it's easier to prove yourself only if you're tested. *The Wire* portrays homosexuals in the following ways:

- **They take on characteristics of the other gender**
- **They put themselves into relationships that are better suited for the pursuit of excellence**
- **They have to overcome more obstacles due to the bigotry that they endure**
- **They can more easily make certain sacrifices that are required to be excellent in their field.**

Traditionally, philosophers have considered gender to include static, unchanging, natural aspects that are directly related to our biological sex. Masculinity has long been perceived as valid through the absence of the feminine, and in turn, the feminine is made valid by the absence of masculinity. However, homosexuality has been long misunderstood partly because it challenges that notion. A homosexual identity not only has, but also allows both the masculine and the feminine to manifest themselves equally. Both Kima and Omar take on a significant number of traditional qualities from the opposing gender.

Kima describes herself as "no lady," and qualifies the statement by often being the most masculine person in the room. In the same scene of "The Buys" mentioned above, Kima describes other female officers and their reactions to dangerous conditions. She says that they won't go into certain situations without their partners and that they are more afraid than she is. Jimmy asks her if she thinks that she is different because she's gay, to which she replies: "I don't know, but is there any other way to police? All I know is that I just love the job."

It's not just that being more masculine makes her braver and better equipped for the more alarming situations. Kima also needs to act more like a man simply to earn the respect of her peers in the male-oriented environment that she lives in. Any police department in the world is a boys' club, and the Baltimore department depicted in *The Wire* is no exception. In the first episode of Season Two, "Ebb Tide," Herc, in a backwards way of complimenting Kima, tells her, "If you were a guy, and actually, in some ways you're better than most guys I know." In Season One, Kima tells Jimmy that "cops are dogs," referring to the way that men can behave when dealing with women (specifically by cheating on their wives).

It doesn't take long for Kima to start taking on these characteristics, and eventually, she even jokes with the other guys about women in the same manner. After Bodie punches an officer in the first season, Kima, in a seemingly out-of-character scene, beats on the criminal who attacked the cop. This is certainly a masculine gesture that is likely performed intentionally so that her colleagues will see her as one of the guys.

Omar, on the other hand, doesn't have to be feminine to impress those around him. He's rather more naturally feminine, which is one of the traits that make him the outcast that he is. He is surely the most patient person, man or woman, in the entire series. His ability to watch over the area that he is going to eventually strike is likely his greatest quality as a drug-dealer-robber. He's also compassionate. In Season Four, when Bunk tells Omar about kids pretending to be him on the streets, he shows a sign of discomfort that reveals his thoughts on the life he has chosen, how he's affecting the children of his neighborhood by being an unseemly model to imitate.

In *Gender Trouble*, Judith Butler talks about sexual and gender identification using two of Sigmund Freud's papers, "Mourning and Melancholia" and "The Ego and the Id," to explain how the lack of the second gender within the heterosexual psyche leads you to incorporate attributes of a lost loved one:

> [Freud] suggests that the identification process associated with melancholia may be "the sole condition under which the id can give up its objects" . . . In other words, the identification with lost loves characteristic of melancholia becomes the precondition for the work of mourning . . . gender identification is a kind of melancholia in

which the sex of the prohibited object is internalized as a prohibition. (p. 79)

More simply, the heterosexual man denies his feminine side to the extreme point where he eventually misses his femininity at the same level of someone who has lost a close loved one—without the benefit of being able to go through a proper mourning process. This could explain a psychological benefit to a male who is more in touch with his feminine side, or vice versa.

Both Kima and Omar use their masculine and feminine traits equally. This use of opposite gender traits gives them a deeper sense of self-awareness, which ultimately gives them an advantage over their peers. The fact that Kima and Omar have had to explore themselves so deeply and have had a constant struggle with issues of gender identity actually allows them to function at a higher level.

This heightened sense of the self that occurs through struggle is demonstrated in the characters' relationships as well. In *Nicomachean Ethics*, Aristotle talks about different kinds of friendship. He says the that highest form of friendship is what he calls a "friendship of virtue," where the two partners are constantly trying to better one another—they challenge and teach each other at the same time.

The first time we see Kima in her domestic life (near the end of the pilot), she and her girlfriend, Cheryl, are very casual: it's not an oh-they're-lesbians scene. It's rather a scene about two people who have been together long enough that they're comfortable with each other. They mostly talk about work, and they are two people who are clearly trying very hard to advance their careers. Their relationship continues this way throughout Season One. In almost every scene that they're in together, they're working together, or talking about work. Their relationship is based on their mutual interest in bettering themselves and helping each other to do the same. Cheryl even pushes Kima to take classes to become a lawyer, and then rides her when Kima doesn't go. This is not to say that heterosexual relationships are wholly unable to work in this manner, but the only homosexual relationship depicted in *The Wire* has this quality, and the heterosexual relationships depicted are usually messy and destructive.

Once this foundation of Kima's and Cheryl's relationship becomes nullified (Cheryl loses interest in Kima's career, starts to talk to Kima only about domestic issues, and becomes pregnant) the relationship sours. Kima doesn't have the mother-instinct. She's a police, and being a mother would only distract her from that. Eventually, their relationship becomes a metaphor for the contrast between someone who is focused on work, and someone who is focused on family. Kima, who is our introduction to lesbian domestic life, becomes scared of a life that isn't focused on work, and starts to drink and cheat. The relationship eventually dissolves, and Kima becomes altogether focused on work. This is not to say that she is without a nurturing side. Kima still feels a responsibility to pay child support, and even wants a small role in their son's life after she leaves.

Kima's ability to leave and to sacrifice parenthood for her career is something that's very out-of-character for a woman. Kima, who is not Elija's biological mother, is able to leave the family for the sake of being a police officer in a way that is a lot easier for her than for most heterosexual women. It's the lack of biological connection that makes it easier for her. That's not to say that there is a specific lack of true parenthood for non-biological parents, but in the case of this character, she is easily able to leave the family, and in fact, says that it is the existence of this child that is the reason for the demise of her relationship with Cheryl.

Sacrificing this domestic aspect of her life is something that Kima needs to do to excel at her job. In Season Two, Kima and Beadie Russell have a conversation about balancing parenthood and work that is vital for Kima's decision to choose the side of work, and not try to balance both:

> BEADIE: I'm working my regular eight, I can handle it, you know? But detail like this...
>
> KIMA: That's what I'm asking. I mean, if something comes up on the job, how would you handle it? I mean, at home, with the kids.
>
> BEADIE: Till now, not much came up.
>
> KIMA: But now, say something comes up. I mean, say we do a raid or something, what would you do?

BEADIE: Guess I'd try to get the sitter to stay. Maybe call my folks, like I did tonight. You know how it is with kids, you gotta be there.

KIMA: But you wouldn't miss it? I mean with everybody rollin' out and you having to head home?

BEADIE: Keeps going like this, I don't know what I'm going to do. ("Stray Rounds")

Kima sighs and thinks it over. She understands that balancing work and family is difficult and she likely won't be able to be great at both. The show complements this thought with the heterosexual example of Kima's partner (and in many ways, her double). McNulty is a better detective when he's all alone. When he's in a relationship, he's unable to give his job the dedication that it needs.

The climax of McNulty's abilities as a police officer is at the end of Season Three, as he comes closer to catching Avon Barksdale and Stringer Bell, who he has obsessed over for years. A couple of episodes before he is actually able to do this, he describes himself and his unit as being the greatest group of police in all of the department. He is not incorrect. But Freamon is quick to tell McNulty that there is more to life than the job, and specifically drives home the idea of a family life being more fulfilling. This is the point where McNulty decides that he needs to become a family man, and the last time that he will ever be as good police as he is at the end of that season.

From Avon's arrest on, McNulty is one form or another of bad police. He either gives up being a detective, which is his true calling (he is a good patrolman in Season Four, but truly wasted talent), or becomes a bad one (as when he invents a serial killer in Season Five). When he attempts to be both cop and family man at the same time, something gives, which is usually his family life because of his alcoholism and infidelities.

Kima sees Jimmy's example, and actively decides to simply dedicate herself to her career. This provides two important strengths for her at work: the first is that she literally has more time, can focus more on the job, and not be distracted by children or marital problems; the second is that she actively chose to make an incredible sacrifice in her life, and this is a great motivator for her career. Every day that she works at her job, she knows that she gave up something important to be able to do that job well, and she had better make that count.

The fact that Kima gives up her domestic life for her career is typically portrayed as "masculine," which helps her out in the male-oriented environment of a police department. However, Kima is not masculine or feminine. She does not play the role of domestic wife because that's not who she is. Kima is a lesbian woman who happened to choose her career as a cop over having family because that's who she is. She is more easily able to move beyond gender stereotypes because she is a lesbian.

The homophobic environment of *The Wire* marginalizes and lessens the worth of Kima and Omar. Herc describes Kima as a "stuck-up dyke bitch," when she takes control of a situation, and Omar is constantly belittled as simply a faggot. In fact, throughout most of the series, he is referred to by his enemies as "faggot," or "cock-sucker," and rarely by his actual name. On top of this, it is their sexuality that is used against them. When Avon wants to attack Omar in the first season, he does so by torturing and killing his boyfriend, Brandon. When a perp that has been arrested wants to attack Kima, he calls her "dyke cunt." Even in her seemingly politically correct environment, the commissioner has no interest in talking to Cheryl when Kima was shot, and she is always going to be simply a "dyke" whenever someone wants to demean her. Due to this, these characters have to excel more than those around them in order to be respected on the same level.

In Kima's case, proving herself is simple: she works hard to become an excellent police. She has to prove herself in two ways, as a woman in this old boys' club and as a homosexual in a homophobic environment. Omar, however, uses homosexuality as a force to react against those who attack him. On top of the simple act of being an open homosexual in defiance of his culture's standard, Omar takes this to its extreme and shows his enemies that his sexuality is the source of his power.

In the Season Four episode, "Unto Others," Omar is in a prison full of violent criminals, many of whom he has robbed. On top of that, there's a bounty on his head. His reaction? He overtakes the first man who tries to kill him, and then, in front of a crowd of inmates, stabs him with a shiv in the ass in a clear resemblance to anal sex, as if to say, "Look at me, the fag, look at how manly I am." This gesture, which is at the same time sexual and incredibly violent is the ultimate act of defiance in the homophobic culture which Omar constantly has to defend himself against.

The Cheese Stands Alone

CARVER: Kima, if you don't mind me asking, when was it that you first figured out that you like women better than you like men?

GREGGS: I mind you asking. ("The Detail")

When Greggs and McNulty discuss personal lives, he asks if she has ever been married. She hesitates to tell him about herself, but Bubbles does it for her. When he asks if everyone else figured it out but him, she says that there was nothing to figure out. She told them, "It's better that than have every police on three shifts hounding you every God-damned day. Cops are dogs. . . . It's just something that I had to put out there to get through the day" ("The Buys"). Greggs would have preferred not to have to discuss her sexuality with others, but she does when Bubbles "outs" her, and she finds it more convenient given the culture of her work.

Kima and Omar are very private, very lone-wolf characters. With Kima, it's about protecting her privacy at work, and being her own person at home. Omar, by contrast, dedicates his life to solitude. He creates a lifestyle for himself that revolves around him being an outsider. On top of that, he has created for himself a set of rules and terms that seem to only apply to him. He is never seen at a gay club; and, when he has a partner, it's monogamous, and he is usually seen only with this partner, except at work.

Although there are a lot of contemporary political issues that bring homosexuality in America to light, the issue of gays in the military has a lot of parallels with some of the themes of *The Wire*. Omar's and Kima's preference for solitude underlines the show's direct juxtaposition to the traditional fraternal nature of the military. Both of these characters live and work in settings that could be easily compared to any army. They are fighting in a "war," with a command structure similar to the military's. The streets of any gang neighborhood, as well as traditional (and most contemporary) police and military settings, have a long tradition of being homophobic and violently hostile toward the homosexuals who penetrate their ranks. All three environments rely on a predominantly male atmosphere, as well as intimacy and passion towards one's fellow 'soldiers'. By having prominent characters for each field flourish the way that Omar and Kima do, the show reflects upon the issue of gays in the military, which was reopened not long after the series concluded.

Although these characters are private toward others in their world, they are raw and unprotected to us. The audience gets to see the intimate details of Omar's and Kima's lives more than most other characters. It is no accident that Omar and Kima are the only two main characters that we see naked in the series (In Kima's case, she is the only lead female who exposes her breasts and in Omar's, he is the only lead male who shows his penis). This literal nudity underlines the metaphorical nakedness that they feel, displayed in front of us at all times, sharing their secrets.

Omar Comin'

In the episode, "All Prologue," Omar is awaiting Bird's trial, for which he is a witness. He sits with a court officer, who is doing a crossword puzzle, and having problems:

> OMAR: It ain't working out for you, huh?
>
> OFFICER: Mars is the God of War, right?
>
> OMAR: Planet too.
>
> OFFICER: I know it's a planet, but the clue is 'Greek God of War'.
>
> OMAR: Ares. Greeks called him Ares. Same dude, different name is all.
>
> OFFICER: Ares fits, thanks.
>
> OMAR: It's all good. You see, back in middle school and all that, I used to love them myths. That stuff was deep, truly.

It's no accident that Omar is familiar with ancient Greece. He is a contemporary version of Socrates, walking through the streets of Baltimore.

Both Omar and Socrates have a unique relationship with the boys (that's boys, not men) that they're intimate with. They are mentors to their lovers, teaching them how to be lovers, how to be warriors, and how to be moral. They both act as protectors over the small boys who they mentor.

During his testimony at Bird's trial, Levy accuses Omar of being amoral (similar to the accusations leveled at Socrates, who would eventually see his end as a result of a trial that he faced for "corrupting the minds of the youth of Athens"). Omar's response is to use the Socratic Method to attack Levy's very position of morality, "I got the shotgun, you got the briefcase. It's all in the game, though, right?" ("All Prologue")

Both Omar and Socrates died to prove their point. They both challenged the systems in the cities that they were unquestionably associated and intertwined with. Omar specifically chooses to stay in a place where he knows that everyone wants him dead, which is as close to a complacent suicide as Socrates's. They both embody the Game to the ultimate end. They play it better than anyone else, and dying is a necessary end to this position. Omar takes the Game to its ultimate, logical conclusion, much like Socrates does with his relationship to Athens.

In *One Hundred Years of Homosexuality: And Other Essays on Greek Love*, David Halperin says that although homosexual sex existed in Greece, it wasn't about homosexual love—it was about power and dominance. Omar identifies himself as gay, but takes this idea of homosexuality as power very seriously. Perhaps his relationship with his sexual orientation is more about observing his power over those around him than corrupting the youth of Baltimore.

"   "

— Anonymous

In philosophy, as in fiction, it's often more important to look at what's not being said over what actually is. In a program that pays as close attention to its dialogue as *The Wire* (to say nothing of starting each episode with a quote from itself), what is omitted is no less than crucial.

At the same time as the airing of *The Wire*, NBC was patting itself on the back for having one platonic kiss between two gay friends on *Will and Grace*. Unlike most television of its time, *The Wire* didn't make a big deal about the fact that two of its characters were homosexual. There was no coming-out episode, no series of gay innuendos, not one storyline where characters realized that homophobia was wrong and changed their ways. Skipping these elementary gay storylines, and presenting something more complex—like Kima's relationship with her partner, its termination, and her subsequent relationship with their son—says more about homosexuality in our time than most other contemporary art, specifically within the medium of television.

There are a couple of other scenes that make the show's take on sexuality stand out: The first is the brief sighting of Major Rawls at a gay bar in the Season Three episode, "Slapstick." Simply noting a character's homosexuality (or bisexuality), and never making reference to it again speaks volumes. It is as if the show said, "Look here is another queer character, who is obviously closeted and it is not even worth our attention to explore that. Instead, let's see what's going on with Kima and Omar." The same can be said about Snoop, who not only displays many stereotypical lesbian qualities, but is loosely based on the actress who plays her, who is an out lesbian. Although the show makes allusions to her sexuality, it never directly tells us where she stands. By avoiding this, the writers step beyond what they do with Rawls, because here the show is saying that it doesn't even matter one way or another. Sexuality is not what Snoop's storyline is about, and thus it is unnecessary to explore this side of her.

This is not to say that the show shies away from showing its homosexual characters being gay. If anything, we see Kima and Omar with their significant others more than any heterosexual character throughout the series. Rather, the show chooses only to focus on the gay characters who make use of their homosexuality to become greater.

The Wire's true strength is its ability to seriously examine its characters and setting. The show is a poem about Baltimore, but, more importantly, it uses Baltimore as a microcosm of early-twenty-first-century America. Where would politics, culture, and social progression be in contemporary America without the rise of gay rights and the debate over homosexuality? *The Wire* took a stand on the issue, allowing us to reflect on Plato's time-tested remark in *The Symposium*, that 'homosexuals' are the best of boys and lads.

LINE 11
Omar the Virtuous Thug

JONATHAN TRERISE

Omar Little sits lazily and relaxed in court, testifying against Bird, a member of Avon Barksdale's organization, who's accused of killing a working man. Omar's demeanor, language, and character stand in stark contrast to the stuffy courtroom atmosphere. His presence, crowned by his intentionally awkward tie, pokes fun at the self-importance of lawyers, judges, and the system as a whole. To top it off, Omar completely shocks the otherwise unflappable "drug lawyer," Maurice Levy. And he does this with his stark *honesty*.

After being asked about his occupation, Omar says: "I robs drug dealers." Levy attempts to cast doubt on the character and veracity of someone who makes a living by taking the money of drug dealers. Omar coolly replies: "Just like you, man. . . . I got the shotgun, you got the briefcase" ("All Prologue").

Though the streets of *The Wire* are filled with terrifying and powerful characters—Avon, Wee-Bey, Sergei, Marlo, Chris, Snoop, and Brother Mouzone—perhaps no one's name rings out quite as uniquely as Omar's. It's known that Avon and Marlo are the kingpins, but Omar is somehow, in not being a kingpin, more powerful. It takes entire drug crews and incredible planning to even touch Omar. You must modify your entire operation to deal with the mere possibility of being hit by him. The streets clear when he comes, and often, corner drug crews willingly give up their package to him.

Such is the character of Omar Little, a stick-up artist who was so good at what he did that he became the terror of the Baltimore streets. Importantly, however, he was not only an

139

accomplished stick-up artist. He was a man of his word. He was a man who shocked the law-enforcement world, by helping on occasion, but also by being a man of *character*. His memorable discussions with Bunk and Butchie showed his sincere thoughtfulness as well as his *code*. He calls out people for their moral imperfections, and he never once did anything wrong to someone not in the Game.

Omar is an enchanting and fascinating character. From a philosophical perspective, however, he's also one of the most *virtuous*. This may seem shocking: how could someone who kills people, someone who robs people, someone who is a terror on the streets of Baltimore actually be a virtuous person?

Virtuous Thuggery

Calling someone "virtuous" has a special meaning in philosophy, one that's closely related to how people usually use the word, but which also refers to the ideas of the ancient Greek philosopher, Aristotle, and some philosophers today who follow him. These thinkers, who are sometimes called "virtue theorists," update or apply Aristotle's views to our contemporary world. They think that the proper way to conduct moral inquiry is by careful investigation into a person's *character* rather than her specific actions. So while some ethical theories try to figure out how we should act, virtue theory tries to figure out what kind of person we should be.

So what kind of person is Omar? Virtue theory asks us to identify specific character traits, with an eye toward their propensity to bring about a happy and flourishing life or *eudaimonia*, to use Aristotle's term for a full flourishing life. People should have these character traits in order to achieve happiness both for individuals and the society or world in which they reside.

Do Omar's characteristics actually lead to a flourishing life of happiness? Other fans could add to this list, but here's how I would describe Omar: fierce, intelligent, consistent, resourceful, honest, courageous, calculating, principled, strong-willed, proud, no-nonsense, vengeful, persistent, and generous. Most of these are "good" traits; in Aristotle's view, these are traits which, generally, will increase the chances of Omar and those around him to live a good life. To see this, compare Omar and his general demeanor with Jimmy McNulty. Jimmy, clearly as skilled as Omar in his occupation as Omar is in his, is not consistent, generous, and principled, except sometimes when pursuing a case. Jimmy's relationships are toxic, even his friends are hesitant to help him, and he seems perfectly miserable, *except* when he stops exhibiting these negative character traits. Omar, by contrast, is generally comfortable, at ease, and respected by his friends *and* enemies.

So it seems pretty clear that Omar is closer to flourishing than Jimmy. But is it true that all of Omar's character traits lead to happiness? Don't some of them, such as pride and vengefulness, sometimes lead to trouble?

Can a Virtuous Person Be a Thug?

Indeed, sometimes living out positive character traits can lead to trouble. But the fact that Omar sometimes portrays character traits that are less than ideal does not mean that he's not a virtuous person.

Aristotle thought that the virtues were essentially traits that exemplified *balance*—he thought that too much and too little of particular character traits would both be bad and would not lead to human flourishing. For example, courage is clearly a virtue which will lead to happiness. The lack of courage, cowardice, is clearly a deficiency, and does not lead to a good life, as the coward does not respect himself nor does he get respect from others. Yet there's such a thing as *too much* courage. Being *brash* or *foolhardy* won't lead to a flourishing life because you're likely to make disastrous mistakes. Hence, having proper courage is, as Aristotle calls it, the "mean between extremes," which is necessary to achieve the goal of flourishing or happiness.

So when I said that Omar portrays character traits that are less than ideal, I was being sloppy. Looking carefully at the above list, the only traits which are possibly negative are ferocity, being strong-willed, prideful, or vengeful. Our question, then, is whether or not these traits are ever good. Clearly, they can be: there are occasions that call for ferocity and vengeance and so on.

To go deeper, we need to ask if Omar ever moved to the extremes with *any* of the aforementioned traits. This is not so with ferocity; around children, he was generally gentle. And, as already mentioned, his ferocity was never turned on a "citizen." Also, note his pride: though he was proud, he wasn't so proud as to not be able to recognize skills in others, as in his respect for Brother Mouzone or for intelligent police like Bunk.

The best candidate that I can see for him venturing too far is that he possibly went to an extreme *seeking vengeance* against Barksdale or Marlo's crew. You might also say he exemplified the extreme of persistence, perhaps to the point of obsession. Maybe the passionate pursuit of vengeance impeded his living a flourishing life. When seeking out these goals, he *was* less happy and less satisfied with life. And maybe his desire for vengeance for Butchie led to his death.

But can we really say that someone in Omar's position and context in life *shouldn't* seek vengeance for these things? And shouldn't he seek vengeance diligently, possibly endangering his life and putting his own happiness on hold? Though Omar is clearly guided by his thirst for vengeance, it's not clear that this has gone to the extreme. In Omar's world, the streets of Baltimore, the only justice for Brandon or Butchie would come from Omar; no one else would dare touch Avon or Marlo. Someone had to stand up to these kingpins; someone did send a message to the world that they are not untouchable. And this allows for some happiness, both for Omar and the others that Avon or Marlo oppress.

After all, what would happen if Omar *did not* diligently seek vengeance? This would clearly not lead to any kind of happiness; not committing himself in this way would exhibit the *deficiency* of the virtue of *seeking justice*. So though Omar's circumstances are tragic, the realities of his life and his world only allow for some measure of flourishing. Omar cannot flourish in the grandest sense possible. However, he can and does flourish insofar as his world allows.

So, in virtue theory, we must give careful consideration to *context*. We must, in analyzing the choices people make and the behaviors they exemplify, be vigilantly aware of the circumstances they are in, as circumstances have an influence on right action. To be clear, this is not to say that there are no right answers; there *are* right ways to behave and right characteristics to portray; or at least there are some wrong ways.

It's just that the determination of what the right answers are will depend on many factors.

It's harder to justify Omar's persistence for vengeance for being set-up by Stringer Bell. His obsession here endangered the lives of people in his crew and got Tosha killed. Going too far, it became unbridled vengeance and did not lead to a flourishing life for him or his loved ones. But Omar admitted his mistake in Season Three ("Dead Soldiers"), and there's room in virtue theory for imperfect people.

You Feel Me?

So, Omar's a decent guy with a code. But he's still a criminal. Can we really say that a criminal is a virtuous person?

I think so. First, we need to make clear that legality and morality are different concepts, and often won't and don't intersect. So the fact that something is illegal doesn't mean it is immoral; and the fact that something is legal doesn't mean one should do it. Just because Omar breaks the law, this doesn't mean he's breaking *moral* laws.

That point is hardly controversial. But you might think: how does this help Omar? Historically, actions which are illegal-but-not-immoral are not actions that Omar performs. An important example here would be Rosa Parks's violation of the law that specified where she had to sit on a bus. In cases like that, the law was quite clearly wrong and discriminatory. Nothing like this is the case with Omar. Omar, in contrast to Rosa Parks, kills, steals, and gives people drugs that will feed their addiction, and more.

But virtue theory forces us to consider the context in which these illegal actions are undertaken. Virtue theory also resists looking at the action of killing in itself, and asks if it is right or wrong given the context. So let's look at whom Omar murders. Omar never hurt a working man (by which he means person); he never turned his gun on someone not in the (illegal) game. Stunningly, even when robbing or extorting someone of drug money (like Proposition Joe), he *pays for Joe's clock-repair services* ("A New Day"). To the extent that Omar interacts with people, even other street players, he interacts fairly and honestly. But, to the extent that he involves himself with players in the Game, *about aspects of the Game*, the rules are different.

Contrast this with someone like Marlo. He treats players
outside the Game as he treats players inside the Game. He
kills citizens as wantonly as he kills other players in the Game.
And, can we imagine Marlo dealing with people fairly with
non-game transactions? Would Marlo pay Prop Joe for his
clock-repair services? I believe not. When Marlo gives money to
children, it's pretty clear that it's about setting up and maintaining his empire. Marlo's actions are about obtaining and
retaining power. Omar's questionable actions have more to do
with disrupting power structures (which, I would claim, are
there unjustly; could we see Omar fighting against a truly
benevolent leader? I think not).

So, while Marlo might claim that his illegal actions are, like
Omar's, part of the Game's being the Game, we first must recognize that Marlo killed non-game players, like the security
guard who simply asked him for a modicum of respect
("Refugees"). But, also, the circumstances of Marlo's killing, for
example of Prop Joe, differ markedly from the circumstances of
whomever Omar kills.

Consider three of Omar's victims and the circumstances
surrounding their murders:

- **Stinkum: a known enforcer of Barksdale's organization who was on his way to kill someone when
  Omar got him ("Lessons").**

- **Savino: when Omar kills Savino, it's a bit unsettling
  at first. Savino seems innocent enough (unlike
  Stinkum, we're not as aware of him *as* a killer). But
  Omar explicitly clarifies that Savino *was muscle* for
  Avon's crew, before switching to Marlo's crew; only
  then does Omar kill Savino ("Took").**

- **Stringer Bell: Omar kills Stringer *after* Stringer
  has set him up, deceived him, and generally tried
  to take advantage of and be dishonest with him
  ("Middle Ground").**

In each of these cases, Omar isn't looking for power. Marlo's
explicit purpose in killing Prop Joe was to become king, and he
saw Joe as an impediment to that. Though Joe was a legitimate
target as a player in the Game, Marlo's killing of Prop Joe

occurred *after* Joe had helped Marlo a great deal, and this killing quite clearly was a consolidation of Marlo's power. So Marlo's killings seem more cruel.

But Omar *steals drugs and money*. And after stealing drugs, he either *gives them away* for free or *sells them* himself for a profit. How can this be virtuous?

To be sure, it's hard for us, sitting comfortably reading about an HBO show that we love to think of such activity as virtuous. But again consider context, as well as how Omar behaves *within* the world he resides in. He does not live in a comfortable world where he can sip wine and watch television shows about people who have hard lives. Omar's activity with drugs only victimizes those who are themselves criminals. The only real challenge here then may be the fact that Omar gives or sells drugs to people. However, even then, when Omar does this, it's to someone who would have obtained them anyway. So it's pretty clear that any otherwise immoral activities Omar participates in are merely conducted against those for whom the rules were already different. In Omar's world, drug behavior is much more normal than in the world we are used to.

When the world you exist in is an unjust world, it changes the moral playing field. Omar was raised on the streets, with crime surrounding him and a lack of justice or opportunity being ever-present. In this world, taking justice into his own hands becomes the only way. Omar is indeed influenced by his world; he can't help but be this way. But what's amazing about him is *how* he exists within that world. The question is not "Does Omar do all the right things?"; it's "What kind of person is he?" He treats people with respect when they deserve it. He takes his grandmother to church. He feels responsibility when he has made mistakes. In so many cases, he shows us how to be within our world, even though his world is so very different from ours. Amazingly, Omar is able to develop a distinct ethical code within the terrible world he was raised in.

And let's not lie to ourselves: our world is filled with illegal activity as well. And there are illegal activities that many of us participate in, in part because that's the world we live in. What seems to matter more, much if not all of the time, is how we live within this world, illegal or otherwise. Omar's illegal activities do not in any way preclude him from being a virtuous person, anymore than anyone else's illegal activities preclude them from being virtuous. In Omar's world, the explanation of his getting involved with the illegal Game is very simple: he grew up in Baltimore in the latter part of the twentieth century. It's amazing that, given those circumstances, he was the good man he was.

Yo! My Turn to Be Omar!

Aristotle's idea was that, until you're virtuous yourself and know how to act, you should emulate the conduct of a *moral exemplar*. So, when in doubt, you should do as the virtuous person does. Should we, following Aristotle, *emulate Omar*?

Many of the characters on *The Wire* would benefit from being like Omar, and could make their world better if they were more like him. He is an exemplar in that sense. But there's one significant catch here: when Bunk reported to Omar that he saw *children playing like they were Omar*, Omar was clearly disturbed. He did not like the fact that children were emulating him; nor did Bunk. So, could a virtuous person really *not* be an example to children? I think this is actually the most significant problem for a view that considers Omar to be virtuous.

Furthermore, remember in the last section that I said it's amazing that, given Omar's circumstances, he was able to become the good man he was. Clearly he gets this recognition from my comparing him to the other fierce characters. He's a better man than Marlo, Avon, and so forth. But is he better than everyone who was on the streets? After all, Bubbles and Cutty were both very much of the street; weren't they more virtuous than Omar was?

It may be that this is the real flaw in Omar's character: though he clearly loves children and is gentle with them, they should not follow in his footsteps. They should instead follow in the footsteps of Cutty, who erected a boxing gym to help teach street kids discipline and keep them away from the Game. We certainly don't think that children should get further involved in the drug world, even if, like Omar, they become virtuous stick-up artists.

And consider one who *does* follow in Omar's footsteps: young Michael. There's something disheartening when this "heir-apparent" to Omar's throne as the most serious counterweight to Baltimore's drug lords appears. Michael, who brandishes a shotgun in his final appearance in the show, consistently showed himself to have a sense of honor and virtue, along with significant skills for street survival and success.

So Michael is the new Omar. This is disheartening because Michael had potential outside of the streets. The inability of Cutty to reach him and mentor him, in boxing or otherwise, is unfortunate. However, undeniably, there's also something exciting about this: Michael can be the new person to challenge the unparalleled authority of Marlo (or whomever). Since Omar's gone, who will check the unjust authorities on the streets of Baltimore? Michael will. It's here that we can see why it's okay for Omar not to be like Cutty; it may even be necessary.

Without someone like Omar, nothing is stopping a kingpin from having complete authoritarian control of the streets. Omar and Michael will force them to be more careful, to take extra steps and, perhaps, also be less dangerous to those outside the Game. It was Omar, after all, who helped the law obtain some justice against the Barksdale organization. Some vigilantism can be virtuous; this is true at least, but perhaps most significantly, on the streets, where justice won't come in any other way.

All of us struggle and are imperfect. At times we exhibit behaviors that we wouldn't want our children to emulate. This doesn't mean that we're not otherwise virtuous. This does not prohibit Omar from being a potential moral exemplar. It just explains his imperfection. It's unclear that "perfect virtue" really exists. Either way, on the streets, Omar is still one of the most virtuous people around.

The Game's the Game

Indeed. But the Game can be played in different ways, and Omar shows us that the game can be played virtuously, even when the hand that you've been dealt by society, bad luck, racism, and poverty is an unfortunate one. Perhaps the real crime in the streets, after all, is not the actual crime that takes place. Those crimes are merely the expression, the details or manifestations of the real crime. The real crime is that the real heroes of the street, its truly virtuous citizens, aren't treated or recognized as such.

They endure a triple injustice. First, they are ignored by the rest of the country and the world. After their death, only those on the street will remember them, in a new kind of oral tradition, passed on (and in some cases distorted) by new players.

Second, the virtuous citizens of the street must perennially fight off the notion that, because they are criminals, they are vicious or bad people. Law enforcement authorities assume that they are. Greater society assumes it, too. But these citizens have a notion that they aren't, for example, like Marlo.

Third, these virtuous citizens, and Omar in particular, when they die, don't get the send-off they deserve. They're hardly noticed for who they were, what they struggled against and triumphed over, and what their contribution to the world was. They're not given a hero's funeral. Omar's body is almost mislabeled in the morgue as being someone else's. A coroner only figured out the mistake when he happened to notice that Omar's body had the wrong name attached, and that another body (an older white man) had Omar's. That is, it was a racial and cultural anomaly that got Omar the very least of what he deserved in death: recognition of *his name*.

So Baltimore's virtuous son Omar dies without fanfare or recognition. On the surface, he's just another criminal caught up in drugs. But one of the great things about *The Wire* is its honesty and realistic understanding of the street and its inhabitants—it does more than look at the surface. This is one of the great things about philosophy also: it looks past the surface. And since we've seen past the surface and accorded Omar his appropriate label as a virtuous person, how else must we look past the surface?

The streets of *The Wire*, while fictional, are representative. There are most likely virtuous thugs out there in the real world. It's unlikely that there will be an Omar in the full sense of his character, but the possibility of him as the virtuous thug is instructive. We are quick to be amazed at how someone could get caught up in drugs, or with how violence becomes so normal to some people. But these are mistakes. Though it would be nice if the world was such that, no matter where you are, the myth of the American Dream and the opportunities it provides were readily available to you, this is not the case. Even for those who are able to escape drugs and violence, the hurdles they've climbed are unlike any those of us lucky enough to enjoy *The Wire* from a distance have experienced.

Perhaps one of the most uplifting moments in the whole of *The Wire* is Bubbles's meal with his sister and her children. This moment is of particular value, not only because this is indicative of a potentially positive future for him, but because we have been with him every step of the way, seeing what he's triumphed over. But David Simon, creator of the show, has noted that Bubbles is based upon an addict who in fact *did not* conquer his disease. Knowing Bubbles and his struggles, viewers of *The Wire* can't help but look deeper than the surface view of the streets. Can anyone who has watched carefully look at an addict the same way as they did before?

The same phenomenon extends to how we view "thugs." Some of them are monstrous, vicious individuals. You need only consider Cheese or Marlo to get a view of truly despicable people. But moral life is vast and complex, and looking simply at the actions that people undertake risks a kind of blindness which is all too common.

When we view Omar, we see that a thug can be a beautiful person, someone with a distinct code that is admirable. Furthermore, we may see someone who is a social necessity, a check on the powers that be in an area where governmental and legal rules and enforcers don't have the power that they need to keep those forces in check. So when we see street violence reported on the news, we on the outside have an all-too-common tendency to shake our heads and sigh. But we truly have *no idea* what that violence was about. It could very well be an Omar showing a Marlo that he is not untouchable—that he may not wear any crown he wants to without paying a hefty price.

And consider the reverse: because someone *isn't* involved in violence and drugs, because someone isn't on the streets, we have a tendency to trust him. But what white-collar scandals and the economic crisis should show us is that there are many vicious people off the streets, too. *The Wire* shows us this, again, in the seemingly upstanding people who are despicable, like Bill Rawls or Clay Davis.

So appearances can be deceiving, and we have a tendency to react viscerally and immediately to violence in the media. But *The Wire* has shown us that these reactions are not always trustworthy. They are often guided by clear and simple self-serving behavior, or by a deeper, more nefarious desire to keep certain power structures in place. As the behavior of some of the powerful in *The Wire* shows us, it's comfortable for a lot of people to restrict other people to certain roles and behaviors. Indeed, sometimes even the powerless are comfortable in their roles. Consider Fruit's reaction to Hamsterdam: "Look we grind and y'all try to stop it. That's how we do. Why you gotta go and fuck with the program? All due respect" ("Hamsterdam"). But this is more of an initial reaction to the disruption of business as usual. If progress is to be made, if justice is to be done, if life is to get *better*, disruption of business as usual is necessary. *The Wire*, Omar, and philosophy each disrupt business as usual.

Philosophy finds in *The Wire* a ready companion, able to look past comfortable truisms, able to look carefully at the situation a person is given, and more carefully evaluate his or her character. Taking a more careful look at our own streets, we should not be so quick to judge *The Wire*'s inhabitants. We really have no idea what's going on there without giving them as careful a look as *The Wire* gives its subject matter.

And that's what philosophy is all about. And when philosophy looks at Omar, it can't help but see a virtuous person in Aristotle's sense, even though Omar is a criminal, a killer and a thief. Omar lived the virtuous thug life.

Fourth Case

The Boundaries

LINE 12
No Women Up in the Game

MONA ROCHA AND JAMES ROCHA

Let's ask you two questions. First, which character on *The Wire* was by far the most frightening, creepiest, scariest thug you'd never want to see in a dark alley? Second, how long did it take you to figure out that she was a woman?

Felicia "Snoop" Pearson is a cold-blooded killer, a perfect soldier, and a woman whose womanhood plays almost no part whatsoever in her character. When the police are openly tailing Marlo Stanfield's people, it's Snoop, more than Chris Partlow or Marlo, who yearns to get back to killing. When Chris observes that Snoop's eager to get back at it, Snoop responds, "Goddam! Right? Too much fucking talking around here." When Marlo gives her someone to kill, Snoop responds with barely disguised satisfaction, "Now we talking" ("Unconfirmed Reports").

Detective Shakima Greggs's womanhood is surely more visible than Snoop's, but she's not very womanly either. Recall when Kima first meets Preston "Bodie" Broadus. Bodie had just punched Detective Patrick Mahon during a police raid, and Officers "Herc" Hauk and Ellis Carver were quick to jump Bodie and begin an ass-whupping. The camera cuts to Kima, who sprints over to the scene in order to step in and prevent a travesty of justice—or so it appears. But we've been fooled; this isn't the NYPD or the LAPD we've seen on television—this is the Baltimore PD of *The Wire*. Kima gives Bodie the biggest ass-whupping of any of the cops, really kicking the crap out of him. Later, Herc points out to Bodie that Kima, "Fucked you up like a cop should," to which Carv adds, "One thing about Kima, she put a hurtin' on you like a man" ("The Pager").

Although there are plenty of women on *The Wire*, there are only two right up in the middle of the Game. There's one on each side: Kima on the side of the law, and Snoop from the street side. One message that comes across quite clearly from these two characters is that you cannot survive, much less thrive, in the Game without embracing violence and rejecting femininity. Each of the women who are in the Game is violent to some extent, and neither embraces stereotypical social norms for women, such as a desire for motherhood, a desire for a man, or a desire to wear fancy Cinderella dresses. (As Felicia Pearson says in the *Funny or Die* spoof, "The Wire: The Musical," where she is made to wear a pretty white dress, "Man, fuck this Cinderella Bullshit"). Based on these two women in the Game, we may wonder whether *The Wire* has a feminist message.

Militant Feminism

Feminism is a complex set of theories, and it's nearly impossible to pinpoint one central tenet that all feminists hold. Perhaps the closest claim to a central message of feminism is that there are no differences between men and women that should matter; there is nothing about men that makes them superior to women in any morally relevant way. Thus, any advantages in life that men have in virtue of being men are undeserved.

That much about feminism—the demand for real equality between men and women—is clear. What's more contentious is what feminists think about different attributes that are socially designated as either masculine or feminine. Stereotypically, our society tends to think of men as smart, strong, and powerful; as violent conquerors who seek to win any competition, whether the prize is money, power, or women. When it comes to women, our society tends to think they should be passive, weak, and emotional creatures, who exist to be won over by men and who are dedicated to selflessly nurturing those men, as wives and mothers.

Feminists tend to differ in response to these attributes. While some feminists think that we should encourage individuals to select whichever characteristics they prefer, other feminists see some feminine attributes as objectively good and some masculine attributes as objectively bad. For example, some feminists would argue that embracing violence and trying to win at all costs are the sort of masculine attributes that we should all disdain—women shouldn't try to become more like men in these ways.

There's at least one group of feminists, however, that would disagree on this point. We label them "militant feminists," since they believe that women can, and should, embrace violence when it can be justified. Militant feminism includes two main ideas. The first is that women can excel at *anything* men can, including using violence. The second is that violence is justified, regardless of the gender of the person using it, if it's used in the pursuit of just ends, especially feminist ends. Snoop works perfectly as an example of the first idea. Since Kima's actions are limited by her sense of justice, she stands as an example of the second one.

Snoop and Kima fit in neatly with the militant feminists from the 1960s and 1970s who formed and fought within militant leftist organizations, such as the Black Panther Party and the Weather Underground. We have in mind women such as Elaine Brown and Kathleen Cleaver of the Black Panther Party, and Bernardine Dohrn and Susan Stern of the Weather Underground. These women wove together feminism and militancy in a quest to change the world for the better by fighting to end sexism, poverty, racism, and imperialism.

In the Black Panther Party, for example, Panther women learned to use guns for self-defense against racist mobs and policemen. As Kathleen Cleaver put it, "When we looked at our situation, when we saw violence, bad housing, unemployment, rotten education, unfair treatment in the courts, as well as direct attacks from the police, our response was to defend ourselves." So, the Black Panthers armed themselves, but they also operated free breakfast programs for school children, collected clothes for the impoverished, and funded medical clinics in ghettos.

For their part, the Weatherwomen protested the Vietnam War vehemently and used violence in self-defense in their encounters with the police. Susan Stern remembered a protest in Chicago in 1969: "I saw a woman from my affinity group wedged up against a park grounds shack. Two pigs were working her over with their clubs as she lay there . . . something in me clicked" (p. 148). She then entered the fray herself and used violence in defense of her friend. Portrayed as prone to violence by the media, the Weatherwomen also led political education campaigns to inform the public of what the United States was up to in Vietnam.

As one of the founders of the Weather Underground, Bernardine Dohrn, in particular, stands out as a perfect example of this instructional and militant mix: Dohrn advocated a platform of outright resistance to US imperialism in Vietnam through the bombing of public buildings on US soil. Even though Dohrn and her organization phoned in warnings designed to clear the buildings in question, her actions landed her on the FBI's Most Wanted list. Dohrn saw her actions as justified: through outrageous, violent behavior she was bringing attention to injustices the US was committing abroad.

These militant feminists were tough, capable, and willing to physically fight for their beliefs, and they did not allow society's gendered expectations to get in their way. They were anything but weak, trembling women. Snoop and Kima are good examples of militant feminist characters because they are strong women who use violence in pursuit of their ends, and Kima does so with a strong sense of justice guiding her.

The Lexus of Hard Ass Soldiers

The first main idea of militant feminism is that women can do anything men can do, which includes being perfect soldiers, killers, and anything else that society usually associates with manhood. Just as Jack Johnson, Joe Louis, and Muhammad Ali proved something tangible and important about race by dominating the violent sport of boxing, women too can prove something to the world about their abilities and potential by excelling in the arena of violence.

Snoop makes strides in this arena. She isn't just a soldier: she's a *natural* soldier, who is sickened by Michael Lee's questioning of orders, such as in this scene:

MICHAEL: Why we doing Junebug anyway?

SNOOP: Heard he called Marlo a dicksucker, talk shit like that.

MICHAEL: You heard? You ain't sure?

SNOOP: [*angry*] People said he said it.

CHRIS: [*calm*] It doesn't matter if he said it or not. People think he said it. Can't let that shit go.

MICHAEL: Why not? I mean, Marlo ain't suck no dick, right? So, if Marlo knows he ain't suck dick, then what he care what Junebug say? What anybody say? Why this boy got to get dead for just talking shit.

SNOOP: Because he's got a big motherfuckin' mouth, that's why, and you need to stop running your own mouth, young'un. ("Unconfirmed Reports")

As we see here, Snoop isn't just a soldier; she is an every-order-following, do-whatever-is-asked-no-matter-what soldier who gets visibly angry with anyone who soldiers differently. Snoop's happy to kill, only requiring an order to do so. Michael wants violence to have a reason—he can't embrace violence for violence's sake. In this way, Snoop surpasses Michael in a cornerstone attribute of masculinity: the ability to embrace violence and use it successfully for one's ends, or for the ends of one's superiors.

As Bernardine Dohrn said in a documentary on the Weather Underground, "There's no way to be committed to non-violence in the most violent society that history has ever created." Snoop fits snuggly into this most violent society of ours, which is seen in the clearest way when she goes on a shopping trip into "decent society." The scene in which Snoop goes to the Hardware Barn to buy a nail gun is quite memorable ("Boys of Summer"). As she listens to the salesperson's advice—"You might want to consider the powder actuated tool. The Hilti Dx 460 MX or the Simpson PTP, these two are my Cadillacs"—Snoop capably follows his explanation of the nail gun's advantages of power with minimal recoil. The salesman's benign smile at Snoop's quick understanding vanishes into a look of disturbed alarm, however, when Snoop explains why she appreciates the .27 caliber charge offered by the nail gun: "Man, shit. I seen a tiny-ass .22 round-nose drop a nigga plenty of days, man. Motherfuckers get up in you like a pinball, rip your ass up." Snoop then decides to buy the nail gun, tipping for the good service she's received: "This is $800," the salesman counters. "So what, man? You earned that buck like a motherfucker. Keep that shit." She walks away, happy with her purchase.

Snoop has repurposed what "decent society" sees as a tool into a weapon. In this scene, Snoop gives new meaning to militant feminist Elaine Brown's words: "I have control over all the guns and all the money of the party. There will be no external or internal opposition I will not resist and put down" (p. 5). Snoop sees the world through eyes tinted in blood, where a nail gun isn't just a nail gun. Yet, by owning that violence, Snoop controls her life and can put down any opposition she faces.

Not just a perfect soldier, Snoop revels in killing. In her first speaking scene, when Marlo tells her it's her turn to hit one of Barksdale's corners, she responds, "Bout time. For real" ("Back Burners"). Though she wears a pink jacket, light blue jeans, and has pigtails with brightly colored barrettes as she shoots up Poot's corner (killing Rico), Snoop *uses* a womanly appearance to make it easier to do the hit. For Snoop, womanhood is a costume, and not her identity: she controls womanly attributes, they neither control nor define her.

Feminists hold that the media push beauty ideals that women then aspire to, influencing women to oftentimes undergo dangerous procedures—such as plastic surgery or starvation diets—in order to look a certain way. Snoop is free from these gendered constraints as she is not worried about fashion or beauty. Only when it works for her strategically does Snoop use fashion or gender norms. Snoop picks and chooses the trends she wants to follow, on her own terms. Gender expectations do not dictate to her who she is.

There is only one moment in the show where Snoop genuinely takes on a feminine attribute: it is the moment right before her death. After telling Michael that "deserve ain't got nothing to do with it" in response to Michael's question about why they are killing Big Walter, the two of them pull into an alley. Michael has actually figured out that he is the one targeted for assassination, and so he pulls his gun on Snoop. She then explains why Michael was the target: "It's how you carry yourself. Always apart. Always askin' 'Why?' when you should be doing what you're told. You was never one of us. You never could be." And then, as Snoop fleetingly touches her braids and looks in the side mirror, she asks, "how my hair look, Mike?" ("Late Editions"). So while there is this distinctly feminine moment at the end, it comes only after Snoop has berated Michael for not being a natural soldier.

For Snoop, Michael isn't a part of something bigger than himself: he doesn't have an identity forged in violence, masculinity, and being a soldier, as Snoop does. Her final moment—asking about her hair—suggests a feminine need to know whether she looks good. But she has no need to ask Michael—it wouldn't make sense to ask him—about her worth as a soldier or a killer. Snoop dies knowing she's as good as any man when it comes to the Game.

If I Hear the Music, I'm Gonna Dance

Snoop's character speaks to the militant feminist view that women can engage in violence just as well as men. But Snoop does nothing to suggest a belief in the position that women, as well as men, ought to use violence in the pursuit of *justified* ends. As Bernardine Dohrn said, "We did not choose to live in a time of war. We choose only to become guerillas and to urge our people to prepare for war rather than become accomplices in the genocide of our sisters and brothers" (p. 156). It was because Dohrn's Weather Underground saw itself as fighting for a bigger cause that its members felt justified in taking up arms. Snoop is not fighting for any such cause. For a more justified militant *feminist*, we have to turn to Kima.

Kima has more femininity in her than Snoop (not that it takes much to have more than Snoop), but she is constantly at odds with her femininity, as if it were a threat to who she truly is. Greggs explains to McNulty early on that it is difficult for women to get out of the car alone on the job:

GREGGS: Not without side partners showing up. They're intimidated, physically. They gotta be.

McNULTY: You weren't?

GREGGS: Yeah. At first. But I'm talking about straight out of the academy type scared. You know what I'm saying? I wasn't about to stay scared. You know, you get your ass kicked once or twice. You realize it's not the end of the world, right? Most of the women they don't want to play that. Some of the men too. They don't want to go there.

McNULTY: You think 'cause you're gay?

GREGGS: I don't know. But is there any other fucking way to police? [*Both laugh*] All I know is I just love the job. ("The Buys")

Kima believes that there's some truth to the social gender identification of women as being physically weaker, but that doesn't mean that only women are afraid. She implies that everyone's scared coming out of the academy, and most women and some men never overcome that fear. But if Kima's going to police, then she must overcome her fear. She must overcome the social attributes that are associated with women, such as being weaker, being emotional, or giving in to fear. Kima has to fight through the fear, just as militant feminists would demand, to play her part—the police part—in the Game.

Even though Kima doesn't fully embrace militant characteristics as much as Snoop does, Kima still struggles with attributes associated with womanhood. She isn't a good spouse because she has "too much dog" in her ("Clarifications"). She takes years to warm up to motherhood. Perhaps she's like Weatherwoman Susan Stern, who said, "I'm no longer content to nurture children, or to give a husband support and strength. . . . I need all my strength . . . to fight" (p. 130). In the beginning, the audience sees an increasingly non-maternal Kima, one who grows more uncomfortable as her partner's pregnant belly increases in size. Eventually, Kima leaves her relationship and her baby, and buries herself in police work and extramarital affairs—playing the classic role of the philandering husband.

The crucial event that spurs Kima to give motherhood a second try is catching a murder—the very murder Michael was objecting to in the exchange above, in which Snoop and Chris kill Junebug and most of his family. It was only because Michael didn't follow orders, as Snoop most definitely would have, that a child was allowed to survive the killing spree (Michael, in a clear contrast to Snoop and Chris, is a killer but has parental instincts due to his love for his little brother, Bug; though, of course, Michael puts much of the motherhood burden onto Duquan "Dukie" Weems, who is unable to take up violence even in self-defense, which leads to the other corner boys feminizing him).

Because Kima is made to feel for this surviving child, her desire to be a mother for her own son is kindled. A multiple-victim homicide leads her to buy children's furniture from Ikea, which she is unable to assemble, bringing about her call to McNulty where she screams, "I don't know how the fuck did you of all people do this shit, huh? How?" While Kima becomes maternal, she cannot avoid who she is deep down. Her proclivity toward masculine traits—violence, aggression—blends with her struggling maternal instincts. We see this mix when she tries to put her baby to sleep. Kima's bedtime version of *Goodnight Moon* is tinged with references to a violent world: "Good night, moon" then, turning to the baby, "You say it. Good night stars. Good night, po-pos. Good night, fiends. Good night, hoppers. Good night, scammers" ("Took").

Come Again, Mama-San

Perhaps it's a coincidence that just as Kima takes on the role of motherhood, she also becomes the moral conscience that reins in Jimmy and Lester. More likely, this moral conscience was always somewhere in Kima's character. Either way, at the end of the series, Kima turns into the feminist heroine. And we mean that in the general sense: all feminists should embrace Kima's representation of moral conscience. Kima does the right thing by turning in Jimmy and Lester when they are abusing the system by creating a fake serial killer in order to catch Marlo. All feminists should applaud her doing the right thing even when it may turn her closest friends against her.

Militant feminists believe that being the moral conscience of the Baltimore PD is not only consistent with, but comes out of Kima's use of violence. Unlike Snoop, Kima's embrace of masculine attributes, including violence, does not undermine her ability to seek justice. The militant feminist though would take the point a step further and say that it's because Kima is willing to take any means necessary to find justice that she is able to keep track of what truly is just.

Some people compromise justice by saying they will not pursue it if that requires violent means. The militant feminist believes that justice requires not only seeking justice but also figuring out when doing the right thing requires using violence and when it requires avoiding violence. Once violence is seen as a means that is sometimes appropriate and sometimes not, then a discriminating ability is needed, and that ability can go a long way in determining what is required to do the right thing.

McNulty and Freamon believe their end (defeating Marlo) justifies their means. Their means include: McNulty harming one homeless man directly by relocating him; a copy-cat business card collector murdering two other homeless men; and the investigation causing emotional harm indirectly to other fearful homeless people and to the humiliated families of the dead homeless men. All of these consequences point to McNulty and Freamon lacking the ability to discern whether the end justifies the means.

On the other hand, Greggs retains that ability to discern whether the end justifies the means. We might see the difference between these abilities by looking at feminist theories of care ethics. Feminist care theorists, such as Carol Gilligan or Nel Noddings, have long charged that traditional ethical theories, which were proposed almost exclusively by men, have overly concentrated on masculine attributes. Specifically, traditional ethical theories tend to focus on an unwavering rationality and a very high valuing of individuality, at the cost of feminine attributes, such as care, dedication to relationships, and a strong sense of responsibility for others. Care ethicists point out that ignoring these aspects of morality can make a theory overly rational in a callous way that isn't sensitive to the plights of others. It is especially worrisome that people who follow masculinized ethical theories learn to rationalize their actions based on their sense of individual self-importance, which sounds eerily like McNulty.

There are controversies among feminists over care ethics: not all feminists agree with some of the theory's stronger claims (for example, many feminists think that rationality is essential to ethics, and perhaps should dominate over emotions). But it is clear that people are wrong for thinking an ethical theory allows them to rationalize their actions based on their individualistic sense of what's important to them. Care ethicists are right to point out that people often engage in cold rationalizations and miss those people who are being harmed at the periphery, which leads to an action that appears to the actor to be permissible, but is actually quite immoral.

Greggs is absolutely right to snitch on McNulty and Freamon; she correctly discerns that justice won't permit the harm that has come to these homeless men to go unspoken. McNulty and Freamon are rationalizing precisely because they lack the ability to care about the people we all have difficulty caring about: the homeless. Greggs will not sacrifice her morality just to catch Marlo. She instead stands up for the less fortunate, much as the Black Panthers did both when they carried weapons to prevent police brutality and provided free breakfasts for hungry children. Because Greggs has a good ability to discern right from wrong, she is able to be the moral conscience for an act that represents an injustice that almost all of us are guilty of: not caring enough about the plight of the homeless.

In the end, Kima, who clearly values friendship and relationships, fesses up to Lester and Jimmy. She risks being ostracized, but she clearly values an honest and true friendship more than a lie. Kima represents the militant feminist's ideal heroine: she is a fighter and a nurturer, who embraces violence when she needs to—all the while making sure that her acts of violence are kept in check with a moral conscience.

We do get a feminist message from *The Wire*. It isn't an obvious one, and it isn't easy to spot. It even comes with violent baggage. But if everything else in *The Wire* is incredibly complex and has some violent baggage, why shouldn't the show's militant feminism?

LINE 13
Capital *Noir*

TOMMY J. CURRY

The Wire has become its own trademark of philosophical pro-
fundity. Hell, you know you've made it to the apex of academia
when Harvard is teaching classes on the series. Mind you this
went down despite the warnings of Ishmael Reed (a recipient
of the MacArthur genius award) that *The Wire* simply reifies
dangerous stereotypes about Black people, Black communities,
and drugs.

Unlike the other chapters in this book, this one doesn't cel-
ebrate *The Wire*. Though Simon's creation is cherished for its
realistic depiction of Baltimore and the decaying urban centers
of America, his focus on poverty and class ultimately distorts
the lens through which we understand racism and Black deprivation in this country. For many white academicians, *The Wire*
offers a critical view of the War on Drugs, urban poverty, and
the police state, but this story is not novel or remotely interesting when viewed from the perspectives offered by Black
prison theorists, or compared with Black films over the last
decade.

Like You Didn't Know!

Since the early 1990s Black filmmakers have explored the
impact of the drug trade on Black urban communities and the
corruption of police departments around the country which
benefit from this war.

Mario Van Peebles's *New Jack City* (1991) started a nation-
wide conversation in the Black community about the impact of

drugs, and the rise of drug kingpins, like Nino Brown, who were able to take advantage of these impoverished and neglected communities. That same year John Singleton brought the tragedy of drugs and violence to the West Coast in his directorial debut, *Boyz in the Hood* (1991). *Boyz in the Hood* was revered as one of the first films to deal with the ongoing drug war, gentrification, and the racist profiling of police who prey on the vulnerability of young Black men.

This was just the tip of the iceberg, because two years later Albert Hughes's *Menace II Society* (1993) showed the realness of the street game where Caine is forced to think about his life as he is dying from a drug deal gone bad. Black people have reflected on the issue of police corruption and drugs so much that we have made historical re-imaginings like *American Gangsta* (2007) as well as comedies like *Harlem Nights* (1989) with Richard Pryor and Eddie Murphy, two movies that speak to the economic and political vulnerabilities described in Kenneth Clark's *Dark Ghetto* (1965).

But we all know that white people don't really watch movies with too many Black people in them—since those movies would be Black movies—and white people just don't do that one. So— *The Wire* then is the next best thing, a cable-access series white people feel comfortable with using to understand urban deprivation—at least that's what *Stuff White People Like* lists as white people's eighty-fifth most favorite thing to do.

The issues taken up by *The Wire* are not new and are more than adequately explained by a racial realist perspective. The reality is that many Black people know individuals that resemble the characters of *The Wire*, and Simon's class analysis simply can't keep up with the complex realities of urban Black life in America.

Who's Really Keepin' It Real?

The Wire is routinely called a "realist series," where realist is meant to convey the closeness the series has to actual reality. Actually, when Georg Lukács developed the theory of literary realism, he meant to convey a deliberate attempt to "penetrate the laws governing objective reality and to uncover the deeper, hidden, mediated, not immediately perceptible network of relationships that go to make up society" ("Realism in the Balance,"

p. 38). With regard to *The Wire*, this definition has largely revolved around the capitalist realism of society, or the reality that money rules and determines everything.

From this perspective, money—capital—is the most objective and dominant object driving individual actions, and institutional interests. Leigh C. La Berge thinks *The Wire* "demonstrates how realism is always economic realism . . . . capitalist realism" where "the entire series is an investigation into how the realistic interpretation of an urban nexus of race and economy reveals forms of social violence—structural and interpersonal—as a kind of metonymic totality" (pp. 548–49). Slavoj Žižek thinks La Berge has it all wrong though. For Žižek, *The Wire* is realist because "it's a real community stating itself," where the city of Baltimore takes up the tradition of the Greek tragedy by allowing the *polis* to determine its own representation—how it actually *is* and how it *is to be seen* to the world.

Simon's realism, on the other hand, as stated by Simon himself, thinks that the oppression in Baltimore is "more about class than race" (*The Wire: Truth Be Told*, p. 45), thereby making *The Wire's* "priority . . . to humanize the underclass" (p. 45). This is puzzling given that the underclass has always, since the dawn of America, been a racialized category kept separate by law and social condition. The economic classes of America have always been divided by race—your defective ancestry, your uncivilized land, your savageness, your curse for not being white. Segregation, Jim Crow, and slavery owed their existence to this logic, and made Blacks the American underclass by definition.

Hell, when Major Rawls tells McNulty that he was upstairs answering questions about "some project nigger who supposedly beat my unit out of ten murders, . . . murders no one cares about" ("The Target"), the audience is introduced not only to this troubling aspect of Rawls's character, but to the calculus the police are applying to impoverished Black peoples in Baltimore—dead or alive. In short, nigger deaths don't matter; it's just part of (police) business. *The Wire* makes the death and incarceration of Black people its primary subject regardless of the road to perdition chosen by the characters: be it drugs, murder, or snitching.

Unlike the Black movies of the 1990s, the death of Black characters was not a spectacle, a plot twist, or an urban tragedy. The deaths of the Black characters were the loss of a college graduate, the decision between being a Morehouse man or murderer avenging the life of Ricky, the question of whether life matters in the hood, or if "you living just enough for the city." In *The Wire*, the murder of Black characters follows a seemingly necessary logic.

When Stringer Bell is killed by Omar Little and Brother Mouzone, it is just good business for Avon. Stringer is killed in the eleventh episode of Season Three, but it's not until the next episode that we understand what his death means to the police. McNulty is upset that Stringer won't ever know that he was caught on the wire, and William "Bunk" Moreland, accepts Bell's death as an unsolvable murder committed by a "B.N.B.G."—Big Negro with a Big Gun.

The death of Snoop follows a similar path in Season Five. Since the police actually caught Marlo and his crew in a drug deal, it follows that someone had to betray the group and had to die. Here again Black death is seen as inevitable, a consequence of the indifference to Black life be it by police or dealers in the Game. At least Michael was nice enough to tell Snoop her hair looked good, before he blast that ass, right? Omar Little's death is just as random and anti-climactic, demonstrating this aforementioned indifference announced by Rawls. The most terrifying aspect of Omar's death in Season Five was the seeming naturalness of his murder. It was as if the audience could see, could realistically conceptualize, a small Black child as a murderer, unaware and unremorseful of his actions; a lil' Negro with a gun that inevitably blossoms into a big Negro with a big gun.

McNulty simply says that these deaths are of no concern for anyone including the police whose job is to at least feign sympathy as a motivation to solve the crime. In Season Three, Brianna confronts McNulty about his visit to Donette. Now remember, McNulty told Donette that D'Angelo's death could not be a suicide, and ultimately reveals to Brianna, D'Angelo's mother, that he went to Donette first, because he was looking for someone that actually cared about D'Angelo. This suggests that the Game is so strong that it erases the bond a mother has for her child. Brianna doubts the truth of his theory, insisting that D'Angelo hanged himself and wondering if anyone else supports the theory that he was murdered.

She asked McNulty: "This is just you talking, right? Anyone else saying anything?" He replies:

> Nah, just me. No one else cares. . . . Look I'm sorry I brought this whole mess up to begin with because frankly nobody's gonna do shit about it anyhow. Whoever killed him wanted to pass it off as a suicide, and the cops are happy to have one less murder to investigate. On top of that the . . . state's attorney don't give a fuck. I'm not supposed to give a fuck. So I guess your son just got squeezed between the sides. ("Moral Midgetry")

This is where the class-based analysis breaks down. Are we to take on faith and presumption that the police state is this indifferent to all economically impoverished lives? Stated differently, is this indifference a demonstration of the indifference the police have to the underclass, or is this in fact one of the manifestations of Rawls's racist logics, which place the prestige and "good police" work of the institution above the Black lives lost in retaining the illusion of police state legitimacy?

The most deplorable aspect of these deaths is that they inevitably act as a catalyst for allegedly critical conversations that link the death of these characters to their conditions. You know, people like Omar, probably actually die like that, randomly shot by a child in a grocery store. The supposed realism of *The Wire* in fact misrepresents urban Black life, and presents caricatures of Black death. Stated differently, now white people will start debating if little Black boys are killing people simply as a function of their ghetto existence. This possibility, which is very much racialized—since we don't have the same popular image of little white boys randomly shooting white people in broad daylight in grocery stores—takes the place of fact. The ignorance of whites who don't know about Black urban segregation can now use *The Wire* to fill in their cognitive and experiential gaps of Black poverty. The danger is readily apparent.

Only the Racial Realist Can Be 'bout That

For the white liberal attracted to the sentimentality of *The Wire*, race is just one amongst many categories of oppression. Today, many academics see race as being equal to class and gender in the great matrix of oppression. This intersectional (race, class, and gender) frame, however, is really a discursive distraction—a way to distract readers from understanding how racism actually operates and determines the life chances of non-whites in America. When intersectionality theorists point to this trinity of bullshit, what they are in fact saying is that there are individuals who are suffering because they're not white, not male, and not rich. That's everyone who is not a rich heterosexual white man.

That view would erroneously have us believe that anyone who is not the rich, straight, white man has a story of suffering to tell. So the educated wealthy white woman is oppressed. The bourgeois gay white man is oppressed. The poor white worker who lynched Black people was oppressed. You see the problem. If everyone can be both oppressed and oppressor, it neutralizes the consequence of actual systemic oppression. What we should be after is an understanding of racism and "actual, not discursive" oppression that describes the actual conditions of the world we live in.

You don't see middle class white women publicly executed by cops on YouTube like Oscar Grant. You don't see white gay citizens shot holding a bag of skittles and a can of Arizona tea like Trayvon Martin. You don't see poor white people shot in the street like animals, like Darius Simmons. There's a difference between usually well-educated and economically privileged racial classes of people who are marginalized for their supposed transgressions against society but still have a platform for voicing critiques, and Black people, mostly Black men, who can't say shit because they are dead. This is not to deny that violence can and does happen to the poor, the queer, the female, and the young, but rather to recognize that racist violence not only results in the death of the individual from the group, but aspires for the death of the group itself.

See, actual oppression would mean that the oppressed are killed without hesitancy and fear of reprimand by their oppressors. Actual oppression is when a historical group of people is evaluated by a calculus that enforces its inhumanity socially, and creates in our material world conditions aiming to reflect how the dominant group sees that peoples' inferiority. In other words, real oppression seeks to make the conditions of wretchedness suffered by the oppressed their essential and natural character.

Most people don't really understand what racism is, or what a conversation about actual racism would be like without appealing to some mythical notion of inter-racial solidarity (integration). Racism, according to Barbara Fields, is the "assignment of a people to an inferior category and the determination of their social, economic, civic, and human standing on that basis" (p. 48). Contrary to the most popular ways of thinking about race after the Civil Rights era, racism, ensuring that allegedly inferior people were condemned to an inferior social position was the basis of pre-1964 Jim Crowism and the urban segregation that arose as a response to *Brown v. Board of Education*. Black theories about white racism were not concerned about how whites thought about them as individuals, but the power and instruments whites utilized to ensure their inferior and impoverished status in America.

At the turn of the century, this racist division between the (inferior) Black and the poor white motivated the white worker in the South toward lynching, murdering, and raping the slave for fear of Blacks taking their jobs and by effect of their earnings elevating beyond their proper place. In the last decade, this phenomenon has again manifested itself as the pinnacle of the neo-conservative backlash of the 1980s against civil rights legislation, which today, in the wake of the conservative resurgence against Obama's presidency, demands for the eradication of affirmative action, the criminalization of Black men as enemies of society, the diminishing (sterilization) of Black women's reproductive capacity, and the erasure of Blacks from institutions of higher education—the upshot of which is the elimination of Black economic competition through unemployment, incarceration, eugenics, or under-education—and by effect the political impotence of Black dissent against America's colonial oppression.

This is where Simon's realism falls short and demonstrates the need for a more *racial realism* and anti-colonial frame. While this call for racial realism certainly draws from Derrick Bell's understanding of the term as the permanence of racism and the perpetual subservience of Black progress (be it political, economic, or legal) to the fickleness of white racial interests, it also reflects the mandate of America's colonial history, namely that the white citizen, both in concept and corporeality, must remain distinct from the nigger.

Nigga Please: You Telling Me Niggers Were the Basis of American Capitalism?

Capital, according to Wilderson, "was kick-started by the rape of the African continent, a phenomenon that is central to neither Gramsci nor Marx" (p. 27). While white scholars continue to ignore this catalyst of modernity, Black scholars since the nineteenth century have made the development of political economics from colonialism their focus. For example, W.E.B. Du Bois dedicated most of his intellectual life to the clarification of the relationship between the colonization of Africa, the industrialization of America, and the creation of the nigger within modernity. In *The Negro* (1915), Du Bois explains that:

> The Negro slave trade was the first step in modern world commerce, followed by the modern theory of colonial expansion. . . . The new colonial theory transferred the reign of commercial privilege and extraordinary profit from the exploitation of the European working class to the exploitation of backward races under the political domination of Europe. For the purpose of carrying out this idea the European and white American working class was practically invited to share in this new exploitation, and particularly were flattered by popular appeals to their inherent superiority to "Dagoes," "Chinks," "Japs," and "Niggers." (p. 141)

Contrary to the class-based sentiment of the aforementioned realists, colonization empowered working class whites, the Marxist proletariat, to claim a racial superiority over darker races (the colonized), and allowed them to not only claim a racial (white) superiority over darker races, but violently enforce their social and economic privilege, no matter how miniscule when compared to other classes of whites, against the new nigger *under-caste*.

Hosea Easton's *A Treatise on the Intellectual Character, and Civil and Political Condition of the Colored People of the United States and the Prejudice Exercised towards Them* (1837) observed that the creation of "the nigger" in the United States was not simply meant as offense—to name Blacks as inferior— it was also used as the measure of improvement for whites, a category that no white should imitate by character or condition. Easton rightly notes that while 'nigger' was used as "an opprobrious term employed to impose contempt upon them as an inferior race and also express their deformity of person" (p.40), the name pointed to a social caste of degradation cemented by skin color that operated as an imperative "to inspire half grown misses and masters to improvement. They are told if they do not do this or that, or if they do thus and so, they will be poor or ignorant as a nigger, or that they will be black as a nigger; or have no more credit than a nigger" (p. 40). America's colonial heritage, the psychological wages of whiteness, held by whites, but most violently enforced by the white worker, makes an appeal to a class based realism untenable.

By seeking to employ a universal class consciousness that includes racial minorities, Simon appeals to a reasoning by synonymy and analogy that breaks so sharply from the realist criterion that it can only be deemed ideological, in that it presupposes, against history, that the present state of American society is purely stratified along a class binary of haves and have-nots. In other words, the disdain and worry that Simon expresses could never be articulated by Blacks as caused by a change in the material conditions and political buttresses of individuality, since for Blacks, their history in America has been their duration for centuries under the conditions that now spell doom for Simon in *The Wire*.

Rather, seeking to refute the analysis of Simon, racial realism acts as a corrective, and demonstrates that the loss in the confidence of whiteness and the vitiation of its material worth that signal the end of American empire, is in fact the conceptual motivation for Simon's diagnosis of objectivity. The niggerization of whites is catalytic; making the white consciousness aware of the failure of American society to protect its white racial status, not of the exponential increase of human debasement which has plagued non-whites for centuries.

By focusing on class, Simon makes poverty the genesis of the nigger, when in reality the nigger is condemned to be impoverished precisely because he was the genesis of capital— *capital noir*—the productive energy of the American empire, and she (his Black queen mother) was the nigger-maker.

The demise of the American empire is not the devaluation and dehumanization of the individual's labor as Simon contests, since Black dehumanization axiomatically opposes their historical (colonial) position as non-human labor for whites;

rather the collapse of the American empire resides in the transubstantiation of white-citizen-laborer to Black-nigger-slave. Though it is nominally impossible for such a change to occur within the politico-jurisprudential parameters of race set forth by America, the economic and social conditions that have been married to the nature of the nigger by the racist logic of white supremacy finds remorse in its invalidity.

Now that the political economics safeguarding the alleged social, political, and cultural superiority of whiteness have failed, whites find themselves neighbors with the economic and social counterparts to what in their minds remain wretched melanin-ated savages—the Black American nigger. The pessimism of Simon is a narration of displacement where whites find themselves to be urban, immersed in conditions that are not their own—conditions that seemed natural to Blackness, but unfit to whiteness.

The War on Drugs

Despite overwhelming sociological evidence showing that whites, especially white youth, are more likely to engage in drug crimes than non-whites, (white) America accepts almost without question that the racial disparity between white and Black incarceration is natural given the War on Drugs (Michelle Alexander, *The New Jim Crow*). The War on Drugs was created in a time when illegal drug use was on the decline (p. 6), and expanded police powers to legally incarcerate non-white citizens upon a whim, especially Blacks. This exponential incarceration of Black and Brown peoples has been "the most damaging manifestation of the backlash against the Civil Rights Movement" (p. 10).

The protections awarded to the state at all levels for the incarceration of Black men has not only sparked the concern of human rights organizations, but empirically validated the argument started by Du Bois's *Black Reconstruction*, and publicized by the Black Panthers, namely that prison is the continuation of Jim Crow by other means. The racial realist position, which admits the permanence of racism against Blacks, is able to establish the continuity of the prison system from slavery to now.

Alexander makes it plain: "The current system permanently locks a huge percentage of the African American community out of the mainstream society and economy"—so much so that "the social underclass is better understood as an *undercaste*— a lower caste of individuals who are permanently barred by law and custom from mainstream society" (p. 13).

For Simon, the underclass concept acknowledges that the "inner city is full of people for whom work has disappeared" and explains why "the drug trade is the factory—the only viable factory in places like West Baltimore, North Philly, and East St. Louis." From his perspective, the disappearance of work led to "an underground economy based on the sale and use of drugs; of narcotizing the self. We don't need you for our economy, but if you can at least narcotize yourself and go to sleep with this heroin, we can sell you that and you can participate in your own destruction and can in turn be destroyed by the war we will then wage to maintain the price of this illegal narcotic" (*Labour in the 21st Century*). Simon's analysis does help demystify the propped up legitimacy of this war. Much like the exchange from the very first episode of *The Wire*:

> CARTER: . . . we are an effective deterrent in the War on Drugs when we are on the street.
>
> HAUK: Fucking motherfuckers up.
>
> CARTER: Right Indeed.
>
> HAUK: Fuck the paperwork. Collect Bodies. Split heads.
>
> CARTER: Split them wide.
>
> GREGGS: You heroic motherfuckers kill me. Fighting the War on Drugs. One brutality case at a time.
>
> CARTER: Girl, you can't even call the shit a war.
>
> HAUK: Why not?
>
> CARTER: Wars end! ("The Target")

The Wire, following Simon, is adamant and correct in pointing out the brutality and injustice created by institutions seeking legitimacy through the death and exploitation of individuals. Where this message falls short is in its erasure of the particular currency and power gained by these institutions from the public through the idea of policing and terrorizing Black people.

The Wire doesn't make sense without Black bodies acting out crime, violence, and drug addiction. Not because these other bodies don't commit crime, engage in violence and are victims of drug addiction, but because America can't see *The Wire* outside of Black people. The public would not accept such images of police brutalization and violence towards any other race. The story just wouldn't seem as real if white people were depicted as Avon Barksdale, Stringer Bell, or Bubbles. The image of the drug dealer, the gangster, and the snitch are ensnared within Blackness. Jared Sexton writes: "Empire thus exceeds its political, economic and military rationalities whenever Blacks are concerned" (p. 198).

Throughout *The Wire* the audience accepts the police and the government expenditure of Black life to catch other Black drug dealers, like with the death of William Orlando Blocker, or simply as the function of ghetto depravity. Black life is shown to be where police surveillance is accepted as natural—part of the Game. D'Angelo's car ride with Roland Wee-Bey Brice is a great example of this.

When Wee-Bey asks D'Angelo what's the rule in response to his questions about how he was released, D'Angelo responds, "I know the rule. Don't talk in the car, on the phone, or any place that ain't ours and don't say shit to anybody who ain't us" ("The Target"). While some may suggest this is simply part of the structure of the Barksdale organization, the audience never gets to make distinctions between the members of the Black community the drug activity plagues, and the drug dealers. When we see innocent people use the phone, or walking by the dealers, they appear to be part of the landscape, moving participants seen by some degree as representative of their environment.

The Wire demonstrates the lack of accountability or justice within government, and law enforcement, but what it fails to clarify is the unnaturalness of these interventions and violence on Black communities outside the drug game. For Blacks, "the police operate as the unaccountable arbiters of lethal violence, the agents of domestic militarism that underwrites all expansionism and interventionism" (p. 198), and while the police are given a central role as an institution in *The Wire*, the Black community, the Black lives extinguished, the terror that would never make sense or be accepted if shown in images of whites and in white communities are codified as urban normalcy. Hell, it's just common knowledge that ghettos are dangerous and full of Black criminals, isn't it?

On the Road to Perdition

The critical awareness birthed by *The Wire* is useless in any real attempt to understand American urban life and poverty, because this alleged awareness continues to gauge itself by the effect it has on a diminishing white middle class torn between an economically dismal reality and its aspirations to white superiority. The danger of such an appeal lies in its dependence on a false hope in the solutions proposed by white radicals to deal with problems they cannot begin to see. Frank Wilderson reminds us that neither the Black slave of the sixteenth century nor the Black prisoner of the twenty-first century can be accounted for by the categories of work or exploitation. In short, "the black subject position in America represents an antagonism or demand that cannot be satisfied through a transfer of ownership or organization of existing rubrics" (p. 29).

Theories based on the ignorance of white radicalism cannot arrest the decline of American empire, nor should they. This road to perdition was set in course by the idea that one group of people were entitled to freedom on the bondage and economic exploitation of the other. The bifurcation of America reflects this and requires theoretical innovation, not appeals to the same paradigms that continue to erase, ignore, and adopt Black suffering for its convenience. The concept of the underclass does nothing to account for the racist caste system justifying the drug war and inner city deprivation in the minds of the American public. Just be real—a racial realist.

LINE 14
Hard Times after Hard Time

ZACHARY HOSKINS AND NORA WIKOFF

AVON: Joint might'a broke him.

WEE-BEY: Boss, you're talkin' about a homie walked up and shot Elijah Davis, broad daylight, at Pennsy and Gold, then picked up the phone, dialed 911, told the police, "I just shot a nigger. Come get him." That dude ain't breakin. ("Time after Time")

On his last day in prison, Dennis "Cutty" Wise already has a job offer.

A former soldier in the Baltimore drug trade, Cutty has reached the end of a fourteen-year prison stint in Jessup, Maryland. ("Cutty" comes from the prison's nickname, "The Cut.") Before he has even been released, a prospective employer seeks him out.

In this case it's drug kingpin Avon Barksdale who offers Cutty his old job as enforcer. Perhaps because he's been off the streets for so long, Cutty is initially reluctant, wanting a fresh start. But the drug game, with its promise of money, women, and familiarity, is a strong temptation, especially given the relative lack of available legitimate alternatives. Over *The Wire*'s last three seasons, we watch him struggle to rebuild his life after prison. In one of the show's few happy endings, Cutty finds fulfilling, legal work running a boxing gym for inner-city boys, but not before falling briefly back into the drug trade.

Cutty's story throws into sharp relief the challenges many former prisoners face in trying to rebuild their lives after their punishments end. Many ultimately return to crime. The

Bureau of Justice Statistics reports that more than forty percent of prisoners released in 2004 returned to prison within three years.

We could interpret this as evidence that those who commit crimes are bad people. It's in their character. Bad people don't change, and so of course they commit crimes again. But here's another suggestion: when we consider the obstacles our society puts in the path of former prisoners trying to rebuild their lives, maybe we shouldn't be surprised by how many wind up committing crimes again in fairly short order.

In principle, when offenders' punishments end, they have paid their debts to society and are restored to full membership as citizens in the political community. In practice, though, individuals leaving prison often find little institutional support, and in some cases steep institutional hurdles, in finding work, housing, or other goods many of us take for granted. What's more, as Cutty comes to realize, the stigma of "criminal" often remains even after punishment ends. The cumulative impact of these factors increases the risk that individuals will fall back into criminal behavior.

Cutty's story raises important questions for moral and legal philosophy about the significance of completing one's punishment. How does a person's moral status change with his transition from prisoner to former prisoner? And what obligations, if any, does society have to citizens who have engaged in wrongdoing but have, at least in theory, paid their debts and thus been restored to full membership in the society?

Cutty and other offenders face steep hurdles upon release from prison—obstacles to employment, housing, education, political participation, and public assistance. Defenders of these restrictions may claim that criminals lose their rights to the same opportunities as everyone else, or that the community has a right to protect its members against these dangerous people. But if we take seriously the commonly expressed notion that ex-offenders have paid their debts to society, then restrictions that target ex-offenders seem unfair.

If Cutty has truly paid his debt, then isn't he entitled to many, if not all, of the same opportunities as everyone else to secure the basic goods of life? Obstacles to goods such as housing, jobs, and education continue punishing ex-offenders, even after their formal sentences have ended.

Paying Down the Debt

When Cutty is released from Jessup, he joins roughly seven hundred thousand people who leave US federal or state prisons each year who immediately face a number of important challenges. Finding a place to live and a job, rebuilding their networks of family and friends, and in general learning to cope on the outside. For Cutty, these challenges loom especially large, as he has spent fourteen years behind bars. For nearly a decade and a half, he lived in a completely controlled environment; he was told where and when to eat, sleep, shower, exercise, and whatever else. Now he must rebuild virtually every aspect of his life.

The rebuilding process is made more difficult by federal and state policies restricting ex-offenders' access to public housing, many jobs, welfare, federal student loans, and the vote. There are plenty of others. Some prevent ex-offenders from holding public office, serving on a jury, or adopting or fostering a child. All of these policies impose limits on ex-prisoners that the rest of us don't face.

Are these policies morally justified? If we take seriously the common notion that, upon finishing punishment, a person has paid his debt to society, then it's not clear how we can justify continuing to discriminate against ex-offenders in all the ways we do now. Imagine instead that on Cutty's last day in Jessup, the warden came to him and said, "Well, you've completed your prison sentence, but we're going to go ahead and keep you in here permanently."

Most of us would find this appalling. It's unfair to keep someone behind bars when he's already served his time, already paid his debt. So why, then, should we think it's okay to restrict ex-offenders' access to jobs, housing, or public assistance, or their right to vote? At least, there should be a strong presumption in favor of treating ex-offenders with equal respect, giving them the same opportunities as the rest of us to secure the basic goods of life. If we are to continue limiting ex-offenders' opportunities, there had better be strong, compelling reasons for doing so.

Safety First

The most commonly cited justification of ex-offender bans is that they help keep the community safe. This argument is a version of consequentialism, an ethical view that holds that actions, rules, or in this case public policies are right or wrong according to the overall consequences they promote. Restrictions on housing, for instance, emerged in part from concerns about the safety of the residents. In the 1990s, faced with growing drug and gang violence in many public housing projects, Congress enacted laws permitting housing authorities to deny housing to anyone with criminal convictions.

We find similar consequentialist concerns motivating support for myriad employment bans on ex-offenders. These laws vary from state to state, but among the jobs restricted under various statutes are teacher, accountant, chiropractor, architect, barber, roofer, cosmetologist, interior designer, land surveyor, and farm labor contractor. Typically, as with housing restrictions, proponents of job bans point to public welfare as the central reason for excluding ex-offenders. If drug dealers and gang members make life dangerous for everyone else living in housing projects, then isn't it justified to exclude drug dealers and gang members? Likewise, isn't it permissible to bar someone once convicted of a sex offense from being a kindergarten teacher?

Maybe. But our intuitions about these cases may differ depending on how we flesh out the details. Makes sense to keep drug dealers and gang members out of the projects, right? But what about Cutty, whose gang activity was decades ago, and who now just wants to get his life back on track? Or what if Reginald "Bubbles" Cousins, during his struggles with heroin addiction, had received a drug conviction? Should we conclude that he represents too much of a threat to be eligible for public housing? Similarly, it makes sense to keep sex offenders out of teaching positions, right? But what about someone convicted twenty years earlier for statutory rape because, as an eighteen-year-old, he had sex with his girlfriend, who was sixteen?

Policies that deny housing or jobs to anyone with a criminal record inevitably restrict not only those who represent a genuine danger, but also others who pose no real threat. These policies cast too wide a net. In other words, they're over-inclusive. Sometimes they may be warranted—if we can't tell the dangerous former sex offenders from the non-dangerous ones, then maybe keeping students safe requires a general ban. But given the significant hardships housing and employment bans place on ex-offenders, we should be very careful about using over-inclusive policies. In fact, the burden should fall to proponents of such policies to explain why they are necessary—why other, more tailored policies are inadequate.

Even if the community's interest in public safety could justify restrictions on housing or employment, it's hard to imagine how such concerns could justify other obstacles ex-offenders face, such as bans on student loans or voting. Imagine that Malik "Poot" Carr, a Barksdale drug dealer who served a prison stint and later left the drug game, wanted to apply for a federal student loan. Does barring Poot from student loan funding really keep anyone safer? Some have argued that there's a danger in letting ex-offenders vote, because criminals may engage in election fraud or vote to support corrupt government officials or weaker criminal law enforcement. But ex-offenders are a relatively small portion of the overall population, and there's no reason to think they'd co-ordinate their votes. Not surprisingly, there's no evidence that states currently allowing ex-offenders to vote have weaker criminal laws or higher rates of voter fraud than states that don't.

Another Rigged Game

Because a consequentialist defense of housing and employment bans claims that these bans promote better overall consequences, it matters whether they actually do this. A central question is whether they promote community safety, but we also need to consider other expected outcomes of these policies. If we're assessing what will promote the best overall consequences, then all of the likely benefits and harms are relevant; as Lester Freamon says, all the pieces matter.

First, we can address the purported benefits in terms of community protection. The bans are intended to prevent ex-offenders from endangering others. In fact, criminological research indicates that ex-offenders who are unable to find housing and jobs are more likely to commit new crimes. This shouldn't seem surprising. If we give people legitimate avenues to secure housing, to work and provide for themselves and their families, then they won't need to turn to crime. When we throw up roadblocks for ex-offenders, well, we see Cutty briefly fall back into his old role in the drug trade when no fulfilling job alternatives seem readily available. And of course, more crime means more victims and less public safety.

There's reason to be skeptical, then, about whether ex-offender bans keep the community safer. Even if the bans did promote public safety, though, this wouldn't necessarily mean they're justified on consequentialist grounds. A consequentialist assessment must also consider other potential consequences.

Consider housing: most obviously, the bans mean that public housing often isn't accessible for ex-offenders. This is an especially heavy burden given that private rentals typically aren't a real option. Most private landlords, motivated by similar safety concerns, require criminal background checks for prospective renters. As a result, many ex-offenders are barred from private rentals and public housing. With other options blocked, many former offenders turn to homeless shelters, which ironically risks violating an explicit provision of their parole: they are prohibited from associating with other ex-offenders.

Here, Cutty's relatively fortunate. He returns home to live with his mother, in a room in her basement. But even living with family isn't always an option for ex-offenders. The public housing bans allow authorities to evict entire households if anyone living in the home has a criminal record, so families are often afraid to house relatives returning from prison. This can cause serious tension within families.

What about the consequences of employment bans? Getting a job, especially in the current job market, would be a challenge for most of us. For ex-offenders like Cutty, the challenge is especially formidable. Most prisoners have little education and lack skills needed to find work. They don't typically learn these skills in prison. Faced with tight budgets, federal and state authorities have cut back funding for prison education and vocational programs. Ex-offenders also must overcome the persistent stigma of "criminal." Employers commonly use criminal background checks to weed out applicants they consider risky.

Other than the standing offer to rejoin Barksdale's organization, Cutty doesn't know about any other jobs or how to find them. His parole officer isn't much help, providing only a standard reminder to get a job, stay away from known criminals, and keep the parole office updated on where he's living. Cutty asks if there are still opportunities for day labor each morning at the market. "I don't know, and I don't care," says his parole officer. "Just get a job, any job" ("All Due Respect").

Against this backdrop, ex-offender employment bans can create especially steep challenges. Ex-offenders are commonly disqualified from positions that have nothing to do with their convictions. And those who did receive vocational training in prison may find themselves barred from doing these jobs once released. Some prisons provide barber training, for instance, but most states ban ex-offenders from being barbers.

The end result of all these restrictions is that former prisoners may not be able to find work for months after release. And here's some irony: in many states, failing to secure a job is a parole violation, which could thus land ex-offenders back in prison. As Preston "Bodie" Broadus once said, "This game is rigged, man" ("Final Grades").

Felon? Move On, Man!

Ex-offender restrictions aren't only defended on community safety grounds. A different sort of argument claims that, whether or not ex-offenders are dangerous, they are often not competent to make the same choices as the rest of us. The competence argument, used in defense of voting bans, claims that by breaking the law, offenders show that they don't have the competence, specifically the moral competence, to be entrusted with the responsibility of voting.

As of 2009, thirty-five states restricted people with felony convictions from voting while they're on parole. So when, on election day in the mayor's race, a canvasser for the Clarence Royce ticket approaches Cutty to solicit his vote, Cutty tells him to move on. He isn't eligible to vote because he's 'on papers' ("Margin of Error").

In eleven states, voting rights aren't automatically restored even after people complete parole. And although many states offer processes for restoring voting rights, these are too cumbersome and time-consuming to be a real option for most ex-offenders.

In the same way, if those convicted of drug-related felonies have shown by their past actions that they don't have the competence to make good decisions, maybe we shouldn't entrust them with taxpayers' money in the form of welfare, food stamps, or federal student loans. In tough economic times, why give ex-offenders public assistance if they're likely to waste it? As former Texas Senator Phil Gramm said in pushing for the 1996 federal law barring drug-related ex-offenders from welfare and food stamps, "Welfare shouldn't be used to support drug habits."

It's just not clear, though, why we should think that having a prior conviction is what shows that a person is incompetent to vote or to be trusted with public assistance. Was Cutty less competent to vote than Detective Jimmy McNulty, who didn't vote in the 2004 presidential race and didn't even know the name of the Democratic candidate? Competence to vote is a matter of political judgment, but there's no reason to think people without a criminal record have a monopoly on political judgment.

We might think the ban on public assistance for drug-related ex-offenders is more reasonable: As Gramm said, why should taxpayers' money be used to support drug habits? And after all, many states, including Cutty's home state of Maryland, allow former drug felons to become eligible again if they submit to random drug testing and, if needed, complete a rehab program. But not all states are so accommodating. As of 2012, at least seven states (Alabama, Alaska, Georgia, Mississippi, Missouri, Texas, and West Virginia) have retained the federal lifetime ban on both welfare and food stamps, with no provisions for ex-offenders to regain their eligibility. In several other states, bans are irrevocable on one program or the other, but not both.

If our concern is to make sure those who receive taxpayer support don't use it irresponsibly, this could open doors we'd rather not open. For one thing, maybe we should start requiring mandatory drug testing for anyone who works in the public sector and so has a salary paid by tax dollars: government officials, public school teachers, public university employees, social service employees, and many others.

But why stop there? People can waste taxpayer money in lots of ways other than drug use. Maybe we should start monitoring how public employees spend their salaries, to be sure tax dollars aren't being wasted. If these sound like bad ideas—if you think we should respect people's privacy and give them the benefit of the doubt in such matters—then maybe former prisoners are entitled to the same consideration.

The fact is, people with or without criminal histories can waste money or vote unwisely. But in a liberal democracy where individual autonomy is valued, we don't typically think it's the government's business to restrict people's personal choices merely on grounds of incompetence. Choices that pose a genuine danger to others may be restricted, but as mentioned before, it's unlikely that allowing ex-offenders to vote, or to receive welfare, food stamps, or federal student loans will endanger the community. In the end, the competence argument isn't convincing.

Ain't Nobody in This City That Lowdown

Appeals to the dangerousness or incompetence of ex-offenders claim that allowing them access to public housing, certain jobs, the vote, food stamps, or other goods will lead to bad consequences. But ex-offender bans aren't always defended on consequentialist grounds. Another common argument for voting restrictions holds that if a person breaks the law, he violates the social contract and so forfeits his right to have a voice in the democratic process.

Judge Henry Friendly, in a 1967 decision upholding ex-offenders voting restrictions, based his view on the classical liberal philosopher John Locke's notion of society as emerging from a social contract. The idea, basically, is that by entering into society people agree to give up certain freedoms and to obey society's laws in exchange for the protections and benefits that come from living under the rule of law. A person who breaks the law, Friendly argued, gives up the right "to participate in further administering the compact" (*Green v. Board of Elections of the City of New York*). In other words, a criminal demonstrates a lack of respect for the rule of law, and someone with no respect for the law has no right to have a voice in what the laws are.

However tempting this rationale may at first seem, it doesn't really hold up. Why should we think that criminal acts demonstrate a lack of respect for the rule of law? Many criminals are just weak-willed or reckless. For that matter, many non-convicts are weak-willed or reckless. Roland "Prez" Pryzbylewski was lucky that when he pistol-whipped a teenager outside the towers in Season One, he had friends on the police force who helped him avoid criminal charges. But suppose he hadn't been so lucky, and he had been charged with assaulting the teen. Should we then have said that Prez had no respect for the rule of law, and so no right to participate in the democratic process? If Prez showed a lack of respect, it was presumably for the poor kid he blinded in one eye, not for the rule of law or the practice of voting. In the same way, the idea that all criminals show a lack of respect for the rule of law, or the democratic process, just isn't convincing.

If we're worried about people showing a lack of respect for the democratic lawmaking process, maybe we should focus less on disenfranchising ex-offenders and more on dislodging corrupt politicians—think Clay Davis. Or if we're concerned about people abusing their voting rights, maybe we should restrict lazy, poorly informed citizens from having a voice. Actually, that's sometimes a tempting idea. But we don't go that far, because we think the right to vote is too important.

Deserve Ain't Got Nothing to Do with It

Many people might simply insist that ex-offenders don't deserve all the same benefits as the rest of us. Criminals have done bad things, they've broken laws while the rest of us have complied with the laws—even when it might've been more convenient or profitable to break them. Especially when dealing with scarce resources, whether it's the limited stock of public housing, scarce jobs, or services provided by taxpayer dollars, isn't it okay to give priority to the law abiders over the criminals?

The point here is that, in distributing society's scarce resources, it's justified to prioritize law abiders over offenders. But why should this be so? Some might say it's because unlike law abiders, offenders have done bad things. If this is the basis for barring offenders from these often crucial goods, then we should again ask about the significance of completing punishment. Again, punishment is supposedly how we hold offenders responsible for their criminal acts—it's how offenders pay their debts to society. But if ex-offenders have already been held responsible, if they've already paid their debts, how can it be justified to continue imposing burdens on them that others don't face? How is it just to continue extracting a debt that has already been paid?

Instead, maybe ex-offenders should go to the back of the line not because of what they've done, but because of who they are. Don't people who commit crimes show themselves to have worse moral characters than the rest of us? Maybe this is the basis for treating them unequally even after they've completed their punishments. This question of character ultimately goes to the heart of the issue of ex-offender bans.

Oh, You're Not That?

When Cutty gets shot trying to convince Michael Lee to leave the drug corners, the ER nurse assumes, given his medical history, that he must still be in the Game. On learning what Cutty did in the past, she draws conclusions about who he is. He was a drug soldier, a criminal, and so that's all he'll ever be.

In fact, by the end of *The Wire*, Cutty has found his calling as a boxing coach and mentor to young boys in the neighborhood (and seems to be getting along much better with the nurse). He has stayed away from the drug game, aside from trying to keep kids off the corners. By all accounts, he's reformed. Wee-Bey and Avon might see Cutty's behavior as evidence that, as Avon predicted, the joint "broke" Cutty. Avon and Wee-Bey have a different perspective on things from most of us, of course. What they call being "broken," we might call reform. Either way, Wee-Bey must've been surprised to learn that Cutty didn't want back into the drug game. He thought Cutty would always be a soldier at heart. Unfortunately, our federal and state policies make the same inaccurate assumption that Wee-Bey made about Cutty, the same assumption that his ER nurse made: that those who commit crimes never change.

It's all too easy to assume that criminals are just bad people, irredeemable. When we assume this, it's easier to rationalize a lot of the restrictive policies we (the "good guys") now impose on ex-offenders (the "bad guys"). But as *The Wire* shows us, things are rarely so clear cut. Jimmy McNulty's one of the "good guys," but he's also deeply flawed. Omar Little is a likeable killer with a strict moral code. Even Wee-Bey, serving a life sentence for numerous murders he committed (and several he didn't), shows depth of character in agreeing to give guardianship of his son, Namond, to Howard "Bunny" Colvin, in hopes that Namond can stay out of the drug game and have a better life.

And as Cutty showed, even murderers can redeem themselves. Not everyone who completes his sentence is thereby reformed, but if punishment really is about paying your debt to society, then those who serve their time earn the right to make a clean start. As they work to rebuild their lives, ex-offenders have to face the same obstacles we all do, but shouldn't be hamstrung by obstacles the rest of us don't face.

Fifth Case

The Loss

LINE 15
The Wire as American Tragedy

AVRAM GURLAND-BLAKER

Fade into an empty building being rehabbed. A man named Russell 'Stringer' Bell lies shot dead on the floor, his expression remorseful but unapologetic. He owns the building, a construction project of his very own B&B Enterprises, a would-be entrance of drug dealers into "legitimate" commerce.

A few months earlier, and only a few miles away, the body of Frank Sobotka was fished out of the Patapsco River. His expression was just as hardened, but its frustration and resentfulness clearer. His life was spent in compromising himself in order to support his own; he tried to repent for some of his sins, but only ended up getting his throat slit.

In a few years, back on the west side of town, a thin, unhealthy boy named Duquan Weems will sit outside a school. An awkward, impoverished ninth grader, he's surprisingly bright and good-natured despite his circumstances. Roland "Prezbo" Pryzbylewski, his sympathetic eighth grade teacher, gave him food, clean clothes, a place to shower. But now Dukie's there trying to pull some cash out of Mr. Prezbo to fund his new heroin addiction.

These vignettes have one thing in common: they're all tragic. David Simon's Baltimore-set drama is the grittiest, most gut-wrenching, most powerful television tragedy. And not by accident: Simon purposely designed it to be just that. In an August 2007 interview, he told *The Believer*'s Nick Hornby that *The Wire* was a contemporary American version of a classical Greek tragedy, but instead of the gods screwing humans, in *The Wire*, it's modern-day institutions like the police, the drug trade, the education system, municipal politics, and the post-industrial urban economy that callously chew people up and spit them out.

But it's one thing to design something to be a tragedy, and another to actually make it that. It's amazing how powerfully Simon realized his design; *The Wire* is a five-season exposé that throws the inner-city life of Baltimore in our face, all with a kind of violent grace that makes it the best work of tragic art we've seen in a long time.

But why do we care so much about the highs and lows of players, police, and politicians, not to mention those on the sidelines, in Bodymore, Murdaland? You think that D'Angelo Barksdale, Bodie Broadus, and Prop Joe Stewart give a shit about our lives? Probably not.

So why do we get caught up in theirs?

It's a surprisingly hard question, and answering it demands the philosophical equivalent of some good poh-lice work: a lot of patience, attention to detail, and some soft eyes.

One lead philosopher in this investigation should be Georg Hegel, who thought that tragedy hooks us by unceremoniously ripping down the front society puts up, showing us the shit that's woven into it. Tragedies build a case around the kind of people we live alongside—in *The Wire*, these people just happen to be the cops, blue-collar dock-workers, white-collar news-hounds, and gangsters, fiends, and corner boys of West Baltimore. But tragedy isn't just about them; it's just as much about us, too. Great tragedies hit hard because they're really about the deep, abiding tensions built into the structure of society. This is exactly what *The Wire* does, blowing away our illusions with the power of Omar's shotgun.

All Prologue

Like good detective work, philosophy's job is to make us aware of what was true all along, just unnoticed. Philosophy isn't the only thing that does this; many would say that art does this, too. Great works of art, tragic and comic, put us in touch with universal aspects of the human condition. They help us see what's too big or too buried beneath the mundane to be recognized, and they speak to all of us, no matter where we're from.

You don't need to be an ancient Greek to identify with Antigone being caught between loyalty to loved ones and an authority's decree. D'Angelo knows what that's like: he almost flips when he finds out that Wallace got capped, and even though he stays loyal, he never really gets back his love and trust for his uncle and the rest of the Barksdale crew.

But how come we relate to lives so different from our own? There's not much I have to relate to with these characters. I'm a young, white, upper-middle class professor, living a relatively secure, comfortable, and rewarding lifestyle. One of my biggest complaints is that I don't have enough time to read what I want.

So you can imagine what it would be like for me to wander into West Baltimore and start telling the corner boys that I can identify with their stories. If you're like me, day-to-day life in the drug trade, not to mention in ancient Greece, is nothing like our 'regular' lives. What part of myself do I see in Bubbles? What do I have in common with Marlo?

When Bunk went to Andre's store and proved that Omar was wrongfully fingered for killing a delivery woman, Bunk showed his talent for seeing past a cover story to find the hidden connections of things below the surface. Hegel had the same talent. And Hegel would have told us that, never mind the fact that *The Wire* is fiction, it's still true, because it shows us the Game.

The Game as it's played everywhere, on and off the streets.

In court, Omar called out Maurice Levy on the fact that they did similar things, just wearing different suits; Hegel would say that we're all made up of the same basic stuff, all motivated by the same basic interests and all a part of the same system. That's why the fictional features of Simon's Baltimore jibe with the facts of our reality. In Hegel's words, "art's vocation is to unveil the truth in the form of sensuous artistic configurations" (*Aesthetics*, p. 55). *The Wire* communes with the stuff that makes us what we are, touches something that goes deeper than the surface of our day-to-day lives or the lives it portrays.

We get hooked on *The Wire* because that shit is real.

It Don't Matter that Some Fool Say He Different

Truth comes from a lot of different places. It can come from the mouths of corner-boys and ex-junkies, or from your lieutenants if they're good. Art and philosophy give you truth in different ways. Philosophy might try to describe the reasons we feel repulsed and incensed by murder. Art, though, shows you the truth, making you see and feel it. Art will take you down into a shipping can with thirteen women's corpses (making us all happy that John Waters's idea of Smell-o-Vision never caught on).

This is what Hegel means when he says that art unveils the truth "in sensuous form." Artists know that people are flesh-and-blood: things get through to us when we literally see, hear, and touch the fundamentally true. Any time you're moved by a song or inspired by a movie, you're feeling this. Whenever you read a book or watch a show, and find yourself identifying with characters, whether you root for them, are repulsed by them, or say to yourself "I know how they feel," you are experiencing what Hegel's talking about. But sensing the truth doesn't have to involve the revelation of some deep, hidden truth about human reality; most of the time, it's just about getting to know better the ins and outs of what human beings are and can be, everything from the good (like McNulty and Barksdale) to the bad (like McNulty and Barksdale).

When we say we "identify" with characters, this identification is a recognition of something we're already familiar with, just in a different form. They may be nothing like us, but not all that different either. We identify with them because what we see in them echoes what we experience ourselves.

Take Frank Sobotka. When you look at the facts of Frank's life, most of us wouldn't see much we could relate to: father of a dysfunctional son, corrupt blue-collar union leader in a struggling industry, dealing with unsavory types behind the backs of law-enforcement and doing so for the survival of unionized labor as much as for power and greed. I hope not too many of you out there know what that's like. But on another level, Frank becomes someone much more similar to us than we realize. He tries to balance the responsibilities he has to his family and to those he works with (and he doesn't always do this well); he gets in over his head, and tries to maintain calm on the outside while panicking on the inside.

Midway through his ordeal, he reaches a breaking point and makes a principled decision, only to give in to financial temptation (a temptation heightened by his dire straits). The culmination of all this is an attempt to clear his conscience and make right, a move that backfires and gets him got. And he does this all against the backdrop of a way of life that's getting harder day by day, while the lives of others who do less work seem to be getting easier. Now, tell me that you can't see a little of yourself in this.

Frank's struggles—his obligations, his determination, and his failures—are something we can relate to, something similar enough to the kinds of struggles we deal with ourselves. However, in Frank's case the struggle is spotlighted and magnified. Frank isn't unique in this respect; what makes so many of the characters of *The Wire* complex and three-dimensional, allowing us to identify with them, is that they go though exaggerated versions of challenges common to us all. So maybe Frank isn't so different from you or me.

Let Them Know Who You Are

That we see ourselves reflected in these characters proves the themes of their lives aren't cut from a different cloth. The difference is, under the lens of *The Wire*, these themes appear starker. But *The Wire* isn't just about the struggles of human life in general—it's specifically about the struggles of contemporary America, about the lives we live and of those around us. Simon slaps down on the interview table the dark side of our world; he pins us with the ugly truth about our society, the things that we know but try to keep down in the hole.

The events of *The Wire* don't take place in a different world. The people who populate *The Wire* aren't different kinds of people. They're products of the same forces that created us and that we deal with everyday. And that's why we feel them.

Simon's ability to give us a realistic portrait of Baltimore really sets the show apart. But realism is hard to achieve. It doesn't hurt that Simon was a reporter for the Baltimore *Sun*, or that many of the people and events portrayed in *The Wire* have some basis in fact. But that alone doesn't give something a sense of realism. If it did, any movie "based on true events" would have realism. Being gritty and unapologetic isn't it, either. Other HBO series such as *The Sopranos* are gritty and unapologetic, but they don't match *The Wire*. Realism needs something more: it needs the kind of unflinching, unapologetic portrayal of events you can't watch without feeling you've been indicted by or are complicit in it—as if the TV just served up a bit of justice the Western District way.

Simon is the real cop providing the beat down, along with Ed Burns and the rest of the writers who made the particulars just right, and the world we've seen is our own hypocritical, post-modern, post-industrial, capitalistic, and media-saturated America. As much as being "factual," authenticity and genuineness are needed for realism. And this is what Simon and his crew give us: they smack us in the face with all those things dysfunctionally true about contemporary America.

All in the Game, Yo. All in the Game

What is tragedy? Asking that is like asking what a real player is: there are different kinds, so different answers. Prop Joe and Marlo were both players, but they played the Game in very different ways; you could call Clay Davis a player too, and even Mayor Royce. It all depends on what you mean by "player." Tragedy is the same way. There are trivial tragedies and there are heavy tragedies. It was tragic when the run of *The Wire* ended. But a favorite show's ending isn't tragic in the same way many of the lives of real people in the real Baltimore are tragic. *The Wire* was dramatic tragedy, but as something that happened it wasn't itself tragic (by contrast, I know a few people who would say that *Jersey Shore* isn't a tragedy, but sure is tragic). I love *The Wire* and am thankful for it; "loving" and "being thankful for" are not things you generally say about real-life tragedies, like someone descending into addiction, living in inescapable poverty, or dying unfairly.

Even when we're talking about dramatic tragedy, there are different defining characteristics. In high school, I learned that a play is a tragedy if "a lot of people die at the end." Aristotle, a bit wiser than my high school teacher, said that tragedy had to arouse pity, fear, and produce a cathartic effect on the audience.

But not just anyone can be a player, and not just anything is tragic. Ziggy sure wasn't a player, no matter how hard he tried to be one, but his end was tragic. In all its different forms, the tragic has certain common features, like a person's fate being undeserved, unforeseen yet inevitable, and involving suffering. Sometimes, it comes out of nowhere, striking down an innocent victim. Like when a kid catches a stray. Other times, tragedy gets back at you, lying in wait, busting out when you least expect it. Daniels was a good cop, a genuine man of conviction, someone who tried to do right. The thanks he got? He's forced to resign because he drew the line at juking the stats.

Fate is often tragic, and if there's one thing you can count on about fate in *The Wire,* it's that fate does what it wants, when it wants. Omar survives the hunt put on him by Barksdale, he survives his trip to prison, but he's shot to death by Kenard in a convenience store. Fate doesn't give a fuck. To fate, life is just being cold-blooded; to the rest of us who care and have emotions, life is downright tragic.

This Game Is Rigged, Man

The most tragic stories in *The Wire* are those where someone's doomed fate slowly and irresistibly unfolds, usually with the complicity of the condemned—like when Bodie falls, even though he played by the rules. It's when you unwittingly dig your own grave, either in spite of your best intentions or even sometimes because of them. We might've done right, done nothing other than what we should have. Our motives were understandable. Our actions were justifiable. And yet we go down.

The Wire thrives on this shit. One reason is practical. These slow-burn tragic episodes are complex and involved; they follow characters' arcs all the way through to their eventual demise. The downfall of a bystander can't be drawn out into multiple acts, let alone an entire twelve-episode arc. By contrast, Stringer's rise and fall took three full seasons.

But if you'd ask Hegel, he'd say that there's another reason why the irresistibly-unfolding-doomed-fate makes better fodder for dramatic tragedy. It's not just that on a structural level the story is deeper and more complex. Dramatic tragedies like *The Wire* illuminate the tensions in the structure of our shared social world. In Hegel's words, drama

> rests entirely on collisions of circumstances, passions, and characters, and leads . . . to actions and then to the reactions which in turn necessitate a resolution of the conflict and discord. Therefore what we see in front of us are certain ends individualized in living characters

and very conflicting situations . . . and we see too . . . its criss-cross movement and yet in its final peaceful resolution. (p. 1159)

Art expresses lived experience, and tragedy portrays misfortune; connect the pieces, and you get the idea that tragic conflict brings us face to face with the pitfalls of our own world.

Most art forms can only give us a single snapshot-like presentation of one underlying aspect of reality. But dramatic tragedy brings together different elements of life, with each character its own concrete, sharply defined expression of what it represents. It's the difference between seeing "Fayette Mafia Crew 4-evah" spray-painted on a brick wall and actually watching what happens to Michael, Namond, Randy, and Duquan throughout Season Four.

Because dramatic tragedies can handle a number of characters at once, giving them the opportunity to interact, Hegel thinks dramatic tragedies show the audience what happens when they step to one another and throw down. Dramatic tragedy is structurally complex, but still concrete and stable; what we get is a deeper, more subtle picture of how different parts of reality run up against each other.

Hegel's favorite illustration of this is the ancient Greek tragedy *Antigone*. What *Antigone* did for ancient Greek life, *The Wire* does for contemporary American society. The story of *Antigone* is the story of two different people with two different codes getting into a beef that takes both of them down. In the play, Polyneices (Antigone's brother) dies leading the losing side in the Theban civil war. With the war over and order restored, Thebes's ruler Creon says that no one can bury Polyneices's body, a direct denial of religious law and an insult to the gods.

Like Marlo, Antigone won't let such a public dis of her people slide. She disobeys Creon and buries her brother. When Creon finds out, he goes after her with about as much mercy as Brother Mouzone. He punishes Antigone by burying her alive. Creon's councilors warn him that he's gone too far, and Creon eventually admits his overreaction. Like in the Season Three finale, "Mission Accomplished," where Avon mournfully confesses to Slim Charles that he gave up Stringer, and that Stringer had been right about Marlo after all. And like the Barksdale-Stanfield gang war, the aftermath of Creon's moves is a string of bodies. Creon leaves to bury Polyneices and save Antigone, but she has committed suicide, along with Creon's son, her lover. Creon's wife kills herself when she finds out that her son is dead. Creon, now faced with the tragic effects of a chain of causes he set into motion, collapses in sorrow.

Antigone, like *The Wire*, portrays a series of characters taking understandable actions based on justifiable motives, then facing fucked-up consequences because the Game is rigged. The truth is, as Prez realizes, "No one wins. One side just loses more slowly" ("Refugees").

Just a Gangster, I Suppose

What Hegel says about *Antigone*, we can say about the characters of *The Wire*. The main players all have justification for doing what they do, but nobody's saved. Antigone fights for loyalty to the gods, for the values of fidelity and tradition. Creon fights for loyalty to society and the law. Avon and Marlo were about street rep, Jimmy McNulty is about showing how smart and how unbeatable a hardnosed Irish cop can be, Stringer Bell is about bringing professionalism and business smarts to the Game. McNulty came at all three; at the end of the day, all four went down. It would be easier to say that one person was in the right and everyone else in the wrong, but that's not the way it was. Everyone held fast to their convictions and took principled stances.

The problem wasn't Antigone or Creon, or Barksdale, Bell, Stanfield or McNulty. The real problem is the incompatible values that animate them. You can stand by good principles and still go down. That's a big part of what Simon was talking about when he said that *The Wire* substituted modern-day institutions for the ancient gods of Greek tragedy. You can be a faithful servant to whatever idealized vision you choose. You can worship whatever god you embrace, whether it's the god of law and order, of the street, the political process or the free press. But those institutions, they're not looking out for you. They're only as trustworthy as the most corrupt individuals who take advantage of them.

The power of dramatic tragedy, says Hegel, is its ability to show us something real and pull the curtain back on its dysfunction. Like all other great dramatic tragedies, from

Antigone to *Hamlet* to *The Godfather*, *The Wire* works by spot-
lighting the way life itself is unfair, how it's cruelly indifferent
to our beliefs about justice, right, and goodness. *The Wire* does
this non-stop: one of the show's enduring themes is its message
that, the way the system is set up, people either become hyp-
ocrites or casualties. It's a surveillance op of contemporary
American urban society, and it puts together a case to show
that the rules of the Game aren't consistent, orderly, or benign;
the structures that "support" us, along with the values we
embrace, are themselves fundamental sources of suffering and
misfortune.

   The Wire covers myriad institutions that make up modern-
day urban society, from the economic underclass, to criminal
organizations and law enforcement, to post-industrial blue-collar life, to local politics, the education system, and the media.
We see the way that these institutions are fated to clash and
create casualties in their wake, including D'Angelo, Frank,
Dukie, Wallace, Johnny, Bunny, Randy, Bodie, and Gus.

   Both Simon and Hegel realize that what contributed the
most to the fates these characters suffered was that they lived
in the world they lived in and were who they were supposed to
be. Their "tragic flaws" were the ones that could be traced
directly to the failures of society.

   For my money, no one from *The Wire* illustrates this better
than Stringer Bell. Stringer is the paradigm example of an
unknowing complicit victim of a callous fate. Some say that
Stringer's ambitions and values symbolize a street version of
pure capitalism, but I think you can even say that Stringer represents the American Dream. Born into the lowest socioeconomic rung, he climbed his way out by the means available to
him, inching his way towards a "legitimate" future of security
and prosperity. He was fueled by unwavering ambition, determination, and intelligence. Some might say that Stringer got
too big a head, that he fell into the classical tragic flaw of
hubris; maybe he did, but you try being a humble motherfucker
and running the streets. Avon'll tell you, you got to be hard.
Stringer was; he was patient and calculating. He held back
where it was best not to go to war (like with Omar), but he took
action without hesitation where it needed to be taken (like
with Wallace, D'Angelo, and later even Avon). He kept an open
mind and made his own opportunities (like with the formation

of the New Day Co-Op). He wasn't perfect. He screwed Donette, he stabbed Avon in the back. But the "good guys" aren't perfect either—no one is.

Stringer was as strong, devoted, and smart as they come. If anyone deserved to do well in the end, it was him. But as Snoop says, "Deserve got nuthin' to do with it" ("Late Editions"). The American Dream is one thing; American reality is something else. Stringer's thoughtful, well-reasoned decisions, those qualities that cemented who he was and what he was about, set in motion events that ended with him facing Omar and Brother Mouzone on the floor of his own construction site. That's cold. Stringer couldn't have been better than he was, and he was only what money, power, and strength, the gods that Stringer worshiped, say is worthy of admiration.

Fuck the Average Reader

We can argue about whether *The Wire* is the greatest television show of all time. But I think it's one of the greatest dramatic tragedies on television or anywhere else. If we see Baltimore through Simon's eyes, we see just how truly and deeply fucked life in America is. And if we watch *The Wire* through Hegel's eyes, we see how and why Simon's vision is so sharp, powerful, and haunting.

But that's not quite the end of the story. Hegel told us what makes dramatic tragedy the thing it is, and why it hooks us with such emotion. But Simon followed his own rules: "My standard for verisimilitude is simple and I came to it when I started to write prose narrative: fuck the average reader" (*The Believer*). Hegel's theory helps us build a case about why *The Wire* makes us jones after it so intensely. But, as a dramatic tragedy, *The Wire* itself goes beyond anything Hegel could have imagined. Simon beat Hegel on two counts: the complexity of *The Wire*, and in his answer to the question, "what's the most tragic ending of all?"

The Wire shows McNulty-sized balls taking on so much of society. For Hegel, if a tragedy took on more than the collision of two codes, it took on too much. What's amazing about *The Wire* is that it calls out everybody. Just think about Season Five: Simon reports on conflicts everywhere, including in the police with McNulty and Freamon versus Moreland and

Greggs and Daniels versus Rawls; in the urban criminal world with Marlo versus Prop Joe versus Omar; in politics with Carcetti versus Campbell and municipal Baltimore politics versus Annapolis; and in the print media with Haynes versus Templeton, Klebanow, and Whiting.

But even these stories get pushed below the fold, as the front-page story of Season Five is the codependent and mutually destructive relationships between these institutions. A policeman uses the media to pressure the mayor for better funding. The mayor uses the police to present himself as an effective and compassionate leader. The media uses both of them to sell papers. The city of Baltimore and its inhabitants, by the way, don't see anything that changes much through all this; they face conditions that continue to deteriorate.

The Wire also steps philosophically to Hegel by saying that the most tragic ending isn't when people die, it's when they go on living. Hegel's "clash of social institutions" theory is a unique spin on dramatic tragedy, but like most classical theorists of tragedy, Hegel thinks that quality-product for dramatic tragedy requires the deaths of the central characters. The main characters' staged deaths are the "sensuous representation" of the dysfunction of the system: since dramatic tragedy is about the contradictions built into the system, Hegel thinks, tragic protagonists necessarily go down.

For Simon, people die, and people suffer, but the beat goes on. The tragic culmination of *The Wire* isn't the death of the protagonist, it's the re-establishment of the status quo: lieutenants becoming colonels, deputy commissioners becoming superintendents, and mayors becoming governors.

Simon constantly reminds us that at the "end," despite the blood, sweat, and tears covered by *The Wire*'s five seasons, nothing really changes. So not only is *The Wire* tragic because it is true, not only does it bring us face to face with the dysfunction inherent in the society on top of it all, *The Wire* reminds us that when things get bad, they stay bad, and if we don't do something about it now, the reckoning will just get worse.

But the tragedy is, it's not like anyone can do shit to stop it.

LINE 16
The Birth of Tragedy from the Spirit of Baltimore

JOHN THOMAS BRITTINGHAM

In the 2007 film *Stranger than Fiction*, Dustin Hoffman's tweedy English professor character asks Will Ferrell's actuarial man-of-not-so-quiet-desperation whether he believes that he's living in a tragedy or a comedy.

The question seems utterly absurd. Comedies are movies I watch with my friends or when I'm folding laundry. Tragedies are what I say I watch so I look cultured and informed, or what I actually see when I watch the Columbus Blue Jackets (a team so inept Bubbles and Johnny Boy could play for them).

Yet, considering whether or not we live in a comedy or a tragedy is not so absurd a question if we think about comedies and tragedies the way that the ancient Greeks did. According to Aristotle, comedy wasn't just playing for laughs but a drama where the slovenly, unctuous loser of the Greek world—basically the ancient version of every character Seth Rogen or Jonah Hill plays—somehow, miraculously, ends up on top. Comedies take characters who know nothing and put them in a situation where they're supposed to know everything. They're screwed and you know it. This is the basic set-up for *Brewster's Millions*, *Trading Places*, *Tommy Boy*, *Burn After Reading*, and even *The Big Lebowski*.

Tragedy, simply, is the other way around. Some dude who appears on the top comes crashing down to the bottom. Think *Oedipus* or *Antigone*. People who are supposed to be cool guys and gals who know things, end up knowing very little and being tossed around by fate like they're rag-dolls.

Americans love comedies. We can make good ones (contrary to what may be playing now at a Cineplex near you) and we tend to root for the underdog on any and all occasions. We might even say that Americans think of themselves as living in a comedy in which the slackers of the world can write a program or build a doohickey and get mega-ultra-rich.

However, there is another America. There is the overtly tragic America that David Simon and Ed Burns show us in *The Wire*. And this version of tragedy is not just Aristotle's idea of tragedy. This is not just about heroes tumbling to their doom or loves being lost. This is tragedy of a Nietzschean magnitude.

What is Nietzschean tragedy? Just to keep you in the loop, Friedrich Nietzsche was one of the "Famous Germans" of the nineteenth century. Famous for what, you ask?

Famous for:

1. **throwing a wrench in intellectual culture with ideas such as the "Will to Power," the "Übermensch," and Eternal Return**

2. **being the second greatest inspiration for one of your college buddies becoming a huge dick for a time—the first being Ayn Rand**

and

3. **having a mustache so big that establishing its origins would require a congressional hearing and multiple tests for HGH use.**

What does this have to do with *The Wire*? And why does it matter if I'm watching a tragedy or a comedy, let alone if I'm living in one? If I'm being an honest tragedian, decent answers are hard to come by.

The King Stays the King, the Queen Ain't No Bitch, and Only Smart-Ass Pawns Survive

McNULTY: . . . Seems Unfair

SNOT-BOOGIE'S FRIEND: Life just be that way. ("The Target")

In a 2008 interview with NPR's Terry Gross, David Simon said, "We've been stealing from a lot of the Greek tragedies and a lot of the characteristics of the characters in those plays are apparent in *The Wire*." Why the Greek tragedies? What makes them so special? Simon thinks that it's the argument you have with your fate.

I mean hubris, that ancient Greek notion of believing oneself to be on equal footing with the gods when one is not. Hubris reveals to the characters and to us watching that said character is doomed. Such an argument is not about personal morality or virtue or love or whatever else Shakespeare crammed into his plays; no, it's about the very simple fact that all of these characters live in a world where forces beyond their control decide their fate. In some cases, the gods deciding the fates of these characters are represented by the social and political institutions that comprise the Greek polis or the modern American city. In other cases, the gods are represented by a simple phrase: the Game.

Aristotle (who was, ya' know, insanely smart) is a guy who would turn to you with a knowing glare and say "All the pieces matter, Detective. All the pieces matter" ("Old Cases"). Aristotle described tragedy in terms of the parts that made it work. In *The Poetics*, he tried to understand how things like plot and character and diction worked together correctly in order to produce a good tragic play.

But Nietzsche thought about tragedy more in terms of the forces at work in the drama itself. We might define Nietzschean tragedy as a drama where the forces of the Apollonian and the Dionysian wrestle with each other and produce the art of tragedy. This view of tragedy is not concerned with the different parts and how they work together so much as the general themes that run through a work's entirety. All this talk of gods and forces and fates might make you think Nietzsche's a little crazy (and you wouldn't be completely off base), but his definition of tragedy is helpful for understanding what's going on in *The Wire*. But first, wtf is an Apollonian or a Dionysian force?

When we think about these forces it's best to think about them as orientations or dispositions, rather than ghosts or spirits or three-headed spaghetti monsters. The Apollonian is an orientation towards order, rationality, and logic. It's also the orientation towards dreams and illusions. In *The Birth of*

Tragedy, Nietzsche sees the Apollonian as the attempt to fight against one's fate by ordering and structuring life in spite of the fact that life is, for him, fundamentally chaotic. We see this Apollonian orientation best represented by the police force bureaucracy—especially in the characters of Major William Rawls and the Deputy Ops Ervin Burrell. There's also something Apollonian in the character of Russell "Stringer" Bell, which eventually leads to his downfall.

Dionysus was the Greek god of music, of primal oneness, and of excess and revelry. Think Heath Ledger's portrayal of The Joker in *The Dark Knight*, or Britney Spears circa 2007, or what people think about when they think about the 1960s. In *The Wire*, the Dionysian orientation is best represented by what the hoppers, dealers and kingpins call the Game. It ostensibly refers to the drug game, but much more than just the buying, selling, distributing, and protecting of illegal narcotics. There's a sense that the entire world of *The Wire* is a game, and all who play it acknowledge its violent and merciless nature. The Game is chaos, changing only in intensity, endless in its performance.

To play the Game is to acknowledge that you're going to suffer and that you can't do otherwise. It's to understand that you must take all you can from life before you die at the hands of the Game. Avon Barksdale and his minions know this truth well. They revel in Dionysian excess knowing that the next day might result in their demise. Detective Jimmy McNulty also revels in excess without an instinct for self-preservation.

As Burrell succinctly summarizes, "This is Baltimore, gentlemen. The gods will not save you" ("Dead Soldiers").

Intoxication, Lies, Damned Lies, and Criminal Machinations

PARTLOW: 'Why' ain't in your repertoire no more. ("Refugees")

PROP JOE: Stir up a hornet's nest, no tellin' who gonna get stung. ("Reformation")

In Greek tragedy, having a primary conflict is not enough. No, if you're going to have a good tragedy you've got to get into some complicated stuff. There must be, in the words of the illustrious Dude, "a lot of ins, a lot of outs, a lot of what-have-yous." It's not enough that we have a bunch of cops on one side and drug dealers on the other. Or that we have as our protagonist a white homicide detective and as our antagonist a black drug kingpin. For there to be good tragedy, and a show as good as *The Wire*, we have to have secondary, even tertiary conflicts.

The best places to find these rising conflicts are within the organizations of characters that represent the Apollonian and Dionysian orientations that Nietzsche says are required for tragedy. Thus, if we're looking at an Apollonian organization like the Baltimore Police Department, we're bound to find ourselves a couple Dionysian characters. And in the BPD, there is no bigger disciple of Dionysus than Detective Jimmy McNulty.

Nietzsche says that the essence of the Dionysiac "is best conveyed by the analogy of intoxication." McNulty is certainly a character who is constantly intoxicated, and with more than just Jameson: he's also drunk on his performance as a homicide detective, his intelligence, and his amazing penchant for self-destructive, drunken one-night stands.

Ideal police officer? Probably not. Ideal protagonist? Absolutely.

Nietzsche describes the Dionysian man: "These Dionysiac stirrings, which . . . cause subjectivity to vanish to the point of complete self-forgetting, awaken either under the influence of narcotic drink . . . or at the approach of spring when the whole of nature is pervaded by lust for life" (*Birth of Tragedy*, p. 17). McNulty is a character that loses himself in his work to the point that he has no sense of self-preservation or any sense of loyalty to others. Whether it's through bucking the chain of command in Season One or by fabricating evidence for the sake of a case, McNulty remains a Dionysian man in an organization that is thoroughly Apollonian.

But what makes the BPD so Apollonian? Aside from being a government institution charged with maintaining order, the police department is an organization that traffics in illusions. So how can the police department both be a place that is the bastion of rationality and of illusion? Don't those things seem opposed to one another?

The police department stands as a bastion of rationality in the sense that it is driven by numbers and data. One of the constant motifs found in every season of *The Wire* is that the bosses in the police department want acceptable stats for their individual units. They want an acceptable, albeit, what appears to be horribly low, number of cleared murder cases, arrests of low-level drug dealers, and a lot of dope on the table. You accomplish all of that and you get to keep your job. Yet, the department also fudges the numbers. The bosses manipulate the numbers whenever possible, so that they can get their clearances, collect their pensions, and live in peace.

The epitome of this Apollonian impulse towards order and the illusion of order is none other than McNulty's commanding officer. Rawls is a purveyor of the illusion that the homicide division he leads does good police work, making the city a better place. In reality, all Rawls wants are his clearances. Thus, in tragic fashion, we have the Apollonian Rawls making life miserable for our Dionysiac McNulty, and vice versa.

Although Rawls is the master of Apollonian action, the orientation towards order and illusion that characterizes the Apollonian as such is pervasive throughout pretty much every social and political institution in David Simon's Baltimore. Rawls is but one of a number of individuals who strives to maintain order and, even more so, the illusion of order. Such an impulse leads to the destruction of those who would balk at this orientation, as we see in the cases of McNulty, Lester Freamon, and their comrades in the Major Crimes Unit.

The Barksdale crime syndicate, on the other hand, is the inversion of the Apollonian structure of the police department. The Dionysian character of the Barksdale organization has a lot to do with the differences between Stringer and Avon—differences that ensure the inevitability of their mutual betrayal. While Avon's organization uses fronts like the strip club and the funeral home, it is fundamentally an orgiastic revelry in the suffering and shortness of life. What makes the Barksdale organization Dionysian, despite that it is organized and Avon imposes discipline, is its lack of any pretense concerned with anything outside the Game.

The organization sees life as suffering: its customers suffer, its employees suffer, even its founders eventually suffer. Rather than fighting this understanding, the Barksdale organization revels in it. It deals in pain and its release. Even amidst discussions of familial bonds and business partnerships, suffering is not to be avoided or eschewed.

Suffering is the way of things, be it within a family unit or the Game. Consider what Avon says when he and D'Angelo visit Avon's brother in the state rehab center in Season One. "This is family," Avon says, "family is what count, family is what it's about. Family gonna always be there 'cause its blood" ("The Pager"). Beyond the dissimulations of criminal organizations and the machinations of fronts for money laundering, Avon sees the real value that binds him to others as one of family and blood. Thus, even though Stringer's assassination of D'Angelo was the right business decision, Avon had to retaliate because there was a deeper bond than business—there was blood.

Avon continues his discussion with D'Angelo at the bedside of his brother, demonstrating a rare moment of reflection upon the Dionysian character of the Game, his organization, and himself. He says:

> Live the life, leave the life, ain't no big thing. . . . If he dead, you know, I could carry it better. Coming up the way we do you kinda expect it. See, the thing is, you only gotta fuck up once. Be a little slow, be a little late, just once. And how you never gonna be slow, be late? You can't plan for no shit like this man. It's life. ("The Pager")

Avon is not running from the violence and suffering of life; rather, he embraces it. Certainly, he shows fear, but he is not about to deny life through illusions in order to prolong it. The Game, for Avon and his organization, is life. We expect a violent end. What does "be a little slow, be a little late" translate into other than "be the fallible human being that you are?" To be human, the Dionysian man says, is to affirm life beyond your ability to control it and to revel in the primal unity you share with all human beings who are subject to the same arbitrariness of existence.

A Man without a Country

While the Barksdale organization is fundamentally Dionysian, Avon's lieutenant and best friend Stringer is fundamentally Apollonian, as he is set on transforming the drug game into a rational, legitimate, and thoroughly organized business.

Such is his folly.

Stringer's concerned with more than just running drugs and keeping corners. He's developing business opportunities beyond the leering eyes of urban law enforcement agents. And yet, he depends upon the very chaos of the drug game to sustain his other ventures. We can see how creator David Simon set up the inevitable betrayal of Avon by Stringer, and vice versa, from the start.

Avon is a family man who lives by the old ways of the game: violence and symbolism. He even wants his own acts of violence to be symbols of the ways of the Game, such as the burned out eye and tortured body of Omar's lover Brandon. Stringer is a man without a country: a business-only power broker in possession of shrewdness and a drive for order. It's Stringer who develops the New Day Co-Op and invests in businesses and properties all over the city. Stringer is what Nietzsche would call a theoretical man.

In *The Birth of Tragedy*, Nietzsche describes the theoretical man as he in whom we find "the imperturbable belief that thought, as it follows the thread of causality, reaches down into the deepest abysses of being, and that it is capable, not simply of understanding existence, but even of correcting it" (p. 73). The theoretical man believes his intelligence, his reason runs so deeply, that, in the desire for reform and a stroke of true hubris, he is capable of changing the world.

Stringer starts the New Day Co-op not because he wants to hang out with other dealers but because he needs a new connect and sees the value in diminishing the violence between the different organizations. He uses reason to attempt to reform a foundational level of the drug game. Yet, the co-op, his real estate investments, all of his conniving and business savvy cannot reform the Game. Stringer Bell's intelligence cannot change his fate.

No one's can.

Them Little Bitches on the Chessboard

FREAMON: You're not even worth the skin off my knuckles, junior. You put fire to everything you touch, McNulty, and then you walk away while it burns. ("Hamsterdam")

Both the Apollonian man in a Dionysian organization (Stringer Bell) and the Dionysian man in the Apollonian organization (Jimmy McNulty), when faced with the magnitude of force embedded within the institutions, have no recourse but resignation. Caught by Omar and Brother Mouzone in his failed real estate project, Stringer offers one last Apollonian attempt, one last rational argument for saving his life.

He offers the two of them money.

But the game's Dionysian core will not allow such an illusion to persist and as Omar and Brother raise their weapons, Omar speaks the Dionysian wisdom that Stringer hasn't been able to hear: "You still don't get it, huh. It ain't about money" ("Middle Ground"). It's about Brandon and the lies that pitted Dionysian enforcer against Dionysian stick-up man. It's about love and blood and revenge: drives that go much deeper than business.

In the end, all Stringer can do is stare them down and, resigned to his fate, tell them to get on with it.

McNulty's "end," less climactic than Stringer's, is no less an act of resignation. Pointing to the futility of his actions, Freamon asks McNulty, "How exactly do you think it all ends . . . a parade? A gold watch?" ("Slapstick").

McNulty's Dionysian character had to revel in the chaos of the streets, to break through the illusions of order found in his line of work. But, as Freamon says, "the job will not save you. It won't make you whole, it won't fill your ass up" ("Slapstick"). So intoxicated with his own ability as a detective, so immersed with the life of being a police officer, Jimmy McNulty's slow to realize that his penchant for being devoid of any instinct for self-preservation is an illusion itself, the illusion of being a self.

Detective James McNulty is his job and lacks anything beyond it.

What he needs is, as Freamon so eloquently puts it, "a life . . . it's the shit that happens when you're waiting for moments that never come" ("Slapstick"). No case, no job, no takedown can save Jimmy McNulty from his demise. Reveling in the chaos of Dionysian life has become a mask that must, in its time, be removed. Finally acknowledging that doing the job he does better than anyone else leads to his own destruction, McNulty resigns himself to being less that he can be. He fully embraces the disorder. In other words, the dog leaves the force, settling down with Beadie Russell. In the end, for Nietzsche and for the residents of Simon's Baltimore, there is no escape from the chaos, suffering, and joy of life.

There is only resignation.

Why Tragedy Matters

BARKSDALE: The game is the fuckin' game. Period.

BELL: Same as it ever was. ("Homecoming")

Nietzschean tragedy is a drama in which the Apollonian and Dionysian orientations wrestle with one another. These two forces do not resolve into a higher reconciliation a la Hegel's system, nor are they understandable apart from one another. Although our culture has been one of a more Apollonian disposition, it has never been without its Dionysian elements and characters. The friction between these two forces produces the brilliance and healing that is tragedy. It's a balm bringing together order and ecstasy, revelry, power and honor, achieving "that magnificent blend" which is the affirmation of life in all its forms. *The Wire* is a tragedy of Nietzschean proportions because it is a tale of struggle between these two impulses in modern American culture. It's a tragic show because, in the end, none of the characters can escape their fate.

And neither can you or me or anyone who watches the show.

The Wire holds a mirror up to our society and tells us that the fate of this fictional Baltimore is our own. This is the world we live in whether we pretend to live elsewhere or not. And yet we're asked to affirm life in all of its chaos and pain and ecstatic joy. If your job will not save you, if your intelligence will not save you, if your violence will not save you, if the gods will not save you, then what will?

For characters like McNulty, Freamon, and Bell, there's only resignation before their fate. In fact, the very idea that these characters need saving is questionable. Only those hostile to life would require salvation from their earthly lot. The Nietzschean characters in *The Wire* recognize the inescapability of their fate and, rather than quaking before it and seeking escape, ultimately embrace it. For Nietzsche, in spite of all of the shit that life throws at us, the only thing left is to affirm life. The rain falls on the just and the unjust, on the righteous and the wicked. All we can do in the face of this is take a deep breath and say yes to life.

This is why tragedy matters. It shows us life as the struggle between order and excess, chaos and control, and asks us to affirm it anyway. To know if you're living in a tragedy or a comedy is really just a secondary way of asking why tragedy or comedy matters. Comedy matters because, to quote Tom Petty, "even the losers get lucky sometimes" and we all, in our own odd ways, wish we were those lucky losers.

But tragedy matters because, in spite of all our efforts to build up eternal kingdoms, to craft spectacular lives, we cannot escape our fate. In the end we die. That's the final act. We might as well affirm life nonetheless because the Game has been, is, and always will be the Game.

LINE 17
The Wire, or, What to Do in Non-Evental Times

Slavoj Žižek

"Who is David Guetta?" I asked my twelve-year-old son when he triumphantly announced that he was going to a Guetta concert. My son looked at me as if I was a complete idiot, and replied: "Who is your Mozart? Google Mozart, you get five million hits, google Guetta, you get twenty million!"

I did google Guetta and discovered that he is effectively something like today's art curators: not simply a DJ, but an "active" DJ who not only solicits but even mixes and composes the music he presents, like the art curators who no longer merely collect the work for an exhibition but often directly solicit its creation, explaining to the artists what they want.

DJ David Simon

And the same goes for David Simon, a kind of curator of the multitude of directors and screen-writers (up to Agnieszka Holland) who collaborated on *The Wire*. The reasons are not simply and only commercial; it's also the nascent form of a new collective process of creation. It's as if the Hegelian *Weltgeist* moved from cinema to TV series, although it's still in search of its form: the inner Gestalt of *The Wire* is *not* that of a series—Simon himself has referred to *The Wire* as a single, sixty-six hour movie.

Furthermore, *The Wire* is not only the result of a collective creative process, but something more: real lawyers, drug addicts, and cops are playing themselves; even the characters' names are condensations of the names of real persons from Baltimore

(Stringer Bell's name is a composite of two real Baltimore drug lords, Stringer Reed and Roland Bell). *The Wire* thus provides a kind of collective self-representation of a city, like the Greek tragedy in which a *polis* collectively staged its experience.

Fuckin' Fuck

If *The Wire* is a case of TV realism, it's not so much object-realism (a realistic presentation of a social milieu), but rather subject-realism—that is, a film staged by a precisely defined actual social unity. This fact is signaled by a key scene in *The Wire* whose function is precisely to mark the distance towards any crude realism, the famous "all-fuck" investigation in "Old Cases," the fourth episode of Season One.

In an empty ground-floor apartment where a murder took place six months earlier, McNulty and Bunk, witnessed by a sole silent housekeeper, try to reconstruct how it happened, and the only words they pronounce during their work are variations of "fuck." They do it thirty-eight times in a row, in so many different ways, it comes to mean anything from annoyed boredom to elated triumph, from pain or disappointment or shock at the horror of a gruesome murder, to pleasant surprise; and it reaches its climax in the self-reflexive reduplication of "Fuckin' fuck!"

We can easily imagine the same scene in which each "fuck" is replaced by a more "normal" phrase ("Just one more picture!", "Ouch, it hurts!", "Now I got it!" and so on). This scene works at multiple levels: 1. it uses the prohibited word on non-satellite TV channels; 2. it serves as the point of seduction (after hours of "serious" stuff, it functions as the point at which a typical viewer will fall in love with *The Wire*); and 3. the pure phallic joke marking the distance towards serious social realist drama.

What's a Wire?

So, again, what realism are we dealing with here? Let us begin with the title: "wire" has multiple connotations (walking on a wire, and, of course, wired), but the main one is clear: "The title refers to an almost imaginary but inviolate boundary between the two Americas," those participating in the American Dream and those left behind (Marshall and Potter, p. 228). The topic of

The Wire is thus class struggle tout court, the real of our times, inclusive of its cultural consequences:

> So here, in absolute geographical propinquity, two whole cultures exist without contact and without interaction, even without any knowledge of each other: like Harlem and the rest of Manhattan, like the West Bank and the Israeli cities that, once part of it, are now a few miles away. (Jameson, "Realism and Utopia in *The Wire*")

The two cultures are separated by the very basic way of relating to the real: one stands for the horror of direct addiction and consumption, while in the other, reality is carefully screened. On the horizon, we can even see the contours of the rich as a new biological race, secured from illnesses and enhanced through genetic interventions and cloning, while the same technologies are used to control the poor. Simon is very clear about the concrete historical background of this radical split when he says things like:

- **We pretend to a war against narcotics, but in truth, we are simply brutalizing and dehumanizing an urban underclass that we no longer need as a labor supply.**

- *The Wire* **was not a story about America, it's about the America that got left behind.**

- **The drug war is war on the underclass now. That's all it is. It has no other meaning. ("The Straight Dope")**

This bleak picture provides the background for Simon's fatalistic worldview: he says that *The Wire* is meant to be a Greek tragedy but with institutions like the police department or the school system taking the place of the gods, the immortal forces that toy with and blithely destroy the mortals below.

The Wire is a tragedy in which the postmodern institutions are the Olympian forces, throwing the lightning bolts and hitting people in the ass for no decent reason. In the last couple of years, we've witnessed the rise of a new form of prosopopoeia, where the thing which speaks is the market itself: the market is more and more referred to as a mythic entity which reacts, warns, makes its opinion clear, and so on, up to demanding sacrifices like an ancient pagan god. Just recall the news headlines in our big media: "When the government announced its measures to combat the deficit, the market reacted cautiously." "The recent fall of Dow Jones, which surprisingly followed the good news in employment, signals a clear warning that the market is not so easily satisfied—more sacrifices will be necessary."

There may be an ambiguity as to the precise identity of these "Olympian forces" in contemporary societies: is it the capitalist market system as such (which is making the working class disappear), or the state institutions? Some critics have even proposed to read *The Wire* as a liberal critique of bureaucratic alienation and inefficiency. It's true that the basic (and often described) feature of the state bureaucracy is to reproduce itself, not to solve the problems it's supposed to deal with, or even to create problems in order to justify its existence.

Recall the famous scene from Terry Gilliam's *Brazil* in which the hero, whose electric wire in the wall malfunctions, is secretly visited by an illegal electrician (Robert De Niro in a cameo appearance), whose criminality consists in simply repairing the malfunction. The greatest threat to bureaucracy, the most daring conspiracy against its order, is a group which actually solves the problems bureaucracy is supposed to deal with (like Hamsterdam, or the conspiracy of the McNulty group, which works to actually break the drug gang). But does the same not hold for capitalism as such? Its ultimate aim is also not to satisfy demands, but to create ever new demands which will allow its continuous expanded reproduction.

Olympian [Market] Forces

It was Marx who formulated this idea of the arbitrary and anonymous power of the market as the modern version of the ancient Fate. The title of one essay on *The Wire*, "Greek Gods in Baltimore" is thus quite appropriate: ancient gods are back! That is to say, is *The Wire* not the realist counterpart of the recent Hollywood blockbusters in which an ancient god or half-god (the title characters in *Percy Jackson* or *Thor*) finds himself in the body of a confused American adolescent? How is this divine presence felt in *The Wire*?

In telling the story of how Fate affects individuals and triumphs over them, *The Wire* proceeds systematically, with each successive season making a step further in the exploration: Season One presents the conflict: drug dealers versus police; Season Two steps back to the conflict's ultimate cause—the disappearance of the working class; Season Three deals with police and political strategies to resolve the problem and their failure; Season Four shows why the education of the black underclass is insufficient; and, finally, Season Five focuses on the role of the media: why is the general public not even adequately informed of the true scope of the problem?

Utopias in Baltimore?

As Fredric Jameson has pointed out, the basic procedure of *The Wire* is not to limit itself only to harsh reality, but to present utopian dreams as part of the world's texture, as constitutive of reality itself. In Season Two, "Frank uses money to build up his own contacts in view of a supreme project, which is the rebuilding and revitalization of the port of Baltimore." Jameson continues: "This is then his Utopian project, Utopian even in the stereotypical sense in which it is impractical and improbable—history never moving backwards in this way—and in fact an idle dream that will eventually destroy him and his family" (p. 371).

Another storyline in Season Two follows D'Angelo Barksdale as he grows more ambivalent about the drug trade. When the innocent witness William Gant turns up dead, D'Angelo is shaken, assuming his Uncle Avon had it done as revenge for Gant's testifying. Later, when arrested again, D'Angelo decides to turn state's witness; however, a visit from his mother convinces him of his duty to his family. Due to his refusal to co-operate, he's sentenced to twenty years in prison. Is the mother who convinces D'Angelo not to testify also not mobilizing the family utopia?

In Season Three, Major Colvin conducts a novel experiment: without the knowledge of his superiors, he effectively legalizes drugs in West Baltimore. By consolidating drug dealing, which he knows he cannot stop anyway, Colvin eliminates the daily turf battles that drive up the murder rates, and dramatically improves life in most of his district.

Also in Season Three, friendship itself is rendered as a utopia. Avon and Stringer betray each other, but just before Stringer's murder, the two enjoy one last drink together, acting as if their old friendship is intact. This is not simply fake or hypocrisy, but a sincere wish for how things might have been— or, as John le Carré put it in *A Perfect Spy*: "Betrayal can only happen if you love."

Plus, in Season Four, focused on education, utopia it is to be found in Pryzbylewski's classroom experiments with computers, and his repudiation of the exam evaluation system imposed by state and federal political entities.

If these utopias are part of reality, what makes the world go round, are we then beyond good and evil? In his DVD commentary, Simon points in this direction: "*The Wire* is really not interested in Good and Evil; it's interested in economics, sociology, and politics." Jameson also moves too easily beyond good and evil, and is too short in his dismissal of the "outmoded ethical binary of good and evil." However, his formula seems all too smooth. If we discount the pre-modern (pre-Christian, even) identification of Good with people like us, is the properly ethical focus of *The Wire* not precisely the problem of ethical action: what can a (relatively) honest individual do in today's conditions?

To put it in Alain Badiou's terms, these conditions, a decade ago when *The Wire* was in the making, were definitely non-evental: there was no potential for a radical emancipatory movement on the horizon. *The Wire* presents a whole panoply of the "types of (relative) honesty," of what to do in such conditions, from Jimmy McNulty and Howard "Bunny" Colvin up to Cedric Daniels who, with all his readiness for compromises, sets a limit on meddling with statistics.

The key point is that all these attempts have to violate the Law in one way or another. For example, recall how McNulty aptly manipulates the fact that (as Jameson puts it) "villainy in mass culture has been reduced to two lone survivors of the category of evil: these two representations of the truly antisocial are, on the one hand, serial killers and, on the other, terrorists" (p. 368).

Eccentric Conspirators

McNulty secures funding for the investigation of Marlo Stanfield by creating the illusion of a serial killer, drawing money and media attention to the police department. He interferes with crime scenes and falsifies case notes as part of his plan. The lesson here is that individual acts are not enough: a step further is needed, beyond the individual hero, to a collective act which, in our conditions, has to appear as conspiracy:

> The lonely private detective or committed police officer offers a familiar plot. . . . It slowly becomes clear that genuine revolt and resistance must take the form of a conspiratorial group, of a true collective. . . . Here Jimmy's own rebelliousness (no respect for authority, alcoholism, sexual infidelities, along with his ineradicable idealism) meets an unlikely set of comrades and co-conspirators—a lesbian police officer, a pair of smart but undependable cops, a lieutenant with a secret in his past but with the hunch that only this unlikely venture can give him advancement, a slow-witted nepotistic appointment who turns out to have a remarkable gift for numbers, various judicial assistants, and finally a quiet and unassuming fixer. (p. 363)

Is this not a kind of proto-Communist group of conspirators, or a group of eccentrics from Charles Dickens's novels or Frank Capra films? Is the dilapidated basement office allocated to them by police headquarters not a version of the illegal conspiracy place? G.K. Chesterton's famous formula of law itself as "the greatest and most daring of all conspiracies" finds here an unexpected confirmation.

Plus we should include in this group of eccentrics as their informal external member Omar Little from the other side of the divide between law and crime: Omar's motto can be rendered as the reversal of Brecht's motto from *Beggar's Opera*: what is the founding of a bank (as a legal action) compared to robbing a bank?

Omar Little should be put in the same series as the hero of *Dexter*, a series which debuted on October 1st, 2006. Dexter is a bloodstain pattern analyst for the Miami police who moonlights as a serial killer. Orphaned at the age of three, he is adopted by Miami police officer Harry Morgan. After discovering the young Dexter's murderous proclivities and to keep Dexter from killing innocent people, Harry begins teaching him

"The Code": Dexter's victims must be killers themselves who have killed someone without justifiable cause and will likely do so again. Like Dexter, Omar is also a perfect cop in the guise of its opposite (serial killer)—his code is simple and pragmatic: don't kill people who don't have the authority to order the deaths of others.

But the key figure in the group of eccentric conspirators is Lester Freamon—Jameson is justified in praising

> the genius of Lester Freamon . . . not only to solve . . . problems in ingenious ways, but also to displace some of the purely mystery and detective interest onto a fascination with construction and physical or engineering problem solving—that is to say, something much closer to handicraft than to abstract deduction. In fact, when first discovered and invited to join the special investigative unit, Freamon is a virtually unemployed officer who spends his spare time making miniature copies of antique furniture (which he sells): it is a parable of the waste of human and intelligence productivity and its displacement—fortunate in this case—onto more trivial activities. (pp. 363–64)

Lester Freamon is the best representative of "useless knowledge"—he's the conspirators' intellectual, not an expert, and as such efficient in proposing solutions to actual problems. So what can this group do? Are they also caught in a tragic vicious cycle in which their very resistance contributes to the system's reproduction? We should bear in mind that there is a key difference between the Greek tragedy and the universe of *The Wire*. Simon himself speaks of the "Greek tragedy for the new millennium":

> Because so much of television is about providing catharsis and redemption and the triumph of character, a drama in which postmodern institutions trump individuality and morality and justice seems different in some ways, I think.

In the climactic catharsis of a Greek tragedy, the hero encounters his truth and attains sublime greatness in his very fall, while in *The Wire*, the Big Bad of Fate rules in a different way— the system (not life) just goes on, with no cathartic climax.

The Absolute

The narrative consequences of this shift from the ancient tragedy to the contemporary are easy to discern: the absence of narrative closure and of a cathartic climax; the Dickensian melodramatic good benefactor fails, and so forth. The TV series as a form also finds its justification in this shift: we never arrive at the ultimate conclusion, not only because we never reach the culprit, because there is always a new plot, but because the legal system fighting crime really strives for its own self-reproduction.

This insight is rendered by the final scene of the series, with McNulty observing the Baltimore port from a bridge, accompanied by a series of flashes of the daily life going on in Baltimore. What we get here is not the final big conclusion, but a kind of proto-Hegelian absolute standpoint of a reflexive distance, a withdrawal from direct engagement: our fights, hopes and defeats are part of a larger "circle of life" whose true aim is its own self-reproduction, this circulation itself. A similar point was made by Marx when he noticed that, although individuals produce to reach a certain set of goals, although, from the finite subjective standpoint, the goals of production are its products, objects which will satisfy people's (imagined or real) wants, from the absolute standpoint of the system as totality, the satisfaction of individuals' wants is itself just a necessary means to keep the machinery of capitalist (re)production going.

The narrative openness of the form is thus grounded in its content. As Jameson put it, *The Wire* is a whodunit in which the culprit is the social totality, the whole system, not an individual criminal (or group of criminals). And how are we to represent (or, rather, render) in art the totality of contemporary capitalism? Is totality not always the ultimate culprit? So what is specific about contemporary tragedy? The point is that the Real of the capitalist system is abstract, the abstract-virtual movement of Capital. Here we should mobilize the Lacanian difference between reality and Real: reality masks the Real. The "desert of the Real" is the abstract movement of capital, and it was in this sense that Marx spoke of the "real abstraction," or, as *The Wire*'s co-executive producer Ed Burns put it: "We only allude to the real, the real is too powerful."

Marx described the mad, self-enhancing circulation of capital, whose solipsistic path of self-fecundation reaches its apogee in today's meta-reflexive speculations on futures. It is far too simplistic to claim that the specter of this Leviathan is an ideological abstraction and that behind this abstraction there are real people and natural objects on whose productive capacities and resources capital's circulation is based and on which it feeds like a gigantic parasite. The problem is that this abstraction isn't only in our financial speculator's misperception of social reality, but that it's real in the precise sense of determining the structure of the material social processes: the fate of whole strata of the population and sometimes of whole countries can be decided by the solipsistic speculative dance of Capital, which pursues its goal of profitability in blessed indifference to how its movement will affect social reality.

So Marx's point is not primarily to reduce this second dimension to the first, that is to demonstrate how the mad dance of commodities arises out of the antagonisms of 'real life'. Rather his point is that one cannot properly grasp the first (the social reality of material production and social interaction) without the second: it is the self-propelling metaphysical dance of Capital that runs the show, and that provides the key to real life developments and catastrophes. Therein resides the fundamental systemic violence of capitalism, much more uncanny than any direct pre-capitalist socio-ideological violence: this violence is no longer attributable to concrete individuals and their 'evil' intentions, but is purely 'objective', systemic, anonymous.

Here we encounter the Lacanian difference between reality and the Real: "reality" is the social reality of the actual people involved in the productive processes, while the Real is the inexorable 'abstract', spectral logic of Capital that determines what goes on in social reality. One can experience this gap in a palpable way when one visits a country where life is obviously in shambles, full of ecological decay and human misery; however, economists' reports inform us that the country's economic situation is 'financially sane'—reality doesn't matter, what matters is the situation of Capital.

So, again, the question is: which would be the aesthetic correlates of such Real, what something like a "realism of abstraction" (to quote Toscano and Kinkle) might be? We need a new poetry, similar to what Chesterton imagined as a "Copernican poetry." Imagine if we used the heliocentric phrase 'early-earth-turn' in place of the geocentric 'early sunrise,' fully embracing Copernican physics into the way we see the world around us. Chesterton speaks of "looking up at the daisies, or looking down on the stars," suggesting a new world is waiting for us (*The Defendant*, p. 6). At the beginning of Monteverdi's *Orfeo*, the Goddess of Music introduces herself with the words "Io . . ." ["I am the music."] Is this not something which soon afterwards, when "psychological" subjects invaded the stage, became unthinkable, or, rather, unrepresentable?

In a famous passage from *Capital*, Marx resorts to prosopopoeia in order to bring out the hidden logic of the exchange and circulation of commodities:

> If commodities could speak, they would say this: our use-value may interest men, but it does not belong to us as objects. What does belong to us as objects, however, is our value. Our own intercourse as commodities proves it. We relate to each other merely as exchange-values.

Can we imagine something like an operatic prosopopoeia: an opera in which commodities sing, not people who exchange them? Maybe, it is only in this way that we can stage Marx's *Capital*.

Here we encounter the formal limitation of *The Wire*: it didn't solve the formal task of how to render, in a TV narrative, the universe in which abstraction reigns. *The Wire*'s limit is the limit of psychological realism: what is missing in *The Wire*'s depiction of objective reality, inclusive of its subjective utopian dreams, is the dimension of "objective dream," of the virtual/real sphere of capital. To evoke this dimension, we have to break with psychological realism (maybe, one of the ways is to engage in ridiculous clichés, like Brecht and Chaplin in their representations of Hitler in *Arturo Ui* and *The Great Dictator*).

But is such a suspension of the psychological dimension, such a reduction of persons to clichés, not an act of violent abstraction? In order to answer properly this reproach, let us turn to Samuel Maoz's *Lebanon*, a recent film about the 1982 Lebanon war which draws on Maoz's own memories as a young soldier, rendering the war's fear and claustrophobia by shooting most of the action from inside a tank. The movie follows four inexperienced soldiers inside a tank dispatched to "mop up" enemies in a Lebanese town that has already been bombarded by the Israeli Air Force.

Interviewed at the 2009 Venice festival, Yoav Donat, the actor who plays the director as a soldier a quarter of a century ago, said: "This is a movie that makes you feel like you've been to war." Maoz said his film is not a condemnation of Israel's policies, but a personal account of what he went through: "The mistake I made is to call the film 'Lebanon' because the Lebanon war is no different in its essence from any other war and for me any attempt to be political would have flattened the film."

This is ideology at its purest: the re-focus on the perpetrator's traumatic experience enables us to obliterate the entire ethico-political background of the conflict: what the Israeli army was doing deep in Lebanon, and so forth. Such a "humanization" thus serves to obfuscate the key question: the need for the ruthless political analysis of the stakes of what we are doing in our political-military activity.

Here, of course, we again encounter the counter-question: but why should the depiction of the direct horror and perplexity at the meaninglessness of combat be a legitimate topic of art? Is this personal experience not also part of war? Why should we narrow the artistic depiction of war just to the great political divisions which determine the conflict? Is war not a multi-faceted totality? In an abstract way, this is true; however, what gets lost is that the global true meaning of a war and personal experience of war cannot exist within the same space: personal experience of war, no matter how "authentic," narrows the scope of war and is as such in itself a violent abstraction from totality. Rude as it may sound, refusing to fight is not the same when you're a Nazi soldier killing Jews in a ghetto or a partisan resisting the Nazis; or, in Lebanon of 1982, the "trauma" of an Israeli soldier in a tank is not the same as the trauma of a Palestinian civilian he was bombing—the first one obfuscates the true stakes of the 1982 Lebanon invasion.

The point is thus that the very psychologically-realist "concrete totality" which would encompass social reality inclusive of the lived experience of individuals that are part of it is in a more radical sense abstract: it abstracts from the gap that separates the Real from its subjective experience. And it is crucial to see the link between this formal limitation (remaining within the confines of psychological realism) and, at the level of content, Simon's political limitation: his horizon remains that of the "faith in individuals to rebel against rigged systems and exert for dignity"; this faith bears witness to Simon's fidelity to the US ideology, to its basic premise that postulates the perfectibility of man—in contrast to, say, Brecht, whose motto is "change the system, not individuals": "Mr. Muddle thought highly of man and did not believe that newspapers could be made better, whereas Mr. Keuner did not think very highly of man but did think that newspapers could be made better. 'Everything can be made better', said Mr. Keuner, 'except man.'"

Snot Boogie's Resistance

This tension between institutions and an individual's resistance limits the political space of *The Wire* to modest social-democratic individualist reformism: individuals can try to reform the system, but the latter ultimately wins.

What this notion of individuals who rebel against institutions cannot properly grasp is the way individuals themselves lose their innocence in their struggle against institutions—not so much in the sense that individuals get corrupted, stained by what they are fighting; the point is that even if they remain honest and good, ready to put all at stake, their acts simply become irrelevant or ridiculously misfire, providing a new impetus to the very force they oppose. How does this individual resistance look in *The Wire*? We get its basic scheme in the very first scene: are McNulty and a black kid witness commenting on Snot Boogie's death not like a Greek Chorus?

McNULTY: So your boy's name was what?

KID: Snot Boogie.

McNULTY: God. Snot Boogie. This kid, whose mama went to the trouble to christen him Omar Isaiah Betts. . . . You know, he forgets his jacket, his nose starts running and some asshole, instead of giving him a Kleenex, he calls him "Snot." So he's Snot forever. Doesn't seem fair. . . .

KID: I'm sayin', every Friday night in an alley behind the Cut Rate, we rollin' bones, you know? I mean all them boys, we roll till late.

McNULTY: Alley crap game, right?

KID: Like every time, Snot, he'd fade a few shooters, play it out till the pot's deep. Snatch and run.

McNULTY: What, every time?

KID: Couldn't help hisself.

McNULTY: Let me understand. Every Friday night, you and your boys are shootin' craps, right? And every Friday night, your pal Snot Boogie . . . he'd wait till there's cash on the ground and he'd grab it and run away? You let him do that?

KID: We'd catch him and beat his ass but ain't nobody ever go past that.

McNULTY: I've gotta ask you: if every time Snot Boogie would grab the money and run away, . . . why'd you even let him in?

KID: What?

McNULTY: Well, if every time, Snot Boogie stole the money, why'd you let him play?

KID: Got to. This America, man.

Here is the tragic vision of a meaningless life and death, redeemed only by hopeless resistance. The underlying ethical motto is something like "Resist, even if you know that at the end you will lose." Snot is, of course, a metaphor for the later central character, Omar Little (Snot's name is also Omar): each time he is beaten, but he does it again and again till he's killed. Snot's death is no tragedy for the same reason that the Holocaust was no tragedy, which is by definition a tragedy of character. The failure of the hero is grounded in his character flaw, but it is obscene to claim that the Holocaust was the result of a character flaw of the Jews. The comic dimension is also signaled by the utter arbitrariness of the name: why am I that name? Omar becomes "Snot" for totally external arbitrary reasons, there is no deep foundation for his name, in the same way that, in Hitchcock's *North by Northwest*, Roger O. Thornhill is in a totally arbitrary way (mis)identified as George Kaplan, But Snot, Omar, McNulty, Lester, and others, they continue to resist. Later in the first season, McNulty asks Lester why he ruined his career by pursuing a politically connected culprit, and

Lester answers that he did it for the same reason McNulty is now pursuing the Barksdale gang against the wish of his superiors. There is no reason, just the presence of an unconditional ethical drive which joins together the members of the conspiratorial group. No wonder that the final scene of the series repeats the beginning: like Snot or Omar, McNulty (and others) persisted in their Beckettian repeated failure, but this time, finally, the loser is not only beaten, he really loses, he loses his job, undergoes professional death. The last words of McNulty are: "Let's go home," or in other words, out of public space.

Surrendering to the Absolute

The reflexive withdrawal in the very last scene of *The Wire* stands for a "surrender to the Absolute." In *The Wire*, this gesture specifically refers to the relationship between law, the legal system, and its violations: from the "absolute standpoint," it becomes clear that the (legal) system not only tolerates illegality, but effectively requires it, since illegality is a condition for the system to function. The crucial dilemma with regard to this relationship between the legal order and its transgressions is not the status of direct crime (drug dealers).

The legal system itself generates the crime it fights. Many books have been written on the interdependence of the legal system and drug dealing. The crucial dilemma is a more insidious and unsettling one: what is the status of (utopian) resistance in *The Wire*? Are those resisting the system also a moment of the totality of the system? These individuals, from Snot and Omar to Freamon and McNulty, fighting the system, clinging to dignity in all its diverse forms, are they just the obverse of the system which ultimately sustains them? If yes, is the answer not an obvious, although weird and counterintuitive, one? The only way to stop the system working is to stop resisting it.

The Wire's Real Enemy

Here a (perhaps surprising) detour can allow us to clarify things. If there is an opponent of *The Wire*, it is Ayn Rand. The true conflict in the universe of Rand's two novels is not between the prime movers and the crowd of second-handers who para-

sitize the prime movers' productive genius, with the tension
between the prime mover and his feminine sexual partner
being a mere secondary sub-plot of this principal conflict. The
true conflict runs within the prime movers themselves: it
resides in the (sexualized) tension between the prime mover,
the being of pure drive, and his female partner, the potential
prime mover who remains caught in the deadly self-destructive
dialectic (between Roark and Dominique in *The Fountainhead*,
between John Galt and Dagny in *Atlas Shrugged*).

When, in *Atlas Shrugged*, one of the prime mover figures
tells Dagny, who unconditionally wants to pursue her work and
keep the transcontinental railroad company running, that the
prime movers' true enemy is not the crowd of second-handers,
but herself, this is to be taken literally. Dagny herself is aware
of it: when prime movers start to disappear from public productive life, she suspects a dark conspiracy, a "destroyer" who
forces them to withdraw and thus gradually brings the entire
social life to a standstill; what she does not yet see is that the
figure of "destroyer" that she identifies as the ultimate enemy,
is the figure of her true Redeemer.

The solution occurs when the subject finally gets rid of her
enslavement and recognizes in the figure of the "destroyer" her
Savior. Why? Second-handers possess no ontological consistency of their own, which is why the key to the solution is not
to break them, but to break the chain which forces the creative
prime movers to work for them. When this chain is broken, the
second-handers' power will dissolve by itself. The chain which
links a prime mover to the perverted existing order is none
other than her attachment to her productive genius: a prime
mover is ready to pay any price, up to the utter humiliation of
feeding the very force which works against him, which para-
sitizes on the activity he officially endeavors to suppress, just
to be able to continue to create.

What the prime mover must accept is thus the fundamental
existential indifference: she must no longer be willing to
remain the hostage of the second-handers' blackmail ("We will
let you work and realize your creative potential, on condition
that you accept our terms"), she must be ready to give up the
very kernel of her being, that which means everything to her,
and to accept the "end of the world," the (temporary) suspension of the very flow of energy which keeps the world running.

In order to gain everything, she must be ready to lose everything. Imagine not a strike of the Randian mythic "achievers," but, rather, a strike of the "inherent transgressors": those who, in "resisting" the system and violating its legal rules, effectively make it viable. Imagine the black marketeers in today's Cuba suspending their activity: we can argue that the system would collapse in weeks. (Something similar is known in Western countries as the "work to rule strike": when state employees in a sensitive branch, like custom-services or hospitals, simply strictly follow the rules, thereby bringing the system to a halt.)

Stop Worrying

And the same goes for *The Wire*: in order to accomplish the step from reformism to radical change, we must go through the zero-point of abstaining from resistance which only keeps the system alive. In a weird kind of release, we must cease worrying over other people's worries, withdrawing into the role of the passive observer of the system's self-destructive circular dance. Or, say, in view of the ongoing financial crisis which threatens to undo the stability of the Euro and other currencies, we should stop worrying about how to prevent financial collapse, about how to keep things going. The model of such a stance was Lenin during World War I: ignoring all "patriotic" worries about the fatherland in danger, he coldly observed the deadly imperialist dance and laid the foundations for the future revolutionary process. His worries were not the worries of most of his countrymen.

If we want a real change, then our own worry and care is our main enemy. So stop fighting small battles to outwit the inertia of the system and to make things run better here and there, and prepare the terrain for the big battle. The standpoint of the Absolute is simple to achieve, one just has to withdraw to the (aestheticized, usually) position of totality, as in the vulgar song "The Circle of Life" from *The Lion King* (words by Tim Rice):

It's the Circle of Life
And it moves us all
Through despair and hope

Through faith and love
Till we find our place
On the path unwinding
In the Circle,
The Circle of Life

Those singing this song are the lions: life is a big circle, we eat zebras, zebras eat grass, but then, after we die and turn into dust and earth, we also feed grass, the circle is closed, ... the best message imaginable for those at the top. The important thing is the political spin we give to such "wisdom": simple withdrawal or withdrawal as the foundation of a radical act.

Can we imagine a slight change in *Life is Beautiful*, where the father would sing to the son a similar song on the Circle of Life? "The Nazis are killing us here in Auschwitz, but you should see, my son, how all this is part of a larger Circle of Life: the Nazis themselves will die and turn into manure for the grass which will be eaten by cows; cows will be slaughtered and we will eat their meat in our pies . . ." Yes, life always forms a circle, but what can (sometimes) be done is not just climb or descend in the hierarchy of this circle, but change the circle itself. One should effectively follow here Jesus Christ who offers the paradox of Absolute (God) himself who renounces the standpoint of the Absolute and adopts a radically "critical" stance of a finite agent engaged in the struggle—this stance is deeply Hegelian, because Hegel's main thesis is precisely that on the Absolute which is strong enough to "finitize" itself, to act as a finite subject.

In other words, the reflexive withdrawal into the standpoint of the absolute does not mean a retreat into inactivity, but opening the space for radical change. The point is not to fight Fate (and thus help its accomplishment, like the parents of Oedipus and the servant from Baghdad who fled to Samara), but to change Fate itself, its basic co-ordinates.

To really change things, we should accept that nothing can really be changed (within the existing system). Jean-Luc Godard proposed the motto "Ne change rien pour que tout soit différent" (Change nothing so that everything will be different), a reversal of "Some things must change so that everything remains the same." In some political constellations, such as the late capitalist dynamic in which only constant self-revolutionizing can maintain the system, those who refuse to change anything are effectively the agents of true change: the change of the very principle of change.

The Wire's Tragic Vision

Therein resides the ambiguity of *The Wire's* finale: how are we to grasp it? As resigned tragic wisdom or as the opening of the space for a more radical act? This stain blurs the bright vision of *The Wire* as "a Marxist's dream of a series," as a sympathetic Leftist critic called it. Simon himself is clear here: when asked if he was a socialist, he declared that he is a social democrat who believes capitalism is the only game in town and as such not only inevitable but unrivalled in its power to produce wealth:

> I accept that [capitalism] is the only viable way to generate wealth on a large scale, I'm not arguing, I'm not. You are not looking at a Marxist up here, but you are looking at somebody who doesn't believe that capitalism can work absent a social framework that accepts that it is relatively easy to marginalize more and more people in this economy. Capitalism has to be attended to. And that has to be a conscious calculation on the part of society, if that is going to succeed. ("David Simon on the End of American Empire")

But does Simon's tragic view not contradict this social-democratic reformist vision? While putting his faith into rebellious individuals, he is

> at the same time doubtful that the institutions of a capital-obsessed oligarchy will reform themselves short of outright economic depression (New Deal, the rise of collective bargaining) or systemic moral failure that actually threatens middle-class lives (Vietnam and the resulting, though brief commitment to rethinking our brutal foreign-policy footprints around the world). ("David Simon on the End of American Empire")

But is it not true that we *are* today approaching an "outright economic depression"? Will the prospect of a depression give rise to a proper collective counter-institution (as Aarons and Chamayou suggest, pp. 86–87)? Whatever the outcome, one thing is clear: it is Simon's very tragic pessimism that outlines the space for a more radical change. Only when we accept that there is no future (within the system), can an opening emerge for different things to come.

Sixth Case

Sentencing

LINE 18
Class Projects and the Project Class

SETH VANNATTA

The way to self-knowledge is a path of despair. We're thrown into a world not of our own making, but we all need recognition. Recognition from others doesn't come easy. The product of desire, struggle, and violence, recognition emerges from a dreadful misrecognition.

When Marlo Stanfield rolls up to Bodie Broadus and gives him an ultimatum in Season Four of *The Wire*, Marlo walks the streets of despair. His ultimatum: take our package and keep your corner, or we'll take it. If Bodie chooses the first horn of this dilemma, Marlo gets his recognition. If Bodie challenges Marlo to take his corner by force, then they'll probably throw down.

Marlo and Bodie's battle represents a crucial moment in the history of the human spirit coming to know itself, at least according to the work of Georg Hegel, the philosophical kingpin of this chapter. In *The Phenomenology of Spirit*, Hegel tells us a familiar tale. Two men meet in the streets of West Baltimore (or in the Black Forest in Southern Germany, it really doesn't matter). Each wants recognition from the other. The very presence of the other is threatening, even baffling. Seeing another person like us shakes our sense of self-understanding and pre-eminence. If we cast our eyes downward and walk by in meek silence, we fail to be recognized. If we stand tall and demand to be seen, (and the other does the same), there's gonna be blood.

In such a situation, a battle ensues with three possible outcomes. If one person kills the other, no one gets recognition.

When Lex, jilted by his former girl, Patrice, blows away her new beau, Fruit, in Season Four, he never gets the recognition he wanted. If both combatants die, neither gets any recognition by the other. Only if one person submits, does the other gain recognition. The cat who gets recognized becomes master, the punk who gives in, slave. Hegel calls the master an independent consciousness, the slave a dependent consciousness. The slave is dependent on the master for his life. The master traded the slave's life for his own recognition, earned through the violence of a bat blow to the head or a gunshot to the knee.

Them Little Bitches on the Chessboard

But that's just the start of the story. Think back to Season One, when D'Angelo Barksdale, hanging out in the pit, sitting on milk crates and discarded furniture, explains the game of chess to Wallace and Bodie by comparing it to the drug game. The slave is like the pawn, or perhaps the knight or the castle, the muscle doing the bidding in service of the king, the master. The slave produces for the master.

Hegel says the slave *others* himself in these acts of production. It doesn't matter whether the slave is cooking or buying a meal, cutting up a new package for sale on the street, or kicking the day's count up to the master. The slave has invested himself in the labor of his production. To put yourself into your work is, as Hegel puts it, to spiritualize some material thing. The production of labor is the investment of spirit into the material which becomes the product of your work—though you don't always get to keep it. Hegel calls this *mediation*.

The German for mediation that Hegel used is also translated as alienation, which really just means separation. And it's not always such a bad thing. God spent three days making the world though a process of alienation, of separation, light from darkness, water from water, and land from water. And in those next three days, he invested himself into the population of the world, making man in his image.

McNulty and McNuggets

But alienation can signal a distortion, too. Adam and Eve were alienated from God, nature, and each other, when they realized they had sinned. Like Jimmy McNulty being cast out on a speedboat to work as a harbor cop or like Lester Freamon being confined to pawn shop detail for thirteen years and four months, Adam and Eve were alienated, cast out of the garden. We feel alienation as a result of our transgressions and social missteps. Dukie is constantly alienated at school (and even at Namond's house by Namond's mom, De'Londa)—because he stinks. To feel alienation is to live as a foreigner in your own skin, separated from the person you think you can be, the person you should be.

Karl Marx was a philosopher who spent a lot of time running with Hegel's gang, but he turned Hegel's tactics upside down and expanded them onto corners Hegel hadn't even imagined capturing. He thought that workers, especially in the work of industrialized capitalism, were alienated or estranged while at work. They cannot be themselves while at work, (in the textile mills of Manchester, England, or at Bethlehem Steel in Baltimore, Maryland). The laborers (wage slaves) work for others (masters), and the product of their labor is not their own. They can't invest their spirit into their work and produce artistically—their uniquely human capacity. Their humanity is turned against them, and they become foreigners in their own skin.

Even the inventor of McNuggets doesn't make mad money. Ronald McDonald doesn't cut him a big check. He's like McNulty, doin' the inventive work down in the cellar while the lieutenants, sergeants, majors, or colonels get the recognition for the toil of the pawns. McNulty, like the dockworkers he investigates, can only hit the bar after clocking out to get shitfaced, drowning the despair that results from the dread of misrecognition and estrangement.

Alienation permeates the world of *The Wire*. The dockworkers in Season Two are alienated. The low-level dealers, the cops working the street, and the newsroom editors, are all alienated. Alienation can also result from the logic of institutions distorting the unity and dignity of the human personality. In Season Four, Lieutenant Marimow, operating under the command of William Rawls who is in turn trying to appease Major Royce, effectively kills Lester Freamon's unit. Marimow closes the wiretap on Marlo's drug operation and directs the unit to hit the streets for quick rips, charging several felonies a week in an attempt to show stats. The entire chain of command is a series of master-slave directives, which culminate in Lester's alienation. Lester knows he's a good cop, meant to work big cases, major crimes. But he's separated from the self he knows he can and should be by the logic of the system.

Fuck Prezbo

The teacher-student relation is a special one on the road to recognition and self-understanding. A teacher can lead a student down the path to self-knowledge, but the dread of misrecognition and alienation threaten their journey. Schools can be organized like steel factories causing students to feel distant from themselves, separated from the people they really are or could become. Or teachers could be allowed to practice the *art* of education—their uniquely human capacity.

Season Four of *The Wire* invites us into the world of urban public education. In that world we're exposed to the school's institutional logic—analogous to that of the police force. But we're also shown various experiments in educational strategies, attempts to overcome the constant threat of alienation and the misrecognition it engenders. But the threat of alienation and the despair of misrecognition loom on the students' paths to self-knowing.

Consider Mr. Pryzbylewski's first attempt to get his students to "think on their feet." He asks them how long will it take to get from point A, Baltimore, to point B, Philly? The kids ask if it's East or West Baltimore, and Prez says it doesn't make any difference—East Baltimore ("Home Rooms"). The students immediately dog Mr. Prezbo because they have contextualized the math problem, showing the novice instructor the error of his ways. The students live in West Baltimore and think of East Baltimore as altogether different, rival place. They don't really have a clear sense of where or what Philadelphia is, just that Allen Iverson plays for 'em, but isn't from there.

Mr. Prezbo's mistake was posing the problem at a level of abstraction first and only sheepishly offering a context as an afterthought. Lawrence Blum points out that if Prez had presented the problem in a realistic, experiential context first, he could have had a fighting chance of showing the students how a math problem involves abstracting from your concrete experience and the importance of regional knowledge in that process.

Prez never quite finished articulating the problem involving the distance, time, and rate of motion from Bal'mer to Philly. He had to break up a fight in the middle of class. At the end of class, reading "Fuck Prezbo" etched on a student desk, he realized that he and his students had not connected. The fact that they needed to connect signals the problem—they began in different places, Prezbo a former Baltimore City police, the students, West Baltimore "Fayette Mafia Crew 4-evah," the Season Four "Boys of Summer." Prez and the kids began their interaction from a place of alienation.

Paulo Freire, who ran Marx's philosophical crew on the corners of Brazil, warned against using alienating language in school. Teachers are often not understood because their language is not "attuned to the concrete situation" of the students they address (*Pedagogy of the Oppressed*, p. 96). Prez is fairly attuned to the concrete situations of the streets of West Baltimore, having worked them as a cop. But Mr. Pryzbylewski is out of his skin in the schoolhouse, alienated from his former world and a foreigner in the students' world.

Class Projects

Mr. Prezbo learns something about the concrete situation of his students and their interests during lunch hour. He tries to deter Michael and Karim from gambling during lunch, but the situation of a card game provides the material for a teaching moment. Mr. Prezbo tells Karim he needs to calculate his odds by counting the number of diamonds in the deck by reference to the diamonds Michael is showing. This grabs their attention, and it turns out the students are even more interested in understanding the odds of dice, which is what they mostly play. When Prezbo sees the innate interest in his students, he knows he has a foothold, some leverage to teach math.

John Dewey, who ran with Hegel's philosophical gang as a youngun' but eventually went out on his own, offered some advice about the purpose and process of education. Dewey's favorite number, like Hegel's, was three. Dewey always seemed to be searching for an elusive third, a middle way excluded by

opposing trends in philosophy. His book titles came in twos—
*Human Nature and Conduct, Democracy and Education, The
School and Society*—but his central message always involved
the synthesis of the two previously (and mistakenly) opposed
concepts.

Dewey feared that educational theories had become split
into two opposing camps, those emphasizing the *child* and
those emphasizing the *curriculum*. One favors "interest," the
other "discipline." The former's calling is "freedom and initia-
tive," the latter's is "guidance and control" ("The Child and the
Curriculum," p. 277). But for Dewey only if you begin with a
concession that the child and the curriculum are two separate,
alien entities, could you be forced to choose between the two. If
we construct a curriculum, which emerges from student experience, their interests and needs, then we see that the dilemma
between the child and the curriculum is a false one. For Dewey,
student experience should provide all of the elements, problems, facts, and truths, of the curriculum.

Mr. Prezbo tries putting Dewey's insights into practice.
Gathering all of the dice from the board games stacked in the
school bookroom (and securing a brand new computer and text-
books for his classroom along the way), Prez takes to teaching
the students some math by way of games of dice. How many
ways can you roll a four? A seven? As he told Ms. Sampson,
"Trick them into thinking they're not learning, and they do"
("Unto Others"). These were his class projects.

Curriculum Alignment

The model of education Dewey criticized suggested that students absorb external material as it is impressed on them as a
ring into malleable clay or poured into their container-minds.
Freire called this the "banking concept of education" (*Pedagogy
of the Oppressed*, p. 72). (Marx had a beef with the banking
crew back in the day, and Freire harbored the grudge). In the
banking approach, the teacher tries to "fill" the students with
the contents of the curriculum. And the content is treated as
motionless, static, petrified, and fixed. Freire referred to the
content as "alien to the existential experience of the students"
(p. 72). Alfred Whitehead, who mostly operated out of Boston,
referred to such content as "inert" ideas (*The Aims of*

Education, p. 1). He claimed that education was not a "process of packing articles into a trunk" (p. 33).

A recent film on education, *Waiting for Superman*, unfortunately used the metaphor in a positive light, showing an image of a teacher actually pouring inert items into students' heads. The bad teachers spilled the contents outside the students' brain-bank vaults. Mr. Prezbo was eventually directed to teach material on standardized exams. The content on the standardized exams was inert and lifeless, and his attempts at pouring them into student heads illustrate the educational uselessness of the practice. Prez had glimpsed the art of teaching only to be thrust back into the confines of standardized test prep.

High stakes testing is the current fashion trend of public education, and it's a total waste of intellectual energy. Whitehead bemoaned the use of standardized tests stating, "No system of external tests . . . can result in anything but educational waste" (*The Aims of Education*, p. 13). He thought that no rigid curriculum, which is not modified by the individual teacher for the needs of particular students should be permissible (p. 14). Mr. Prezbo's attempt to modify the curriculum for the needs of his students was right-minded, but the logic of the system among other obstacles, stood in his way. He's told in the teachers' lounge, "The thing is it's your curriculum, and you have to stick to it." ("Corner Boys").

PREZBO: I can't, it's absurd.

He's then advised, "Look. You don't teach math. You teach the test." (We learn that the new buzzword for this is "curriculum alignment.")

PREZBO: And what do they learn?

He's not comforted by his colleagues, one of whom says, "The first year isn't about the kids. It's about you surviving" ("Corner Boys").

We wonder what the use of such lifeless content on standardized exams is. Can students reach into their mind as a storage cabinet and retrieve the formulas of mathematics when a situation calls for their application? Can students make a withdrawal from their bank deposits when they're running short on mental credit? Further, do situations even call for their application? When Prez drilled students in preparation for the standardized test, as if they would need to apply this later in practice, he alienated the students and himself from the curriculum.

We do not learn passively in order to do actively; rather, our doing is learning. The active precedes the passive in the development of the student. Mr. Prezbo's curriculum is effective because he transforms an originally given subject matter of student interests (shooting craps) into more intelligent habits of action. His attempt to get the students "to think" is a matter of habituating the students to direct their actions effectively. Math is just one way of learning to order actions effectively. The knowledge Mr. P. teaches does end in the students acquiring smart and effective habits of activity. Randy actually makes a lot of money throwing dice with some older kids on the block, getting them to follow his mathematically informed bets along the way.

To his credit, Prez does begin with student interests, the necessary condition for the possibility of educational growth. But he "tricks" them into learning, something both Dewey and Whitehead warned against. And what was the greater aim in his project? Dewey identified several criteria for good aims in education. First, they must emerge from student experiences. Second, they must be flexible. Third, they must end in the freeing of activities. Their new modes of behavior must shake off the conceptual or physical confines which previously bound them. Prezbo's aims appear to pass the first criterion, but not the next two. His endeavors are often forestalled by the need to teach to the tests (for curriculum alignment) and so we don't know how he could have revised the initial aim if it were tested more freely. But it does not appear that the learning of odds ends in freeing the activities of the students.

Dewey's emphasis on practice in the classroom did not necessarily involve a turn away from contemplation, reflection, symbolization, and abstraction, which are relevant in math education and genuinely freeing educational goals. Dewey did not want to turn away from curriculum toward the self-interested and spontaneous student. The question is, has Mr. Pryzbylewski? Dewey wanted to break down the strict distinction between the child and the curriculum, but also that between the school and society. Dewey feared that the psychological (or intellectual) component in education, the development of the mental powers of the student, and the sociological component in education, the goal of adjusting the student to social needs and roles, had been separated. The institutional logic of Edward Tilghman Middle School, its demand that its teachers prepare the students for standardized tests, focuses only on the psychological and intellectual components in education at the expense of the sociological. Such a tendency almost guarantees the alienation of the student from the curriculum and a widening gap between child and curriculum, where the goal should be to narrow that gap.

If you buy Dewey's product, the sociological and psychological components are organically related, and should not be separated ("My Pedagogic Creed," p. 85). The unnecessary separation of these components implies that our arenas of learning are isolated and separate from each other, that we're not continuously learning, as if Tilghman students didn't walk past drug corners on their way home every day to all sorts of dysfunction in those homes, learning and acquiring habits of self-preservation along the way. The social situations students find themselves in, including working on the corner and rolling dice, stimulate their powers, and the ensuing activities result in adjusted habits, based largely on the success and failure of their function in those environments.

The question for Mr. Prezbo is: *How can he give due attention to the experiences of the students, their life on the corner and their games of dice, without recreating students adjusted for those social modes of existence?* We know that his spiritual task of educating the students, of leading them down the path of self-knowledge, of helping them become the people they can be and should be, is stifled by the institutional demands of teaching to the test. But even his piecemeal class projects fail to tackle one of the goals of education, that of imaginatively transforming the world they live in.

Adjusting students to the world is one matter. But Dewey warned against trying to achieve an ideal form of association, which merely repeats the traits of the one actually found in student experiences. What if all Prezbo does is get his students adjusted to the world of the West Baltimore drug trade with its violent crimes and familial disintegration?

Dewey wanted students to recreate imaginatively the world they lived in as part of their growth in school, a growth whose only goal was to promote more growth guided by "ordered richness" ("Creative Democracy," p. 229). I'm not sure Mr. Prezbo even scratches the surface of this monumental task. He fails to put the students' social situations into clear relief by showing that they're problematic and trying to raise awareness of their objective situation, so that they do not internalize the norms of its operation and repeat its cycle endlessly.

The Project Class

Dr. David Parenti, the sociology professor at the University of Maryland, who researches violent offenders, attempts to do just that in Season Four. Having received a grant for a pilot study aimed at reducing recidivism, he plans to target eighteen-to-twenty-one-year-olds for "inoculation." Fortunately, the West Baltimore church deacon puts him in contact with retired police officer Howard "Bunny" Colvin, whose experiment in legally ignoring the drug trade and drug use in Hamsterdam, while getting him fired, has earned him some street cred with the academics.

Parenti's Parentalism

The project is not without obstacles. First, Parenti uses "alienating language" when approaching Colvin. The language is so foreign to Colvin that the deacon has to translate. Their first encounter runs as follows:

PARENTI: With this grant the mandate is not only to rethink the way we utilize institutions, but to help us start getting past having to rely on jail and drug rehab as our only responses. We're looking for a specific target group to inoculate, epidemiologically speaking.

COLVIN: Doctor, and pardon me. I'm not an academic, not by a long shot. But what exactly are you, you saying here?

DEACON: [*translating*] He's saying he's got a lot of money to come up with some way to go at those boys out there banging on the corners.

PARENTI: That's exactly what I'm saying.

COLVIN: So where exactly do I come in?

PARENTI: Well, if the salary arrangements are suitable, your duty would be to perform as a field researcher, a liaison operating in the urban environment.

DEACON: [*translating*] You go out in the hood and get him some corner boys to mess with.

PARENTI: This is why I need someone like you to be paired up with me. I go out there on my own . . .

COLVIN: [*interrupting*] And they sell your tenured ass for parts.

PARENTI: In so many words. ("Home Rooms")

Parenti at least has insight into his own limitations. But the entire project is threatened by the fact that it is constructed in an academic environment and thus comes from the outside-in or from the top-down. Freire's foremost concern was revolutionary liberation through education. Insofar as Dr. Parenti is an elite, and lives by the privileges of his elite status, he's an oppressor. His attempts to liberate are humanitarian, and that, for Freire, is the problem, not the solution. Freire writes:

Pedagogy which begins with the egoistic interests of the oppressors, (largely the egoism [of getting published] cloaked in the false generosity of paternalism [Parenti's parentalism]), and makes of the oppressed the objects of its humanitarianism, itself maintains and embodies oppression. It is an instrument of dehumanization. (p. 54)

For the very same reason, Freire warns against treating the oppressed as objects to be studied, Dr. Parenti's very project.

The false generosity of paternalism gets perpetuated by Hollywood films about education year after year. Consider the film *Dangerous Minds*, in which Ms. LouAnne Johnson, a white woman, takes on the task of saving the black and brown students from their own familial and social environment, which is portrayed as backward, irrational, and generally pathological. Her whiteness (as Blum points out) is an index to her individuality, rationality, authority, and missionary task. Her educational project is one of salvation. Similarly in *Waiting for Superman*, the featured underprivileged students' only hope is to be saved by a charter school, and their admission is determined by a lottery system.

Freire explicitly warns against salvation as a genuinely liberatory educational task. Season Four of *The Wire* conveys the darker truth, that Mr. Prezbo or any sociology PhD, cannot "save" the students at Tilghman Middle School, even though Mr. Prezbo desperately wants to save Dukie from social promotion into high school, and despite the fact that Bunny eventually adopted Namond, whose family life was, dare I say, backward and pathological. (His mom's dream for her son was for him to become a soldier like his dad Wee-Bey, and she recommended to Carver that Namond be sent to baby booking as an educational step toward that goal).

Colvin, whose experiential knowledge outruns Parenti's academic knowledge of sociology, shows Parenti first hand the error of his attempt to target eighteen-year-olds by introducing him to an eighteen-year-old criminal who attempts to assault him for taking notes during an interview. Colvin and Parenti instead turn their focus to the eighth graders at Tilghman Middle School. They separate children with behavioral difficulties into their own class, the project class, targeted for study and intervention. The forms of association, the habitual ways of interacting, of these "corner kids" provide the material for their educational project.

Misrecognition on the Road of Despair

The project class instructor, Miss Duquette, a "young, but good" PhD candidate whose thesis work was on social alienation analysis, deftly lures the students down the path toward self-knowledge. She asks: "Who are you?" Moments later: "Let me ask, and I want everybody to write this down: where do you see yourself in ten years? Come on, pencil and paper. This isn't schoolwork. This is about y'all" ("Corner Boys"). She even gets some ambitious responses. Albert wants to be "a pediatric neurosurgeon, like that one nigga." When told he'll need to go to medical school, his response says a lot, "Whateva." Then she walks the students down the road of despair. "How many wrote down *dead*?" Namond, having raised his hand says, "Shit. You saw that comin' huh" ("Corner Boys").

The piecemeal successes of the project class are due to the fact that they use the ways of associating with one another on the corner (a Deweyan method) to foster the social skills that will enable them to, at least, return to a normal (albeit oppressive) classroom, and at best, resolve conflicts conversationally rather than violently (a Freirean aim).

We see Namond flexing his critical skills during group discussion. He says, "We do the same thing as y'all. Except when we do it, it's like oh my God these kids is animals. It's like it's the end of the world comin'. Man that's bull shit. A'yight. Cause it's like, what's it? Hypocrite? Hypocritical"? ("Corner Boys").

ZENOBIA: I mean, we got our thing, but it's just part of the big thing.

COLVIN: This uh corner boy thing, right? You know y'all did all this talkin' up in here. You think you could sit down and write the laws to your thing?

NAMOND: Hell yeah, I'll do it right now and shit.

COLVIN: No I'm talkin' about can y'all do it together? ("Corner Boys")

The project class has moments of success, and Parenti, Colvin, and Duquette have reason to be optimistic. Miss Duquette remarks, "I've never seen students like these so animated." Parenti chimes in, "Focused. The corner culture kids at least." But Miss Duquette knows the obstacles that block their road to self-knowing: "The ones with deeper problems, they act it out. We're not just up against corner logic in there. I'm seeing oppositional defiant disorder, clinical depression, post-traumatic stress, and with the girl DeChandra, borderline psychosis maybe." But the corner kids came alive. Colvin says when they talk about what they know, they speak from the heart, even taking turns talking. They began to engage in genuine dialogue, a first step in liberatory education.

The upside to the method in the project class is that it begins in student experiences and builds on their forms of associations in an effort to teach social skills, such as ordering from a menu in a restaurant. Miss Duquette teaches the class, "When you are polite, people treat you better" ("Know Your Place"). Colvin even takes the students out to dinner as a reward for their successful efforts at socialization. The project class takes one mode of association on the corner, working together, and applies it to a classroom assignment, working in teams to build models. The winning team got the fancy dinner. At Ruth's Chris, Namond, Zenobia, and Darnell are a veritable case study in alienation, foreigners in their own city, (much like D'Angelo felt on his fancy date in Season One). By the time the students ride home with Colvin, they've fallen back into their habits of action, defiant and angry.

Freire wrote that liberatory education must begin in dialogue, and that dialogue is founded upon love, trust, hope, and faith. The students are guided in their practice of dialogical skills, and they engage in the practice of trust-building, by doing exercises such as the trust fall.

But obstacles stand in their way. Albert presents perhaps the toughest case. Anger and disrespect permeate his being. One of his rants is telling enough: "This is bull shit. And I ain't readin' no mu-fuckin' book either. I don't even know nothin' 'bout the damn book. You always gettin' on my ass and shit about some book. Fuck you, cheese-faced bitch" ("Corner Boys"). Later, when the teachers see that Albert is still struggling to join in and still bursts out in profanity at his teachers and peers, they realize the despair that plagues his path to self knowing. They learn that his mother has died on his couch at home, but that no one has come to get her for days. The teachers of the project class learn the social and emotional strains that limit their project are profound and seem insurmountable.

Ultimately, the institutional logic shuts down the project class. Colvin and Parenti are confronted with a challenge that resurrects one of the dichotomies in education that Dewey warned against. The area superintendent accuses them: "You're not educating them, you're socializing them" ("Misgivings"). In her charge, she equates education with the psychological and intellectual component only, and her discourse reveals that she doesn't consider the sociological component to be real education. Colvin does his best, more diplomatically than Parenti, (who calls her "obtuse"), to challenge the system. He pleads: "But it's not about you or us or the test or the system. It's about what they expect from themselves . . . We can't lie, not to them."

Colvin's despair and frustration run counter to that of the outsider, Parenti, who is genuinely excited about the attention the research will receive from academics. Colvin can't believe it: "Academics? What, they gonna study your study? When do this shit change?" ("Final Grades") When we see Colvin depart the academic lecture Parenti gives in the final montage of Season Four with its fancy title, "Dynamic Socialization Analysis Learning Adverse Group," heading a graph that challenges common sense, we're left wondering whether these two worlds will ever enter into genuine dialogue in service of the revolutionary liberation Freire called for.

Both the class projects and the project class fell short of living up to Dewey's and Freire's educational methods. Dewey pointed out that the terms *society* and *community* are ambiguous. First, a community *describes* a form of association common to a plurality of societies, both good and bad. He writes:

> There is honor among thieves, and a band of robbers has a common interest as respects its members. Gangs are marked by fraternal feeling, and narrow cliques by intense loyalty to their own codes. . . . Any education given by a group tends to socialize its members, but the quality and value of the socialization depends upon the habits and aims of the group. (*Democracy and Education*, p. 88)

Second, society is conceived as a unity, a praiseworthy community of public purpose of well-being, where mutual sympathies are expressed among its members. The problem, for Dewey, was to educate the young such that neither meaning was entirely dominant. The forms of association taught should not be overly ideal, as coming from the top-down, nor overly real, as repeating the norms of the isolated and narrow group.

The virtue of Prezbo's class projects was that they began from student interests and proceeded outward to the development of math skills. The virtue of the project class was that it began in a genuine dialogue about the forms of association of life on the corner and proceeded outward to the development of social skills. The failure of both was that they did not show how the forms of associated life on the corner were problematic. Freire's task, and I think Dewey's as well, was to educate in an effort to raise awareness of objective reality in service of the broader goal of self-awareness.

But the way to such self-knowledge is a path of despair. We all long for recognition, but our striving for recognition is assaulted by constant misrecognition. The institutional logic of the school system threatens to distort the unity and dignity of human personality where we may end up alienated and estranged, foreigners within our own skin. Our desires and violent struggles to know ourselves may not be successful. The dread of misrecognition threatens our need for hope.

The Wire does not teach the lessons of naive optimism. For that, watch *Dangerous Minds*, where white folk can save black and brown kids from their own social and familial illnesses. Or mindlessly consume *Waiting for Superman* with its praise for the banking concept of education and the salvation of the underprivileged by lottery balls and charter school admissions.

However, *The Wire* is not without hope. And every genuine educator is a prisoner of hope. The road to all liberation through self-knowing is a path of despair, but all roads have their empty horizons and infinite beyonds. We educators are travelers on that path, struggling to transform what lies beyond.

LINE 19
You Gonna Get Got

KODY W. COOPER

If you walk through the gardens of Baltimore, you better watch your back. That goes for those on the path to destruction as well as for those who walk the straight and narrow track.

Whether or not you walk with Jesus, the devil is not the only one to fear in Baltimore. The bosses in the precinct, city hall, newsroom, and the Game also have the fire and fury at their command. To have fire and fury at one's command is to have *power*. And politicians, cops, journalists, stevedores, and gangsters in Baltimore all seem to be after it. But, what is power? How does life in the city of Baltimore shed light on this nebulous concept?

The Wire presents us with two rival pictures of power and honor that have been defended by classical and early modern philosophers, what we can call the "Old School" and "New School," respectively. The Old School connects power and honor to perfection—that is, power is understood as essentially coupled to human flourishing or virtuous living, regardless of whether it lines one's pockets or makes one famous. It included the notion of power to change one's life, to cultivate the intrinsically loveable qualities of virtue, and to live well. The New School measures power and honor in terms of riches and reputation in a way that is indifferent to loveable or fearful qualities. Let's first consider the New School.

Hobbes on the Harbor

When Wallace asks how pawns become king, D'Angelo responds, "The king stay the king" ("The Buys"). But staying king is evidently not a foregone conclusion. On the streets, Avon Barksdale got jacked twice and Stringer Bell and Proposition Joe were both betrayed and killed. In city hall, Mayor Royce was defeated by Tommy Carcetti. In the precinct, Burrell successfully obtained a full term as police commissioner only to be forced out early.

To stay king you must maintain your power. In the pursuit of riches and reputation, the bosses in *The Wire* present us with the New School's vision of power.

In his masterpiece, *Leviathan*, Thomas Hobbes (1588–1679) formulated the New School view in this way: "the power of man is his present means to some future apparent good." Hobbes, moreover, perceived a general inclination in modern humans: "a perpetual and restless desire of power after power, that ceaseth only in death" (Hobbes, p. 58). The character of this desire is not precisely a ceaseless seeking after more and more intense pleasures. It's not precisely a heroin addict's incessant desire for a fix. It's rather a continued seeking of the *means* to secure your future happiness because whatever power you have at the moment will never be enough.

The power sought is always for the sake of some future good. What is the good? Hobbes's rap was New School when he claimed that there is little or nothing objectively good. This is due to the fact that people disagree over what is reasonable. Hence, Hobbes's claim that "whatsoever is the object of any man's appetite or desire; that is it, which he for his part calleth good . . . there being nothing simply and absolutely so; nor any common rule of good and evil, to be taken from the nature of the objects themselves" (pp. 28–29).

The object or thing desired is always *apparently* good because it's always sought through the prism of a person's subjective wants. The good is relative to individual desires because, by various customs, education, and temperament, diverse persons differ widely in their tastes. And, Hobbes notes, even the *same* person may not always desire the same thing: "the same man, in diverse times, differs from himself; and one time praiseth, that is, calleth good, what another time he dis-praiseth, and calleth evil" (p. 100). Bubbles, for example, continually waffles back and forth in calling dope good or evil. So the desire for power is a desire to secure the means to attain whatever one might happen to desire in the future.

The upshot is that New School power has a twofold character. First, power is *indifferent* to rival visions of human happiness, fulfillment, or well-being in the city because the good is relative to individual desire. Therefore, and secondly, power becomes measured in riches and reputation because these can serve as a means to getting most anything one might want. Frank Sobotka used riches to buy influence and get new legislation to dredge the canal; his son Ziggy used riches to buy a $2,000 leather jacket . . . and a duck.

Regarding reputation, Hobbes pointed out that our power or present means is essentially dependent upon the opinion of others: "what quality soever maketh a man beloved, or feared of many; or the reputation of such quality, is power; because it is a means to have the assistance, and service of many" (p. 51). But "to show any sign of love, or fear of another, is to honor" (p. 52). In the modern city of Baltimore, power and honor can be had equally from love or fear.

Riches and reputation had a place in the Old School. But, the peculiarly novel New School move is to unhitch these forms of power from an objective account of human well-being. In the new view, power is *equally power* inasmuch as money is equally money or reputation is equally reputation, regardless of whether the game is being played in the streets or the courthouse—whether it is in the hands of a Commissioner Daniels or a Marlo Stanfield, of a Rhonda Pearlman, or a Maurice Levy.

My Name Is My Name

The desire for power after power becomes a desire for riches after riches in bosses like Clay Davis, Stringer, and Prop Joe. For them, reputation is good inasmuch as it is a means to lining their pockets. Stringer even comes to see the struggle for street rep as a potential obstacle to running a good business. The violence of beefing over corners is not conducive to a profitable business because dead bodies bring the business-killing scrutiny of the Five-O. So he tells his dealers: "We're gonna handle this shit like businessmen. Sell the shit, make the profit. And later for that gangster bullshit" ("Time After Time").

Stringer and Prop Joe form the New Day Co-Op with other high-level dealers who agree to put aside petty grievances, bring disputes to the group, and collectively bargain for a better discount on the New York package. Stringer sums up the benefits of the co-op: "We gonna make more money together. . . . No beefing, no drama, just business" ("Straight and True"). Stringer and Prop Joe contrast with the two other major drug kingpins, Avon and Marlo. For them, the modern desire for power manifests more sharply as a desire for reputation as the principal goal.

In Hobbes's formulation of the new view of power, any reputation that attracts the service and assistance of many others is equated with honor. Honor is the "manifestation of value we set on another" and value is shown when service or assistance is rendered by word or deed (p. 51). But, as we have seen, this can come just as easily from love as from fear. Hence, New School honor is indifferent between a fearsome and loveable reputation. As New School power is indifferent to rival visions of the good life, so New School honor is indifferent to fearsome and loveable qualities.

Avon's and Marlo's concern for their respective reputations is apparent throughout their stints as kingpin—particularly in their conflicts with Omar. For both kingpins, fear is the key ingredient in the thermodynamics of reputation.

After Omar robs a Barksdale stash house, Avon puts a hit out on him. But, he does not seek a quiet hit in the night. Just as "crackers" kill deer and put them on their truck "tied up and stretched out so everybody can see it," Avon wants Omar put on display to send a message "so people know we ain't playin'" ("Old Cases"). The point is to send a message: anybody who robs Avon gonna get got. Later, Avon's lieutenants get Omar's partner Brandon and leave his mutilated body on display. D'Angelo confesses to McNulty that the body was dropped out in the open in order "to send a message to the 'jects" ("Sentencing"). The message is that if you dishonor Avon in word or deed, you will have a brutal fate to fear. You'll have Avon's *power* to fear.

Marlo's conflict with Omar is incited by Omar's robberies of Marlo's poker winnings and package resupply. To Marlo,

Omar's actions aren't so much a monetary menace as they are a threat to muffle his name ringing out on the corners. Hence Marlo's unflinching judgment is that Omar has to get got. Marlo offers exorbitant sums of money for Omar's head and goes so far as to have Chris and Snoop torture and kill Omar's blind friend and mentor to bait him out of retirement. Omar takes the bait and roams the streets of Baltimore hitting Marlo's stash houses and corners and flushing or burning Marlo's dope and money. Omar repeatedly calls Marlo a punk for not coming to face him in the streets. Yet, none of this reaches Marlo's ears until after Omar is killed.

When Marlo learns the truth, it is one of the few times we see him lose his calm and collected demeanor. He immediately orders his lieutenants to go out on the corners and tell the people that word never reached him about Omar's challenge. Later, after Marlo agrees to give up the kingpin crown in order to get out of jail, he returns to the corner to find that it is *Omar's* name being glorified. The corner boys do not even recognize Marlo and fearlessly attack him. While Marlo successfully protects himself, his face is full of regret—regret that Omar has killed his (no longer fearsome) name.

Before the death of his name at the hands of Omar, Marlo's name rang out on the corner as Avon's did before him: it struck fear into the hearts of all its hearers. Kima makes this point during her investigation of a home invasion and triple killing. Marlo had ordered a hit on Junebug solely on the basis of a rumored slander. When Michael questions whether this is sufficient basis for a hit, Chris replies: "It doesn't matter if he said it or not. People think he said it. Can't let that shit go" ("Unconfirmed Reports").

While investigating the killing, Kima remarks: "People out there are so scared" of Marlo, "I can't get close to an eyewitness on any of it" ("React Quotes"). The fearsome fire and fury at Marlo's command were embodied in Chris's uncanny ability to carry off targeted witnesses and mopes to their deaths with little protest. In Namond's words, "Chris got the power. He tell them to come and they gotta come. Like the devil do with the damned" ("Alliances").

The cultivation of ruthless and murderous reputations was for the sake of personal honor. While Hobbes himself would have deplored this sort of violence—Hobbes preferred to direct

the restless desire for power into nonviolent channels as
enforced by an absolute sovereign—his idea of honor as including whatever quality would make one feared indicates the
rationality of the Stanfield organization's ruthlessness, especially given the conditions of West Baltimore. Through their
fearsome reputations, Marlo was able to control the corners
and Chris was able to make people follow him to their deaths
without putting up a fight. But, are Marlo's and Chris's reputations really *honorable* as the New School suggests? One
could only rightly judge such a reputation to be honorable on
the supposition that power is essentially indifferent to fear-
someness and lovability. The lives of a few others in Baltimore
suggest the Old School alternative.

Gotta Keep the Devil Way Down in the Hole

Aristotle (384–322 B.C.) and Thomas Aquinas (1225–1274 A.D.)
most famously kicked it Old School. On the older view, human
power is not indifferent to but essentially oriented toward perfection or human flourishing. Bosses in Baltimore—Carcetti
and Burrell in city hall, Sobotka at the docks, Klebanow and
Whiting at the newsroom, the drug kingpins in the game—
have an active power to move other persons and things. But
our active powers are also capacities to move *ourselves*. The
active powers that make us human—reason, will, physical
strength, etc.—are oriented toward the well-being or flourishing of the human person. Power is and ought to be directed
toward actual (and not merely apparent) goods.

In contrast to Hobbes, Aristotle and Aquinas held that anyone who reasons rightly will see there are objectively desirable
goods, including healthy bodily and spiritual life, family, friendship, and knowledge or truth. When you deploy your reason,
will, and strength to pursue objects that destroy life, family,
concord, and truth, you have failed to live well or virtuously.
Beginning to live well requires doing away with bad habits
(vices) and acquiring good ones (virtues) because good habits
direct power to the good. But acquiring the virtues is not easy
in the modern city. We have seen that many find themselves
carried away on the wide path of modern ambition characteristic of the New School. Few are on the straight and narrow
because it is a difficult path to follow. Consider McNulty.

McNulty was at one point married with children and enjoyed working as a patrolman in the Western District. When he became a detective, he found his marriage and family falling apart as he indulged inordinate pleasures of body and mind. He boozed, slept around on his wife, and obsessively worked cases against Avon and Stringer not primarily for the sake of justice, but to indulge his vain desire to display his intellectual superiority. Yet, McNulty eventually came to see the wisdom in Lester's words: "The job will not save you Jimmy. It won't make you whole. It won't fill your ass up" ("Back Burners"). Cases, even great ones, come to an end—and there's little recognition for the vain detective who solves them. One-night stands and liters of Jameson didn't fill him up either. So McNulty resolved to leave detective work, cease restlessly pursuing his own vanity, and to give up "the drinking and the whoring" ("Mission Accomplished").

During this period, McNulty is seen to be effectively policing his beat and pursuing a healthier relationship with Beadie Russell and her kids. McNulty's ex-wife Elena remarks that McNulty is the happiest she has ever seen him. But McNulty's happy life unravels when he returns to his vicious habits. McNulty's story of attempted redemption and relapse contrasts with Cutty's, Bubs's, and Walon's. Each of their stories manifests the Old School view of power-for-perfection.

With a Solemn Left and a Sanctified Right

Cutty's initial attempt to live a virtuous life also proved abortive. Cutty, a legendary soldier in the Game, returns to the streets after serving a fourteen-year prison sentence. When initially faced with the prospect of deploying his powers to do honest but backbreaking work in landscaping, Cutty backslides into the Barksdale organization. But when it comes time for Cutty to kill again, he cannot return to the murderous path of enforcers like Chris. Cutty comes to see such a life as incompatible with his true happiness and dedicates his life to making an honest living and helping to get boys off the corner by getting them into his boxing gym.

The young'uns' participation in the sport of boxing is set in stark contrast to the hopper's life of drug dealing. On the one hand, hoppers are beat on and ordered around by dealers in a way that habituates them to act viciously in a cutthroat game of play or get played. Meanwhile, their participation contributes to the further erosion of civil society by supplying addicts with the means to their own self-degradation and self-destruction. On the other hand, boxing is a social practice of employing one's power in pursuit of the objectively desirable goods of play and friendship, and it requires disciplined habits of mind and body in order to succeed.

Specifically, the good boxer needs the cardinal virtues, those four habits that were classically considered as necessary for living well. He needs *fortitude* so that excessive fear or daring will not obstruct that which excellent technique requires. He needs *moderation* not to indulge in delectable pleasures inordinately, which would impede his training regimen. He needs *justice* to fight fairly. And he needs *prudence* to fight smartly. Moreover, concord is the natural effect of competitors exercising their powers in this way. Cutty's training regimen illustrates self-reform to live virtuously and in harmony with one's community. Each of the four cardinal virtues direct power to the path of perfection or flourishing by helping the person to avoid what reason forbids and to do what reason demands when one's emotions would lead one to do otherwise. The stories of Walon and particularly Bubs provide further examples of reforming oneself to direct one's power toward the good through acquiring the virtues.

Walon's is a story all too common for the dope fiend. As Walon tells it, his drug addiction led to two bouts of endocarditis, Hepatitis C, the loss of his wife, "and the respect of anyone who ever tried to loan me money or do me a favor" ("One Arrest"). He pawned his pickup, bike, National steel guitar, and a stamp collection his granddad left him. And even then, when on the corners where he "didn't have a pot to piss in" and no friends, Walon told himself: "Walon, you're doing good . . . God's own drug addict." But Walon came to see that he was not *actually* doing good. He came to see that "it's good to be anywhere *clean* . . . even Baltimore." In other words, Walon came to see the drug-free lifestyle as objectively better, happier, more fulfilling—more *reasonable*—than living as an addict.

Bubs similarly lost his family and became alienated from his daughter and sister. His life of scraping and scrounging in the streets was a day-to-day struggle aimed at that next high. But Bubs was impressed with Walon's testimony and expressed his sincere desire to live well. He even got clean for a few days, banking on Kima's promise to loan him money to start anew. But Bubs's chances at recovery were literally stopped by a bullet when Kima got shot and could not keep her promise. Bubs returned to the needle and remained an addict until the fateful morning when he woke to find that he had unintentionally poisoned his friend Sherrod.

A year after this incident, we find a Bubs who has been clean ever since, regularly attends Narcotics Anonymous meetings at Saint Martin's Church with Walon, is gainfully employed distributing papers for the Baltimore *Sun*, and volunteers his free time at the Catholic Worker's Viva House, serving and feeding the poor and homeless. By the end of the series, Bubs has a breakthrough at an NA meeting and his sister has invited him to break bread with her family.

Bubs embodies the Old School vision of power-for-perfection in his cultivation of virtuous living. Each of his reforms manifests one of the cardinal virtues—those good habits that help one to direct one's powers to living well. Bubs exercises the virtue of prudence by rightly reasoning that he should give up street vending for a job at the Baltimore *Sun*, not only because the latter is a steadier job, but also because off the streets there will be less occasion to be tempted by the needle. He displays the virtue of temperance by checking the desire to get high. He displays the virtue of justice by performing good works for the impoverished and those still ensnared by drugs. And finally, Bubs displays the virtue of fortitude by facing both his grief and his fear of talking about Sherrod.

Crucially, Bubs does not acquire the virtues merely as a means to a good reputation. When, through circumstance, a *Sun* reporter meets Bubs and writes up a story on his life, Bubs is apprehensive about it being published. Walon asks Bubs if he is afraid of being called good. Bubs points out that the reporter "make me sound special for doin' what I need to be doin'" ("–30–"). In other words, Bubs has taken the *intrinsically* honorable and loveable path because it was good for its own sake, regardless of whether or not it brought him fame or fortune. Indeed, the message of Gus Haynes's fight for truth and journalistic integrity in the newsroom of the Baltimore *Sun* suggests that virtue in the modern city may require foregoing fame and fortune.

Assessing the Dark Corner of the American Experiment

In the end, I believe that *The Wire* presents us with a sober vision of the modern American city. It is rife with the ambition for New School power. Many people in city hall, the precinct, the docks, and the streets are driven to gain money and fame, to securing the means to satisfy their capricious desires. And yet, there are glimmers of Old School virtue in the modern city. Even in Baltimore—the city Landsman describes as "the dark corner of the American experiment"—virtue has the power to move ("Dead Soldiers").

The power of virtue is evident in the stories of Walon, Bubs, and Cutty. Walon and Bubs would be the first to admit along with Cutty that "I ain't no angel" ("Margin of Error"). But the virtues of each, their *loveable* qualities, have an intrinsic power to move others to act *well*. Walon's testimony and sponsorship move Bubs. Cutty attracts young'uns off the corners. Bubs inspires a *Sun* reporter to write a story that makes the front page, which potentially inspires others to better their lives as well. Cutty, Walon, and Bubs are a testimony to the power of every person to exit a destructive and vicious lifestyle and begin to live well.[1]

---

[1] I would like to thank Brandon Dahm for reading and commenting on an earlier version of this chapter.

LINE 20

Is Our Thing Really a Part of the Big Thing?

NATHAN ECKSTRAND

> **NAMOND:** We do the same things as y'all. Except when we do it, it's like oh my God these kids are animals. It's like it's the end of the world coming. It's like Man that's bullshit. . . . Hypocritical.
>
> **ZENOBIA:** Yeah, we got our thing, but it's just part of the big thing. ("Corner Boys")

There is a telling moment in *The Wire* when one of the main characters, charged with a crime, threatens to go to the police and tell them everything. He's immediately warned against taking that step by another character, who says, "You can have yourself a pity party, talk all kind of shit to some prosecutor. You know where you'll be then? Out in the damn cold. No connections, no allies, nowhere to hang your hat in this damn town. Or you carry this for all of us" ("React Quotes").

As *The Wire* follows the lives of numerous criminals, there are many who could have said this. But who was it? Brianna Barksdale talking to D'Angelo? Spiros Vondopoulos cautioning Nick Sobotka? Prop Joe admonishing his nephew Cheese?

Surprisingly, it's none of them—it's not even someone from the street at all. The interaction occurs between State Senator Clay Davis and City Council President Nerese Cambell. When we're first introduced to the language of 'carrying this' (an expression that conveys taking a charge rather than betraying the Game) it comes from established criminals like Avon Barksdale and Stringer Bell, so the presence of street language in the Baltimore State House should be disconcerting.

Ideally politicians should be honorable, trustworthy individuals whose interest is in serving the people—their world
should be as far removed as possible from the world of crime,
which exploits the disenfranchised of Baltimore's poorest districts. Yet, as *The Wire* shows, no matter what part of the city
we're in—be it the street, the docks, the schools, the news-
rooms, or the courthouse—the same sorts of statements, people, practices, and habits recur again and again.

When Bubbles says "there's a thin line between heaven and
here" ("Old Cases") to describe the difference between the West
Side and the suburbs where McNulty's kids live, he's also
describing the pretend difference between legality and illegality when it comes to the influence of drug money in politics.

There's Games Beyond the Game

Almost everywhere we look in *The Wire*, we see the exercise of
power. Prosecutors indict drug dealers and, occasionally, politicians; Marlo runs West Baltimore with an iron fist, going so far
as to set in motion Herc's eventual firing; even Bubbles is able
to apply force over Barksdale's crew after they assault Johnny
by siccing the police on them.

Michel Foucault, a twentieth-century French philosopher,
has a lot to say about power. Foucault rejects the theory that
power flows only from the top to the bottom. Contrary to the
"fecal gravity" theory of power—"bang on the right people and
the shit rolls downhill" ("Straight and True")—those on the bottom can exert power over those at the top, compelling the
wealthy and influential to respond to them. Wallace, a pawn in
the Barksdale organization, controls Stringer Bell's fate and
the fate of the Barksdale investigation for a time. Despite his
humble position in the drug food chain, he has drug lords,
police captains, and prosecutors running around after him
because he can connect Stringer to a murder.

Everyone in society has access to power, even if they don't
recognize it, from the lowliest drug dealers to the mayor of the
city. This is because power is not something you have, but
something you use. Foucault writes that "power is exercised
rather than possessed; it is not the 'privilege,' acquired or pre-
served, of the dominant class, but the overall effect of its strategic position" (*Discipline and Punish*, p. 26). Were this not the

case, we would be hard pressed to explain how drug dealers and fiends are able to render parts of Baltimore uninhabitable, or laws unenforceable by the police.

Power relations form networks that can operate in myriad ways (p. 27), including actions, statements, or thoughts. This is why Jimmy McNulty, whose pursuit of criminals is often stymied by those above him, is not without recourse to pursue Marlo Stanfield during Season Five after Major Crimes is shut down. McNulty uses deaths in the homeless community to fabricate a serial murderer, exploits the Baltimore *Sun* (and Scott Templeton's zeal for attention) to draw media coverage, through which he puts pressure on the bosses to provide manpower, money, and resources for a long-term investigation of Stanfield. The network of power relations between the police, the *Sun*, politicians, and lawyers, is employed by McNulty to force those who control the purse strings to respond to him.

I've Been Here Before

Power runs deep in society. So deep, in fact, that Foucault says our knowledge of the world is intricately connected with the exercise of power. The concepts we use to describe the world, the strategies we use to solve problems, even our language— it's all influenced by networks of power. Think of the 'stat game' played by Baltimore's finest. Police bosses like Burrell and politicians like Clarence Royce claim it helps to rid the city of crime by letting the police know where and when crimes are occurring so that they can respond proactively. In actuality, police officers learn to reclassify incidents to make them appear less serious, and to only go after easy arrests instead of major crimes. This produces statistics that make politicians and bosses look like they're being 'tough on crime' without actually having to tackle the underlying social and economic problems. Daniels eloquently illustrates this when refusing to juke the stats: "But the stat game—that lie—it's what ruined this department. Shining up shit and calling it gold, so majors become colonels and mayors become governors. Pretending to do police work while one generation . . . trains the next how not to do the job" ("–30–").

The 'stat game' produces a knowledge of criminality which emphasizes crimes that are easily traceable and solvable, hiding systemic or persistent crimes like conspiracy, money laundering, and racketeering. This knowledge does not illuminate the connections between poverty, lack of education, and crime. Bunny Colvin, who admirably tries to fix some of these underlying issues when he carves Hamsterdam out of abandoned neighborhoods, is chastised by the bosses when his experiment is discovered. Not because people can't recognize the good that Hamsterdam does (Mayor Royce tries to keep it going), not because there aren't powerful people speaking in its favor (both the Deacon and the Johns Hopkins academics were strong advocates), but because the systematic way in which Colvin's project tries to confront criminality is antithetical to the war on drugs, its zero-tolerance policy, and the statistical method embraced to wage it.

Focusing on the exercise of power can uncover such networks and hidden connections, revealing unseen biases that underlie the modern world. Foucault's work, which focuses on what he calls 'games of truth' surrounding the mad, the criminal, and the perverse, parallels *The Wire*'s emphasis on different parts of the city with every season, from public schools to the docks. And, just as *The Wire* critiques the stat game, standardized tests, and certain uses of anonymous sources, Foucault critiques the ways society talks about and treats the insane, prisoners, and deviants. In one of his most famous examples, Foucault argues that the treatment of prisoners as lifelong delinquents has led to the formation of an inferior class in society, leaving millions of people like Cutty unable to vote because of prior felony convictions.

Foucault argues that by showing how power functions, it will be possible to identify, criticize, and change pernicious parts of modern networks of power. His books draw attention to the statements of previous thinkers and the practices of earlier ages, showing the ways statements and practices can lead to unanticipated results. With each season of *The Wire*, David Simon similarly draws our attention to dangerous practices and ideas, though he does it by illustrating the effects in a dramatic narrative rather than writing what Foucault calls "a history of the present." In Season Two, *The Wire* asks how economic forces have led us to dismiss or deride unions, and what effects that has had upon working people. Season Three makes us think about how treating drug users as criminals to be jailed, rather than as patients for rehab, changes our perception of drug users. Carcetti's tragic journey from reformer to pro-establishment politician demonstrates how even the most idealistic among us can become tamed by the desire for personal advancement and the pressures of the political system. Like Foucault, *The Wire* does not provide easy answers to these problems, but shows us ways in which the beginnings of solutions can be formed.

Similar networks of power reverberate up and down society, so that the most disenfranchised in the city end up exercising almost identical powers as those on the top. Former Officer Roland Pryzbylewski becomes aware of such repetition after beginning his career as a teacher, when he encounters a 'stat game' similar to the one at work in the police department. When he asks what standardized tests assess in students, the response from another teacher is blunt: "Nothing, it assesses us. The test scores go up, they can say the schools are improving." Prysbylewski's response was equally candid: "You juke the stats, and majors become colonels. I've been here before" ("Know Your Place"). It's a sentiment Foucault could echo, as he illustrates how the networks of power operating in prisons were adapted for use in mental asylums, military barracks, and even schools—a fact hardly lost on the students at Tilghman Middle (*Discipline and Punish*, pp. 210–15).

The Wire illustrates this in other ways too, as no matter where you go in Baltimore you find similar systems, people, and operations at work. Jimmy McNulty, Omar Little, and Michael Lee are all individuals talented at their jobs but whose moral codes put them at odds with their bosses or co-workers. The New Day Co-op, Tilghman Middle School administration, and Baltimore *Sun* executive editors are all concerned with properly structuring their organizations hierarchically so they can control the distribution of drugs, education, and news, respectively. Foucault's revelation that systems reverberate throughout society can help us understand why there is today such an institutional demand for quantification (such as No Child Left Behind), job performance reviews, and measurements of racial or gender diversity. We have all adopted similar 'games of truth'.

With this characteristic of power understood, it's no longer startling that the language of City Hall, of mayors and state senators, has influenced the language of the street. The same networks of power and games of truth that Avon, Prop Joe, and Marlo participate in are those familiar to Campbell and Davis. *The Wire*'s illustration of the drug war's effects on people from all professions, ages, and socioeconomic classes, finds a basis in Foucault's demonstration of how networks of power ripple out, entangling institutions and individuals in their web. If we can recognize these systems, perhaps we can develop alternatives to the problems we face.

Game's the Same, Just Got More Fierce

So, how does power function in society today? Foucault believes it trains or disciplines us to act in conformity with the specific ways networks of power operate. Discipline 'produces' us as individuals who feel compelled to comply with a variety of social norms, from banal ones like how to sit in school and what to eat to stay healthy, to dangerous ones such as how to run a drug corner, or those that favor certain races, genders, and sexualities over others. Training occurs through three primary means: hierarchical observation (the constant surveillance of individuals), normalizing judgment (social and internal pressure for individuals to conform to what is normal and acceptable), and examinations (the regular testing of our behavior and knowledge to see whether we're conforming).

Many of the dangers *The Wire* identifies, whether in the schools, the courthouse, or in the police station, Foucault would argue, stem from these three means of discipline. Hierarchical observation organizes objects and people to make them visible, identifiable, and knowable (p. 170). Similarly, administrators at Tilghman Middle School are often seen observing teachers and students in their classrooms through a conveniently placed window in the door, just as the cubicles in the Homicide department in the Baltimore Police Department provide for supervision by Landsman and Rawls. When *The Wire*'s protagonists step out of line, they're often observed doing so, which leads to sanctions or reprimands (Nickolas Sobotka's theft of cameras brings Frank Sobotka's wrath down upon him). Even when they're doing their jobs as the bosses want them to, police, drug dealers, union leaders, and teachers update those in charge. Lieutenant Daniels attends Comstat meetings where he reports to Major Rawls, who reports to Commissioner Burrell, who reports to the mayor; Pryzbylewski reports to Vice-Principle Donnelly; even Omar checks in with Butchie and the police from time to time. The characters of *The Wire* are constantly observed and appraised.

This may not in itself seem like such a terrible thing, but when it's combined with the second characteristic of power in the modern era, normalizing judgment, it starts to have an insidious effect—especially when that effect goes unnoticed. Normalizing judgment is how we learn to police ourselves and others. Minor crimes that would have been ignored earlier in history take on a larger significance and lead to more severe penalties, and massive sets of codes and regulations are drawn up that every individual is compelled to follow. Those who act according to these regulations are rewarded, while those who are even a little bit off are corrected with sanctions, fines, written warnings, or worse (p. 183). Watch out, change your behavior now—or these misbehaviors will end up on your permanent record.

McNulty, who does things his own way, is regularly penalized even when he does a good job, while hacks like Burrell who follow rules to a T are promoted time and time again. The sanctions McNulty faces ultimately have an effect, as in Season Four McNulty begins to police himself by leaving the detective squad, and for a while he does not run afoul of the networks of power in Baltimore.

Namond Brice is judged in a way similar to McNulty, although the code of rules he is expected to follow is different. Namond is reprimanded several times by various teachers and administrators for failing to wear the proper shirt, using bad language, and ignoring instructions. Namond also hears about it on the corner when Bodie criticizes his work ethic. When Colvin takes Namond and several other students to dinner at a fancy restaurant, Namond's lack of knowledge regarding the proper code of behavior leaves him feeling dejected and angry. Normalizing judgment compels us to act in accordance with the code of rules and behaviors that society sets down for individuals in our position. As Colvin puts it when describing the students' behavior to Dr. Parenti: "They're not fools. They know exactly what we expect them to be" ("Know Your Place").

The third characteristic of power, the examination, both classifies and corrects individuals. Exams require individuals to display their knowledge for others to see, allowing those others to separate individuals into groups of better and poorer performers. Exams can be dangerous when used to identify nonconformists in society and to compel such individuals to follow societal norms. Throughout Season Two, union members are subjected to examination by the government. Their books are perpetually open to prosecutors and they are forced to testify before a grand jury to confirm that they are doing things properly.

When Frank Sobotka and the other dockworkers fail the exam, the federal government steps in to run the union. Not because the government wants to save the union but because they want to discipline it, to make it act in accordance with the codes of behavior set out for it. With regards to the crimes of the union, the government has no intention of catching all the criminals (as we see, they let the Greek go). The important part of busting the unions is to subject Nick Sobotka and the remaining dockworkers to harsher regulations so that they learn to behave and act properly. Exams are a constant ritual in our society, one which makes it easier to constrain those who step out of line (*Discipline and Punish*, p. 184).

Don't Matter How Many Times You Get Burnt, You Just Keep Doin' the Same

There's a danger facing those of us who are interested in reforming the system, and it is a danger that *The Wire* illustrates well. Lester Freamon's personal experience tells us something about how Baltimore treats those truly interested in fixing the city, as his early efforts led the Deputy Commissioner to send him, for thirteen years and four months, to the one place Freamon didn't want to go—the pawn shop unit. *The Wire*'s reformers are constantly stymied, threatened, and punished. The few actual reforms that are pushed through are quickly undercut so that they don't endanger the networks of power and games of truth at work in Baltimore.

Foucault can help us understand why true reform is more often avoided rather than embraced, or embraced only to be avoided. Systems of power and games of truth often are difficult to root out because they are so embedded within our ways of thinking and acting. They become great edifices upon which we build our society, and would require a fundamental reorganization of society to uproot. In speaking of how deeply entrenched prisons are in our society, Foucault writes that "rooted as it was in mechanisms and strategies of power, it could meet any attempt to transform it with a great force of inertia" (*Discipline and Punish*, p. 305). Our reformers in *The Wire*, when they attempt to arrest Avon Barksdale or convict Clay Davis, are not just threatening the interests of individuals but the interests of the economic, social, and political systems at the heart of our community. Against the reforms of people like Freamon and Colvin, those economic, social and political systems push back using the power and authority exercised by people like Clarence Royce and Irving Burrell.

There is another danger connected to reforms: they are often appropriated by the networks of power they are meant to undo; the work done to achieve reform ultimately ends up supporting the systems it opposes. The stat game and standardized tests are two examples of this; in both cases, they were originally envisioned as solutions to the problems of crime and lack of education, but over time they became the problem.

Drug lords like Barksdale, Bell, and Stanfield accommodate themselves to the stat game by hiring low-level dealers to stand tall and take a charge, while schools teach to the test and end up making education irrelevant to students' actual experiences. By the time we come across them in *The Wire*, the stat game and standardized tests have become obstacles to police work and education, not solutions.

Even mechanisms we use to incentivize admirable behavior can become harmful over time. Consider Templeton, the reporter at the *Sun* who covers the homeless murders in Season Five. He's motivated in part by his desire to win an award, and in doing so to escape to a better newspaper with a better byline, better pay, and more visibility. Yet to achieve this, Templeton ends up selling out his journalistic ethics and professional duties to win a Pulitzer. Because of the newspaper's desire for an award, Templeton's sensationalism trumps the seriousness and rigor that journalism is ostensibly about. Gus Haynes comments on this in the last episode of *The Wire*, saying "Get some profile, win a prize—maybe you go to a bigger newsroom somewhere. Whiting, Klebanow, Templeton—they snatch a Pulitzer or two, they're up and gone from here. For them, that's what it's all about." ("–30–"). What is it that allows reform to turn against goals?

Foucault uses power to explain how this happens. In his books on sexuality, Foucault claims that within the last couple centuries there has been a virtual explosion of discourse about sexuality, with much of it centered on how sexuality is repressed (*History of Sexuality*, p. 17). In response to this supposed repression, there has been much ink spilled about how to free sex, or at least how to properly reform it. Yet the moment of freedom never seems to come. Are we constantly coming up short in our attempts at reform, or is there something else at work? For Foucault, the discussion about freeing sex is actually part of the system that enslaves it. Foucault writes:

> If sex is repressed, that is, condemned to prohibition, nonexistence, and silence, then the mere fact that one is speaking about it has the appearance of a deliberate transgression. A person who holds forth in such language places himself to a certain extent outside the reach of power. (*History of Sexuality*, p. 6)

There is a thrill one gets from saying sexuality is repressed, that it is something that should be brought out from the dark and opened for all the world to see. Pretend reform—whether it is applied to sexuality, education, or crime—can make us feel that we are doing the right thing, distracting us from the depth of the problem we are facing and the steps needed to fix it. The 'stat game' and standardized tests make us think we are moving forward, allowing politicians and administrators to claim they are addressing the problem, but they are actually a way of insulating networks of power and games of truth from genuine change.

The Gods Will Not Save You

Within our society, there is no one person who is in charge, no puppet master pulling all the strings. Power is exercised from numerous points and can be seen in both large and small practices. Yet power works best when it is unseen, when the people implementing it speak grandiosely about the principle of reform.

Everyone in society both exercises and is subject to power by virtue of their participation in the networks of power relations that compose our community. We're hooked on power the same way a West Side fiend is hooked on yellow tops. Only occasionally are drugs seen in *The Wire*, but they structure or influence every event in the show, from the actions of Carcetti's campaign for mayor to D'Angelo's decision to go to jail.

Many of Foucault's statements about power could have been uttered by a character on *The Wire* were one simply to replace the word 'power' with 'drugs.' It is not hard to imagine Carcetti, talking to Tony Gray about the problem of drugs, saying "[drugs are] tolerable only on the condition that [they] mask a substantial part of [themselves]" (*History of Sexuality*, p. 86). Neither is it farfetched to imagine Lester Freamon, in mentoring one of the younger detectives, saying, "[Drugs are] everywhere; not because [they] embrace everything, but because [they] come from everywhere" (p. 93). In *The Wire*, drugs, even if not always present in physical form, are ever-present as a force and motivation for each character we meet.

The possibility of shaking off the restrictions of networks of power and games of truth is, for Foucault, about as easy as it would be for Baltimore's fiends, kingpins, dealers, hoppers, and cops to give up drugs. If we are to ever get to a better world, it will be through a constant struggle to undo the influence that power has on our lives. Those in *The Wire* who continue the fight despite the constant pressures from above to conform never win outright, but do achieve small victories. Accumulate enough of them and, perhaps, the pernicious forces identified by *The Wire* and Foucault will gradually start to change.

LINE 21
Stop Snitching, Screw the System

MYISHA CHERRY

JOHNNY: No Bubs, I mean, there gotta be rules or else things get fucked up.

BUBBLES: Ain't no rules for dope fiends.

JOHNNY: When the police got you shackled up, you make a move, right, you help yourself out. But to just start snitching for no reason doesn't make no sense . . .

BUBBLES: Whoa, whoa, whoa, let me track this. You populating like you can tattle tell when you locked up but you can't do it straight up for the money? No offense, son, but that's some weak-ass thinking. You equivocatin' like a motherfuck.

JOHNNY: 'Kay, so a snitch is a snitch, right?

BUBBLES: There you go!

JOHNNY: So why be one, man? I mean, we getting by with our capers.

BUBBLES: 'Deed, we getting by out here every damn day, rippin' and runnin,' but ain't got shit to show for it.

JOHNNY: That's part of being a soldier! I mean, that's you, right? That's what you say.

BUBBLES: Yeah, that's why I put all this mileage on these feet. You wait, you wait till you ain't a pup no more. See if you ain't looking for something a little more steady for your own self. . . . Look, we hook up with my girl Kima, we get paid, you gonna be better.

JOHNNY: No, fuck that, Bubs, alright? I'm not fucking a snitch.

BUBBLES: You know, I can argue the other side. Say that you drop a
dime to duck a charge then you a snitch. You do it as a living, you
a professional! ("Straight and True")

We don't often expect drug fiends to engage in ethical debate,
but so opens the fifth episode of *The Wire*'s Season Three. In
"Straight and True," drug addicts Johnny and Bubbles are
walking down the streets of Baltimore engaging in an ethical
debate about snitching. Bubbles has been a confidential
informer, or CI, for Detective Kima Greggs for some time. He
tells Johnny about it after Johnny is beaten within an inch of
his life by the Barksdale gang for trying to use counterfeit
money to buy drugs. Bubbles, thinking the dealers went too far,
decides to get even with the drug dealers by helping "his girl
Kima" identify members of the Barksdale crew.

However, when Johnny finds out that Bubbles is still snitching to Kima, he argues that there are rules that must be followed and not snitching is one of them. From Johnny's
perspective, to provide information to the police voluntarily is
just wrong. To Bubbles, there are no rules. Snitching is a way
to get easy money instead of rippin' and runnin', collecting
scraps, and having nothing to show for it.

Johnny suggests that giving up information to the cops to
get yourself out of trouble is morally preferential to providing
information for money. Snitching to avoid a charge is part of
the game for a fiend. Bubbles argues the opposite, saying that
snitching while in custody is breaking a code of the street and
showing weakness, but informing for financial gain is like a job
or a profession. (I'm pretty sure Bubbles has taken a logic
course before. He's certainly a product of the Baltimore City
Schools in their better days.)

Listening to drug addicts philosophizing about the ethics of
snitching makes you wonder why they would worry about
ethics. If they are willing to commit 'capers' like shaking down
a man on a ladder, to get money, why worry about selling information? Makes you wonder why people like Johnny, not hardened criminals like the drug dealers, or those under the same
rules as them, would stick so faithfully to the 'no snitching'
code.

The threat of police infiltration, the promotion of loyalty,
and the demonizing and ill treatment of 'rats' show the tradi-

tional importance that the no snitching rule has held in the crime business. But in *The Wire*, viewers see that both those in the Game (drug-dealers) and those not in the Game (civilians) are obliged to abide by this rule. This can be confusing to street outsiders: if the business of drug dealing is so dangerous and detrimental to society, why would law-abiding citizens refuse to help the police get rid of the mess by withholding information? There are a few reasons to consider why people like Johnny and ordinary residents in *The Wire* refuse to snitch.

Fuck the Police

Don't sell us on process, Mr. Mayor. We've had years of this kind of treatment from city police.

—Minister ("A New Day")

One reason why the characters in *The Wire* abide by the no-snitching code is because they experience personally how unjust law enforcement is. Though the police cars patrolling their neighborhoods say "protect and serve," the people know what's really up. Cops come in different flavors: the most popular and dangerous are corrupted (Walker), overzealous (McNulty), disinterested (Polk and Mahon), violent (Colicchio) or a mixture of all four.

'Citizens', or people not in the drug game, don't think that the police care about the people in their districts or that they genuinely try to make their neighborhoods liveable. So they show little interest in helping the police who either ignore them or mistreat them. Rather than work with the cops, we see characters like Namond, in the Season Four episode "New Day," get the police back for the dirt they do. But instead of throwing yellow paint on a corrupt cop, like Namond and his crew did, people use their silence.

The police do lots of dirt in the show and the residents, citizens and players alike, take note. An individual can be in her neighborhood, minding her own business, and the police can come looking for trouble—like when Carver, Herc, and Prez go to the Towers and start a riot. The only purpose for their presence at the Towers late that night is to "let those motherfuckers know who you are" ("The Detail"). When the officers arrive to the housing projects, they approach two residents who happen to be outside, not engaging in any crime. The police harass them by forcing the men to lie on the ground. They then order one guy to take his clothes off, while strewing both men's possessions all over the ground. Officers Hauk, Prez, and Carver believe that their badges give them this right.

In *Democracy Matters*, Cornel West suggests that this is an example of "evangelical nihilism," when those in power believe that their might makes them morally right:

> The classic expression of *evangelical* nihilism is found in Plato's *Republic* in the person of Thrasymachus, the Sophist who argues that might makes right. Thrasymachus mocks truth, integrity, and principle by claiming that power, might, and force dictate desirable political action and public policy. Raw power rather than moral principles determine what is right. For him, the terms of what is just must be dictated by imperial elites because such exercise of power is necessary in order to ensure national security and prosperity. (*Democracy Matters*, p. 30)

This term, *evangelical nihilism*, is really just a poetic way of saying that those who have power believe that they are always right simply because they have the guns and badges. However, such reasoning is a blatant appeal to authority, assuming that those with power and those in positions of authority make right whatever they say or do. Because those, like Thrasymachus, who think that might makes right, brook no dissent in the vein of 'You're with us or against us,' West characterizes this stance as evangelical. On this particular night at the Towers, the officers are far from being in West's neighborhood of right, the one of truth, integrity, and principle. Instead, they're all about might, engaging in the sort of twisted, violent behavior that only turns citizens against them.

The Slave-Master Relationship

Why do the police in *The Wire* treat the criminals and "suspicious" people this way? We might look to the history of race and prisons in the United States for an answer. Angela Davis notes in *Racialized Punishment and Prison Abolition*, that when blacks got their freedom after emancipation, they were no longer subject to the slave-master relationship as traditionally understood. The criminal justice system, however, became an institution whose purpose shifted from solely reforming white criminals to also confining free blacks and reminding them they might as well still be slaves, thus creating a new system. Former slaves became identified as "criminal" with the state as their new "master." The penal system moved into the position the master once occupied: having full control over black lives and bodies.

In *The Wire*, we see police use their power to control where dealers can go, what they can do, and what they can say, even if the dealers are not engaging in a crime, such as when Michael and his crew were eating Chinese food in a different neighborhood. Although they were behaving themselves, when Officer Walker saw them, he told them to "get back on the reservation where their black asses belong" ("A New Day").

To Walker and other cops in the series, their badges give them the power to limit the actions of their subjects. These officers believe that, because they are cops, they are justified in going out on the streets, busting heads, and treating people like they are less than fully human. It's known as the "Western District Way." If their victims resist, the police can threaten them with bodily harm or arrest. In fear, some citizens are quick to obey, as Randy does when Officer Walker takes the money he got from Chris Partlow ("Soft Eyes"). Speaking up for himself would have put Randy at risk. Thus, Walker makes sure any rebellion against his evangelical nihilism will have dire consequences.

This slave-master relationship reoccurs throughout the series. Back at the Towers, the police search for individuals to target and arrest for any reason, which mirrors the rapidity with which newly free blacks were arrested under the Black Codes of the early twentieth century. Similarly, Walker's harrassment of Michael and his friends reflects the fact that vagrancy was often used as an excuse to arrest and imprison newly freed blacks during the post-Reconstruction reign of Jim Crow in the South.

Angela Davis describes these codes as petty violations that could get a black man arrested, but which were not criminal for whites. They included not coming to work or making "intimidating gestures" toward a white person. Davis compares the southern Black Codes to modern legislation such as the

Rockefeller Drug Laws, which gave mandatory sentences for possession of narcotics. In both instances there is the intentional creation of policy that makes it easier to exercise authoritative control over not only blacks, but also other minorities and poor people. Carver, Herc, and Prez's off duty sweep of the Towers to accost and antagonize innocent residents is just one example of this unjust, racial targeting and the continuation of the slave-master dynamic.

Fists Are for Fools

Historically, according to Davis, blacks have been perceived as not having a soul. During the era of slavery, Blacks were considered animalistic, irrational creatures, who only understood brute force and therefore didn't deserve respect. When the slaves were freed, the inclusion of blacks in the criminal justice system prompted a shift in its purpose. The justice system was no longer used to reform souls (since blacks did not have them) but rather to physically punish bodies. Like the former slave master who used force to control, the new criminal justice system resorted to punishing the body of blacks through the institution of chain gangs and corporal punishment.

Today excessive physical violence by police is labeled brutality, but it is really a form of punishment designed for those criminals (minority and poor), whom authorities believe can't be changed, and like other beasts, are too stupid to understand anything but physical violence. When a police officer, such as Officer Walker in "New Day" or Prez in "The Detail," uses physical violence as a form of punishment, it tells you exactly what they think of those individuals: they are soulless and beyond reform. It tells those who witness the act that the only way to correct criminals is to treat them like animals and use force in the same way the master formerly punished his slaves. Officer Walker's breaking of Donut's fingers demonstrates a rejection of Donut's humanity and reminds the "criminal" that he is a second-class soulless fool not worth the trouble of an official, sanctioned investigation and prosecution.

Back at the Towers, the police's plans go sour when a young man leans on a police car and refuses to leave. Prez pistol whips the teen in the eye, and those witnessing the brutality from the towers' windows disapprove loudly and actively, throwing bottles, a TV set, and firing gunshots from above as they scream, "Fuck the Police."

While their superior officer, Lieutenent Daniels, berates Herc, Carver, and Prez for their folly, he also covers for them. The young man Prez hit is a fourteen-year-old who ends up in critical condition. Daniels tells Prez to change his story from "He pissed me off" to "He made me fear for my safety" to avoid trouble with Internal Affairs. The fact that Prez is put on desk duty and not charged with brutalizing a child illustrates Davis's argument: there is a greater chance of going to prison (or the hospital) for simply being black than for actually committing a crime. Thus Davis argues people are disproportionally punished in relation to their race and class.

It would be natural to assume that cops only approach the drug dealers with this sort of treatment. However, in "Transitions" from Season Five, while police are arresting kids on truancy charges (another example of a frivolous cause to arrest black kids), a citizen asks politely (twice) for the police to move their vehicles so that he can drive through. In front of other cops and witnesses, Officer Colicchio charges at the citizen, chokes him while yelling, "Who do you think we are? We're the Police." This event shows how even law-abiding citizens are treated like slaves, expected to recognize the master's power. Any sign of non-conformity on this matter is cause for a brutal response, letting the community know exactly what the police think about those they abuse.

To Dirty Cops: The Streets Are Watching

Throughout the series, the residents witness the violent, selfish, and dehumanizing actions of the police. Even the "respectable" and "elite" blacks are aware of it and can find themselves victims of this mistreatment. When a fellow minister is harassed and mistaken as a criminal by Herc in "A New Day," black ministers go to the Mayor to protest.

The incident makes it clear that no one black is immune to police brutality. Why? Because the war on drugs continued the power dynamic (between the criminal justice system and black and poor citizens) of the Jim Crow South in the urban centers populated by the southern black diaspora. As Major Colvin admits to Carver in "Reformation" from Season Three, drug related police work creates an environment in which criminals become the enemies, and neighborhoods become occupied territory. This war analogy, though different from the slave-master relationship, conveys the same point: citizens can be sacrificed, no one will be trusted, and collateral damage cannot be avoided.

If the war on drugs ruined the police's job, according to Major Colvin, it also ruined the citizens' willingness to see police as anything but enemies. If this is the nature of police-civilian relations, it becomes easy to understand why citizens in *The Wire* refuse to snitch to police. Citizens wonder "Why would I want to help a policeman do his job and get promoted as a result of my tip or testimony?" There is no desire to snitch on criminals who sell drugs while at the same time helping the police, many of whom act like criminals themselves. Instead, the citizens maintain their silence, which clearly communicates their message: "Fuck the Police."

The Audacity of Despair

Distrust in the ability of the criminal justice system to protect black and poor citizens is another reason why citizens in *The Wire* abide by the no-snitching code. In *Race Matters*, Cornel West defines nihilism as a feeling of hopelessness, worthlessness, lovelessness, and social despair that citizens feel in America. This feeling is not caused by a deep-rooted self-hatred, but because of what he calls in *Democracy Matters*, "paternalistic nihilism," when those who are in power think that their efforts to change things are futile, and they begin to work for special interest groups instead of for everyday citizens.

Paternalistic nihilism happens when Commissioner Burrell is more interested in reducing crime numbers to satisfy and help re-elect Mayor Royce than in reducing the factors (unemployment, school drop outs, lack of extra-curricular activities and fatherlessness) that are the main causes of the drug epidemic. In response, citizens recognize that they are not a priority. What results is a sense of neglect and a loss of trust and hope in the system that is supposed to protect and provide ways for them to flourish.

Citizens recognize that they cannot walk freely up and down their own front steps because drug dealers crowd their stoops and the police fail to intervene. They know that even when dealers are arrested, they're often back on the streets the next day. If the police do not have enough power to provide basic neighborhood safety or to prosecute criminals, then citizens become nihilistic about the police's ability to protect them.

When Major Colvin attends a community meeting, a Sergeant tells the attendees that the police cannot fight the drug war alone: "When you see illegal activity, pick up the phone." Yet the Sergeant fails to acknowledge the extremity of the challenge in the request. As one man notes, "My cousin Wiley co-operated. He went downtown and he testified. Now he's deader than Tupac today" ("Hamsterdam"). The citizen's response points to a loss of faith in the ability of the police or justice system to protect the citizens who do decide to help police fight the war on drugs.

The state knows the power of a witness testifying in court to get a conviction, but in *The Wire*, it becomes evident that the police do not protect the citizens in exchange for witness testimony. In Season One's "The Target," William Gant is one of two who witnesses D'Angelo Barksdale shoot Pooh Blanchard in the Towers. Although Barksdale is acquitted, Gant is later killed. At his autopsy, McNulty notes: "It sends a hell of a message" ("The Detail").

We're quick to assume that what McNulty means is that the dealers are telling project residents not to testify against drug dealers at the risk of being murdered. However, this statement can also be interpreted in another way. Gant's murder may not necessarily prevent the residents from snitching on the Barksdale gang, but instead may make them scared to trust the police's ability to protect them if they do testify. The result is a loss of trust, and citizens begin to feel the pull of nihilism. Police power is rarely exercised in the protection of citizens. If citizens don't trust the police, then they don't snitch to the police.

But consider the difference between fear and nihilism. It is one thing to be scared of people hurting you, and another to have a sense of hopelessness about being protected by the very people who have the power to stop criminals from harming you. Fear is a passive feeling. Nihilism lacks hope, not reason or strength. When a citizen says in a community meeting that she calls the cops lots of times but the dealers are back on the streets the next day, this is not fear speaking, it is her under-standing of the system and a knowledgeable response. Just as you and I know that one plus one equals two, she also knows that if you call the cops, things will not change. The community understands that testifying to the police does not guarantee protection from either the dealers or the police. So, instead of risking their lives, the citizens take this knowledge and either refuse to snitch, or they change their story like Nakeesha Lyles, the second witness in D'Angelo's trial. Despite changing her story, Nakeesha is killed by the Barksdale gang in Season One's "Cleaning Up" to prevent her from testifying about the bribe she received.

No, nihilism is not a weakness or fear. It is being hopeless because you have every reason to be. It's about recording infor-mation, processing the data, and coming to the conclusion that the police cannot or will not do their job so there is no need to risk your own life to help them.

West argues that nihilism poses a threat to the community because it causes people to become disconnected from the world, gives them no hope for the future, and makes them cold-hearted. Although nihilism can produce these results in the long term, in the short term, the form of nihilism that citizens in *The Wire* display is not destructive but healthy. It is healthy because the loss of hope is not in life itself, but in the police, the criminal justice system, the government. It is an affirming nihilism because it makes constructive, one might say prag-matic, use of knowledge and produces self-reliant citizens with strong bonds between neighbors. In other words, the no snitch-ing code says "I don't need or want your help." It says, "We care about ourselves too much to be deceived by empty promises."

Wising Up to the Game

We succumb to nihilism as a result of learned experiences. In "Margin of Error" from Season Four, Randy's youth and naivety allowed him to trade his knowledge of Lex's murder to avoid Assistant Principal Donnelly's wrath. However, Officer Hauk divulges Randy's identity to Little Kevin, a member of Marlo Stanfield's gang. Fulfilling the role of a paternalistic nihilist, Herc is more interested in solving his case than protecting his source, Randy, and the word spreads in the streets that Randy is a snitch. Although a detail is put outside Randy's house, the police car leaves to answer a fake call and, once again, the police neglect their duty to protect a citizen. As a result, Randy's house is firebombed. The police were supposed to protect Randy, but that was a joke. When Carver visits him in the hospital, Randy's words echo the jaded perspective of many:

> You gonna help, huh? You gonna look out for me? You gonna look out for me, Sergeant Carver? You mean it? You gonna look out for me? You promise? You got my back, huh? ("That's Got His Own")

The answer is NO. The police in *The Wire* will not protect you when you snitch. The best thing to do is to stop snitching until they start protecting. A year later we see Randy refuse to get caught in the trap again; he has learned the lesson well. Bunk visits him in a group home, trying to convince him to snitch again, but now Randy, more informed about how the Baltimore City Police operate, knows the police will not help him. Randy replies, "that's what y'all do huh, lie to dumb ass niggas" ("The Dickensian Aspect"). Randy is no longer naive. He appears physically older, stronger, and perhaps meaner, and his outlook is different. He no longer has confidence in the power of the police to protect his interests. His days of co-operating have disappeared with his youth.

An Act of Rebellion

To outsiders, law-abiding citizens who refuse to snitch may be seen as cowards who have no respect for the law or victims who do not want their communities to change. Their silence may also appear to condone the drug dealers' actions. But those who do not snitch are not apathetic. We see examples of this in *The Wire* when residents attend community meetings, even sparsely. Residents do in fact care, they just do not think law enforcement can or will do anything. Refusing to snitch is not merely an act of passive resistance. Rather, it's a type of non-co-operation similar to Gandhi's philosophy of non-violent protest. Not snitching is as active as co-operation because it takes effort, heart, can produce results, and sends messages to the police that they have failed at their job. The act of not snitching should be seen not as retreat, but rebellion, not against one's own community, but against the injustice of the police and the government they represent.

According to Gandhi, the philosophy of non-co-operation is a rebellion against the government's need to control citizens through their dependence on the state. Similarly, not snitching is a way to let the police know that the citizen will no longer be dependent on the police for protection or change. As Randy spoke to Bunk in that room in the group home, his refusal to be dependent on the police any longer is evident. It was time for him to rebel.

Not snitching is rebellion against the systematic failure of the legal system. According to Gandhi, the philosophy of non-co-operation with the government was justified because it was morally right to withdraw co-operation from the state since the state had become corrupt, oppressing rather than protecting citizens. Not co-operating with the police forces citizens to find alternative methods to solve their problems. Cutty's mentorship and boxing group serve as examples of the community helping itself without being dependent on the police to solve its problems.

Although in *The Wire* those who refuse to snitch are not as organized as Gandhi's followers, their stance is very political. Like other non-violent resistance, "Stop Snitching" is a courageous way for citizens to undermine a system that does not have their best interests at heart. Instead of rioting, they rebel through silence. This sort of rebellion, rather than being unpatriotic, is as American as hell.

Our Connect

Alexander, Michelle. 2010. *The New Jim Crow: Mass Incarceration in the Age of Colorblindness.* New York: The New Press.

Alvarez, Rafael. 2010. *The Wire: Truth Be Told.* New York: Grove Press.

Aristotle. 1999. *Nicomachean Ethics.* Second edition. Indianapolis: Hackett.

———. 2006. *Nicomachean Ethics.* New York: Oxford University Press.

Atlas, John, and Peter Dreier. 2008. Is The Wire Too Cynical? *Dissent* 55.

Beckett, Katherine, Kris Nyrop, and Lori Pfingst. 2006. Race, Drugs, and Policing: Understanding Disparities in Drug Delivery Arrests. *Criminology* 44.

Bell, Derrick. 1976. Racial Remediation: An Historical Perspective on Current Conditions. *Notre Dame Lawyer* 52.

———. 1989. *And We Are Not Saved: The Elusive Quest for Racial Justice* . New York: Basic Books.

———. 1992. Racial Realism. *Connecticut Law Review* 24.

———. 1993. The Racism Is Permanent Thesis: Courageous Revelation or Unconscious Genocide. *Capital University Law Review* 22.

Benforado, Adam. 2010. Quick on the Draw: Implicit Bias and the Second Amendment. *Oregon Law Review* 89.

Berkman, Alexander. 1912. *Prison Memoirs of an Anarchist.* New York: Mother Earth Publishing Association.

Blum, Lawrence. 2011. "B5—It Got All the Dinks": Schools and Education on *The Wire. Dark Matter.* <www.darkmatter101.org/site/2011/04/29/b5-it-got-all-the-dinks-schools-and-education-on-the-wire>.

Bowden, Mark. 2008. The Angriest Man in Television. *Atlantic Monthly* 301 (January–February).

Brown, Elaine. 1993. *A Taste of Power: A Black Woman's Story*. Anchor.

Burdeau, Emmanuel, and Nicolas Vieillescazes, eds. 2012. *The Wire: Reconstitution Collective*. Les Prairiers Ordinaires–Capricci.

Butler, Judith. 1990. *Gender Trouble: Feminism and the Subversion of Identity*. New York: Routledge.

Butler, Judith, and Catherine Malabou. 2010. *Soismon corps: Une lecture contemporaine de la domination et de la servitude chez Hegel*. Paris: Bayard.

Camus, Albert. 1954. *The Rebel: An Essay on Man in Revolt*. New York: Knopf.

Chesterton, G.K. 1901. *The Defendant*. <http://www.online-literature.com/chesterton/the-defendant/6>.

Cleaver, Eldridge. 1968. *Soul on Ice*. New York: McGraw Hill.

Cleaver, Kathleen. 2001. Women, Power, and Revolution. In Kathleen Cleaver and George Katsiaficas, eds., *Liberation, Imagination, and the Black Panther Party*. New York: Routledge.

Cottingham, John. 1986. Partiality, Favouritism, and Morality. *The Philosophical Quarterly* 36.

Davis, Angela. 1998. Racialized Punishment and Prison Abolition. In James 1998.

———. 2003. Political Prisoners, Prisons, and Black Liberation. In James 2003.

Dewey, John. 1972. My Pedagogic Creed. In *The Early Works of John Dewey, Volume 5, 1882–1898*, Carbondale: Southern Illinois University Press.

———. 1976. The Child and the Curriculum. In *The Middle Works of John Dewey, Volume 2, 1899–1924*. Carbondale: Southern Illinois University Press.

———. 1980. Democracy and Education. In *The Middle Works of John Dewey, Volume 9, 1899–1924*. Carbondale: Southern Illinois University Press.

———. 1988. Creative Democracy: The Task Before Us. In *The Later Works of John Dewey, Volume 14, 1925–1953*. Carbondale: Southern Illinois University Press.

———. 2002. *Human Nature and Conduct*. New York: Dover.

Dohrn, Bernardine. 2002. *Weather Underground*. Documentary. Sam Green director.

———. 2006. Fall Offensive. In B. Dohrn, B. Ayers, and J. Jones, eds., *Sing a Battle Song: The Revolutionary Poetry, Statements, and Communiqués of the Weather Underground, 1970–1974*. Seven Stories Press.

Du Bois, W.E.B. 1915. *The Negro*. New York: Holt Press.

———. 1998. *Black Reconstruction in America: 1860-1880.* New York: The Free Press.

Easton, Hosea. 1837. *A Treatise on the Intellectual Character and Civil and Political Condition of the Colored People of the United States and the Prejudice Exercised towards Them.* Boston: Isaac Knapp.

Fallis, Don. 2011. The Many Faces of Deception. In Josef Steiff, ed., *Sherlock Holmes and Philosophy: The Footprints of a Gigantic Mind.* Chicago: Open Court.

———. 2012. It Is a Great Crime to Lie to a King. In Henry Jacoby, ed., *The Game of Thrones and Philosophy: Logic Cuts Deeper than Swords.* Malden: Wiley-Blackwell.

Fields, Barbara. 2001. Whiteness, Racism, and Identity. *International Labor and Working-Class History* 60.

Foucault, Michel. 1978. *History of Sexuality: An Introduction.* Pantheon.

———. 1979. *Discipline and Punish: The Birth of the Prison.* New York: Vintage.

Fraley, Todd. 2009. A Man's Gotta Have a Code: Identity, Racial Codes, and HBO's *The Wire. Darkmatter: In the Ruins of Imperial Culture* 4.

Franklin, Judd. 2009. Common Ground: The Political Economy of *The Wire. Darkmatter: In the Ruins of Imperial Culture* 4.

Freire, Paulo. 1993. *Pedagogy of the Oppressed.* New York: Continuum.

Freud, Sigmund. 1960. *The Ego and the Id.* New York: Norton.

———. 1966. Mourning and Melancholia. In *The Standard Edition of the Complete Psychological Works of Sigmund Freud,* Volume XIV (1914–1916). London: Hogarth.

Goff, Phillip Atiba, J.L. Eberhardt, M. Williams, and M.C. Jackson. 2008. Not Yet Human: Implicit Knowledge, Historical Dehumanization, and Contemporary Consequences. *Journal of Personality and Social Psychology* 94.

Green v. Board of Elections. 1967. 380 F.2d 445 (2d Cir. 1967), *cert. denied,* 389 U.S. 1048. <http://law.justia.com/cases/federal/appellate-courts/F2/380/445/314856>.

Green, Sam (director). 2002. *Weather Underground* [documentary].

Halperin, David. 1990. One Hundred Years of Homosexuality. In *One Hundred Years of Homosexuality: And Other Essays on Greek Love.* New York: Routledge.

Hegel, G.W.F. 1966. Who Thinks Abstractly? In Walter Kaufmann, ed., *Hegel: Texts and Commentary.* New York: Anchor.

———. 1975. *Aesthetics: Lectures on Fine Art,* Volumes 1 and 2. Oxford: Oxford University Press.

Hobbes, Thomas. 1994. *Leviathan: With Selected Variants from the Latin Edition of 1668*. Indianapolis: Hackett.

Hornby, Nick. 2007. Interview with David Simon. *The Believer* 5 <www.believermag.com/issues/200708/?read=interview_simon>.

Jackall, Robert. 1988. *Moral Mazes: The World of Corporate Managers* Oxford: Oxford University Press.

James, Joy, ed. 1998. *The Angela Y. Davis Reader*. Malden: Blackwell.

———, ed. 2003. *Imprisoned Intellectuals: America's Political Prisoners Write on Life, Liberation, and Rebellion*. Boulder: Rowman and Littlefield.

———, ed. 2007. *Warfare in the American Homeland*. Durham: Duke University Press.

Jameson, Frederic. 2010. Realism and Utopia in *The Wire*. *Criticism* 52 <www.mediafire.com/?w8bikt8gu9l543d>.

Kahn, C.H. 1979. *The Art and Thought of Heraclitus*. Cambridge: Cambridge University Press.

Kant, Immanuel. 1959. *Foundations of the Metaphysics of Morals*. New York: Macmillan.

———. 1998. *Groundwork of the Metaphysics of Morals*. Cambridge: Cambridge University Press.

Keneally, James M. 2010. Jury Nullification, Race, and *The Wire*. *New York Law School Law Review* 55 <www.kelleydrye.com/publications/articles/1500/_res/id=Files/inde x=0/1500.pdf>.

Kirk, G.S. 1954. *Heraclitus: The Cosmic Fragments*. Cambridge: Cambridge University Press.

La Berge, Leigh Claire. 2010. Capitalist Realism and Serial Form: The Fifth Season of *The Wire*. *Criticism* 52.

Leonnig, Carol D. 2006. *The Wire*: Young Adults See Bits of Their Past. *Washington Post* (December 11th) <www.washingtonpost.com/wp-dyn/content/article/2006/12/10/AR2006121001034.html>.

Lewis, David. 1983. *Philosophical Papers, Volume 1*. New York: Oxford University Press.

Locke, John. 1988. *Two Treatises of Government*. Cambridge: Cambridge University Press.

Lukács, Georg. 1964. *Studies in European Realism*. New York: Grosset and Dunlap.

———. 1980. Realism in the Balance. In Ernest Block, ed., *Aesthetics and Politics,* London: Verso.

Marshall, Courtney D. 2009. Barksdale Women: Crime, Empire, and the Production of Gender. In Tiffany Potter and C.W. Marshall, eds., *The Wire: Urban Decay and American Television*. New York: Continuum.

Marx, Karl H. 1974 [1867]. *Capital: A Critical Analysis of Capitalist Production*. Volume 1. New York: International.

Mill, John Stuart. 1979. *Utilitarianism*. Indianapolis: Hackett.

Newton, Huey P. 2003. Prison, Where Is Thy Victory? In James 2003.

Nietzsche, Friedrich. 1966. *Beyond Good and Evil: Prelude to a Philosophy of the Future*. New York.

———. 1978. *Thus Spoke Zarathustra: A Book for None and All*. New York: Penguin.

———. 1996. *Human, All Too Human: A Book for Free Spirits*. Cambridge: Cambridge University Press.

———. 1998. *On the Genealogy of Morality*. Indianapolis: Hackett.

———. 1999. *The Birth of Tragedy and Other Writings*. Cambridge: Cambridge University Press.

———. 2001. *The Gay Science*. Cambridge: Cambridge University Press.

———. 2005. *The Anti-Christ, Ecce Homo, Twilight of the Idols, and Other Writings*. Cambridge: Cambridge University Press.

O'Rourke, Meghan. 2006. Behind the Wire: David Simon on Where the Show Goes Next, *Slate* (1st December).

Parfit, Derek. 2011. *On What Matters*. Oxford University Press.

Peterson, James Braxton. 2009. Corner-Boy Masculinity: Intersections of Inner-City Manhood. In Potter and Marshall 2009.

Plato. 1989. *Symposium*. Indianapolis: Hackett.

———. 1992. *Republic*. Indianapolis: Hackett.

Potter, Tiffany, and C.W. Marshall, eds. 2009. *The Wire: Urban Decay and American Television*. New York: Continuum.

Read, Jason. 2009. Stringer Bell's Lament: Violence and Legitimacy in Contemporary Capitalism. In Potter and Marshall 2009.

Reed, Ismael. 2010. Should Harvard Teach *The Wire*? No, It Relies on Cliches about Blacks and Drugs. *Boston Globe* (September 30th) <www.boston.com/bostonglobe/editorial_opinion/oped/articles/2010/09/30/no_it_relies_on_clichs_about_blacks_and_drugs>.

Roberts, Dorothy. 1998. *Killing the Black Body: Race, Reproduction, and the Meaning of Liberty*. New York: Random House.

Ryan, Maureen. 2008. Barack Obama on His Favorite TV Show. *Chicago Tribune* (January 14th).

Saner, Emine. 2010. *The Wire* Star's Racism Claims. *Sydney Morning Herald* (July 1st).

Sepinwall, Alan. 2008. *The Wire*: David Simon Q & A. (Blog post, March 9th). Retrieved from: <http://sepinwall.blogspot.com/2008/03/wire-david-simon-q.html>.

Sexton, Jared. 2007. Racial Profiling and the Societies of Control. In James 2007.

Simon, David. 2000. *The Wire: A Dramatic Series for HBO*. Retrieved from <http://kottke.org.s3.amazonaws.com/the-wire/The_Wire_-_Bible.pdf>.

———. 2007. David Simon on the End of American Empire. Freag.net <http://www.freag.net/en/t/xxq4/david_simon_on_>.

———. 2008. The Escalating Breakdown of Urban Society across the US. *The Guardian* (September 5th) <www.guardian.co.uk/media/2008/sep/06/wire>.

———. 2008. Presentation at UC Berkeley Townsend Center for the Humanities' Forum on the Humanities and the Public World, September 10th <www.youtube.com/watch?v=nRt46W3k-qw&feature=related>.

———. 2009. *Labour in the 21st* Century. Video Interview, December 28th <www.youtube.com/watch?v=6wsMEeoXXOY>.

———. 2011. The Straight Dope: Bill Moyers interviews David Simon. *Guernica* (April 1st) <www.guernicamag.com/interviews/2530/simon_4_1_11>.

Singer, Peter. 1972. Famine, Affluence, and Morality. *Philosophy and Public Affairs*1 [revised edition] <www.utilitarian.net/singer/by/1972———.htm>.

Skyrms, Brian. 2010. *Signals: Evolution, Learning, and Information*. Oxford: Oxford University Press.

Sober, Elliott. 1994. *From a Biological Point of View: Essays in Evolutionary Philosophy*. Cambridge: Cambridge University Press.

Stern, Susan. 2007. *With the Weathermen: The Personal Journey of a Revolutionary Woman*. New Brunswick: Rutgers University Press.

Stocker, Michael. 1970. Intentions and Act Evaluations. *Journal of Philosophy* 67.

———. 1976. The Schizophrenia of Modern Moral Theories. *Journal of Philosophy* 73.

Sverdlik, Steven. 1996. Motive and Rightness. *Ethics* 106.

Talbot, Margaret. 2007. Stealing Life: The Crusader Behind 'The Wire'. *New Yorker* 83 <www.newyorker.com/reporting/2007/10/02/071022fa_fact_talbot#ixzz2GSiRc/22>.

Toscano, Alberto, and Jeff Kinkle. 2009. Baltimore as World and Representation: Cognitive Mapping and Capitalism in *The Wire*. *Dossier* <http://dossierjournal.com/read/theory/baltimore-as-world-and-representation-cognitive-mapping-and-capitalism-in-the-wire>.

Wallace-Wells, Ben. 2012. Girl on 'Wire'. *Rolling Stone* (February 5th).

Weber, Max. 1958. *The Protestant Ethic and the Spirit of Capitalism*. New York: Scribners.

Wells, Ida B. 1997. *Southern Horrors and Other Writings: The Anti-Lynching Campaign of Ida B. Wells 1892–1900*. Boston: Bedford.

West, Cornel. 2001 [1993]. *Race Matters*. Boston: Beacon.

————. 2004. *Democracy Matters: Winning the Fight Against Imperialism*. New York: Penguin.

Whitehead, Alfred North. 1967. *The Aims of Education and Other Essays*. New York: The Free Press.

Wilderson, Frank, III, 2007. The Prison Slave as Hegemony's (Silent) Scandal. In James 2007.

Žižek, Slavoj. 2012. *The Wire* or the Clash of Civilizations in One Country [podcast]. London: Birkbeck Institute for the Humanities (February 24th).

Hoppers, Fiends, and Natural POH-lice

Spending his days slinging philosophy at the University of Memphis, **WILLIAM ALLEN** keeps off the corners by working on a dissertation analyzing contemporary liberal political theories and ways of integrating the underclass while promoting self-determination in such communities. Even though he'd never juke the stats in his research, he finds himself more and more trapped in the Game of philosophy.

DAVID BZDAK is an Assistant Professor of Philosophy at Onondaga Community College in Syracuse, New York. His academic career started late in life, after his invention of the Chicken McNugget failed to get him out of his basement cubicle at McDonald's headquarters. Inspired by *The Wire*, he often conducts his philosophy classes using nothing but curse words, while drinking Jameson and blasting music by Steve Earle and the Pogues. At home, he dominates games of hide-and-seek with his three children, Sophia, Eli, and Zak, who are quite sick of his proclamation that "The king stay the king."

While a PhD candidate at Southern Illinois University Carbondale, **JOHN THOMAS BRITTINGHAM** moonlights as an Adjunct Professor of Philosophy at Greenville College. His main areas of philosophical interest are Phenomenology and Philosophy of Religion. When he is not busy teaching or dissertating, he occupies his time by consuming profane amounts of pop culture. This young soldier considers himself to be something of a "smart-ass pawn."

A former resident of Northeast Baltimore, **MYISHA CHERRY** received her BA in philosophy from Morgan State University and her Master of Divinity from Howard University. Successfully avoiding all the

West Side mishegas, she moved to New York City in 2006. Unable to avoid the mishegas of academia, Cherry is a "super adjunct," juggling courses in ethics and social and political philosophy at John Jay College of Criminal Justice, York College, St. John's University and Long Island University. When she's not teaching, she's playing instruments, obsessing about LeBron, praying she gets into a PhD program before this book is published, and writing about philosophy and religion at *Huffington Post* and myishacherry.org.

W. Scott Clifton is a PhD candidate at the University of Washington-Seattle, hoping to graduate in 2013 before the academic gods shoot a lightning bolt in his ass. He has interests in aesthetics, philosophy of mind, ethics, and Nietzsche. Does he think that Omar Little may have become a permanent part of his subconscious as a result of his investigations of Nietzschean themes in *The Wire*? Indeed.

Kody W. Cooper is the only known person to have watched all five seasons of *The Wire* while simultaneously reading Aquinas's entire *Summa Theologiae*. Luckily, he, like McNulty, still prefers Catholic whiskey over Protestant. Currently, he's completing a PhD in Government at the University of Texas-Austin. Like Wee-Bey, his word is still his word . . . wherever you find him, in Austin or in Baltimore, it'll be his word that finds you.

Convinced that assessment is really just another form of jukin' the stats, Joanna Crosby is particularly grateful for tenure and junior colleagues who get stuck with the shit detail. When not in the classroom, endless committee meetings, or fomenting discontent, she's in her garden, writing about Foucault or Confucius, dreaming of a 100 harness draw loom, or planning her next undergrad study tour to China. Her husband and fellow *Wire* aficionado, Michael, fell in love with her all over again when she pointed out they needed a re-up on cat food. Luckily for their four furry fiends, they maintain a solid connect.

Policing the corners of the Philosophy Department at Texas A&M University, Tommy J. Curry is infamous for keeping it real and giving a fuck, whether or not it's his turn. As such, he's constantly giving it to the racist American and Continental enterprises and the white philosophers that sustain the current ideo-racial apartheid of the discipline. He has published over two dozen essays on American racism and white supremacy, and specializes in Critical Race Theory, specifically the work of the late Derrick Bell. He is working on several book projects currently: a republication of William H. Ferris's *The African*

Abroad, a manuscript on the failure of American integration entitled *Nationist Dawn*, and a book on Derrick Bell's political philosophy entitled *At the Dawn of Shadows*.

NATHAN ECKSTRAND is a PhD candidate in philosophy at Duquesne University. Like David Simon, he grew up south of Baltimore in the suburbs of Baltimore County. Unlike David Simon, he developed an interest in philosophy while studying at Earlham College in Richmond, Indiana. He currently studies social and political philosophy, which he hopes to put to use understanding some of the issues examined in *The Wire*. He's co-editor of the book *Philosophical Reflections on Violence: Essays from this Widening Gyre*. In his spare time, he likes kayaking and hiking. Rumor has it, he recently read that book, *Things White People Like*.

PROF JOE teaches at a small school in Baltimore, Maryland. He would give more failing grades, particularly to that burdensome nephew on his sister's side, but it's not like he wouldn't hear about it come Thanksgiving time. Grade inflation is a small price to pay for peace and quiet. A man who likes to stay busy, Joe moonlights at Normals where he tries to hook neighborhood kids on books. Reading, he says, is fundamental.

TY FAGAN is a Visiting Assistant Professor in the Philosophy Department at Elmhurst College. His research focuses on the philosophy of mind and cognitive science, in particular the power and limits of nonlinguistic thought. He also writes on animal cognition, early Greek philosophy, and moral psychology. He has definitely not written a pilot script for *Cool Lester Smooth*, a prequel spin-off to *The Wire* that follows Lester Freamon's early days on the force in 1970s Baltimore (unless you are David Simon and you like this idea, in which case he has totally written that script and would love to hear from you).

Splitting his time between Information Resources and Philosophy, DON FALLIS is Professor at the University of Arizona. He has written several philosophy articles on lying and deception, including "What Is Lying?" in the *Journal of Philosophy* and "The Most Terrific Liar You Ever Saw in Your Life," in *The Catcher in the Rye and Philosophy: A Book for Bastards, Morons, and Madmen*. His hero is Major Howard Colvin of the Western. Although "Bunny" lies a lot, he only lies to do good, and he often lies with the truth—such as when he says, "I thought I might legalize drugs," intending that his colleagues think that he is just joking.

A Central-Canadian, **KENN FISHER** hails from Toronto. The editors have worked hard not to hold his access to universal health coverage against him. With a bachelor's in Political Science and Philosophy from the University of Toronto and a post-graduate certificate in Television Writing and Producing from Humber College, Kenn currently works as a writer-producer in Toronto's film and television industry. He first watched *The Wire* in its entirety over a period of about five weeks in the spring of 2010. It easily became one of his favorite shows, and he is oft quoted as saying that it is the funniest TV show ever made. A fiend for reform, his favorite season is the third, and his favorite character is The Bunk.

JASON GRINNELL is Assistant Professor of Philosophy at Buffalo State College. His primary philosophical interests are in bioethics and professional ethics, as well as ancient philosophy. This is his third foray into the world of popular culture and philosophy, having contributed to *The Philosophy of Joss Whedon* (2011) and *Clint Eastwood and Philosophy* (forthcoming). He loves his job, but lately has been feeling a bit too much pressure to capture the Dickensian aspects of philosophy.

AVRAM 'OZ' GURLAND-BLAKER is a PhD candidate at Temple University, currently finishing his dissertation—the professional philosophy equivalent of running a corner, only instead of drugs, money, guns, projects, and fiends, there are books, books, computer screens, books, and nitpicky dissertation committee members acting like you just got the count wrong, again. He teaches, writes, and spends a lot of time thinking, which suits him just fine because he's much more of a stoop kid than a corner kid. He lives in New York with his wife and son.

A research fellow in the Robina Institute of Criminal Law and Justice at the University of Minnesota Law School, **ZACHARY HOSKINS** writes on moral, political, and legal theory. As a philosopher, he was initially intimidated by the sartorial conventions of a law school. But unlike Bunk Moreland, he's resisting becoming "strictly a suit and tie motherfucker."

SEAN MCALEER is a gaping asshole. We all know this. Fuck if everyone at the University of Wisconsin, Eau Claire, where he teaches philosophy, doesn't know it. But fuck if I'm going to stand here and say he did a single fucking thing to get his philosophical work to appear in *American Philosophical Quarterly*, *Pacific Philosophical Quarterly*, *Utilitias*, *Studies in the History of Ethics*, and *Film and Philosophy*. This is not on him. Believe it or not, everything isn't about him.

When **MONA ROCHA** is not writing her dissertation on militant feminism, she is completing home improvement projects with her powder-actuated nail gun, which happens to be the Lexus of nail guns. She has written on violent women and militant feminists ranging from Black Panthers and Weather Women to Snoop, Kima, Buffy and Irene Adler. She is currently a PhD candidate in the history department at Louisiana State University.

While **JAMES ROCHA** grew up on the hard streets of South Central Los Angeles, his only association with hoppers was the occasional basketball game, and he only came across drug fiends as they walked by his house while he sat inside, reading Immanuel Kant, ethics, feminist philosophy, and philosophy of race. If LA had stoops, James would'a been sitting on one. Having since graduated to teaching and researching these subjects as an Assistant Professor at Louisiana State University, he sees his number one job as ending weak-ass thinking and stopping students from equivocating like motherfuckers. James is unlikely to get his tie snipped while napping as he doesn't wear the things; he's just a philosopher, who likes to think that philosophy is the Game beyond the games.

JIM THOMPSON teaches philosophy, religion, and applied ethics at Presbyterian College. He fears that his daily existence is closer to *The Office* than *The Wire*, but he prods his students to give a fuck nonetheless. As he rarely uses profanity, he tries to make this point more gently. His favorite character in *The Wire* is Dukie Weems. Jim has a PhD in religious ethics from the University of Chicago.

JONATHAN TRERISE originates from the Western (US, not District), but is currently professing philosophy at Coastal Carolina University in Myrtle Beach. He's interested in political philosophy and applied ethics. He's convinced that when it comes to social and political issues, *The Wire* is the best show of all time. Another fiend for reform, he thinks Season Three is best. No doubt, Omar is, in his mind, one of the best characters ever conceived. But he also can't help but smile when Bunny, Bubbles, or Dukie smiles. You feel me?

SETH VANNATTA is an Assistant Professor of Philosophy and Religious Studies at Morgan State University in Baltimore. He's the editor of *Chuck Klosterman and Philosophy: The Real and the Cereal* (2012) and author of several book chapters including "The Most Dangerous Rock'n'Roll Band in the World" in *The Rolling Stones and Philosophy: It's Just a Thought Away* (2011). He travels outside of Baltimore, where the radio stations are different, to present papers on American pragmatism among other topics. When asked by his department chair to turn in his travel receipts, he always responds quoting his favorite *Wire* character, Clay Davis, "Sheeeeeeit! In West Baltimore, I'm all cash and carry."

NORA WIKOFF, like Bodie Broadus, often suspects that the Game is rigged, that she's a pawn, just one of "them little bitches," on the academic chessboard. A doctoral student in the George Warren Brown School of Social Work at Washington University in St. Louis, she's working on a dissertation exploring the financial impact of incarceration on former prisoners. When she's not writing, she spends time teaching her two terriers the finer points of "front and follow."

SLAVOJ ŽIŽEK is a senior researcher at the Institute of Sociology, University of Ljubljana, Slovenia, and a visiting professor at a number of uppity American Universities. Žižek is most known for his work on psychoanalysis, political theory, and film theory. He absolutely disregards the distinction between high and low culture, referencing *Home Alone 2* in an essay on Friedrich Schelling and quoting the *Lion King* in his chapter on *The Wire*. His original bio was written using only variations of the word fuck, à la Bunk and McNulty, but we rewrote it to include several of his fucking book titles, including *The Indivisible Remainder, The Sublime Object of Ideology, The Metastases of Enjoyment, Looking Awry: Jacques Lacan through Popular Culture, The Plague of Fantasies,* and *The Ticklish Subject.*

Index

NOTE: Episode titles are followed by numbers showing the season and place within that season. For example, the notation (1.5) after an episode title indicates that that episode was the fifth episode of the first season.

Achilles, 7
addiction, viii, 37, 39, 89, 103, 143, 176, 182, 193, 198, 219, 262
Aeschylus, 13
Alexander, Michelle, 174, 289
Ali, Muhammad, 156
alienation, 220, 240–43, 247, 250, 252
"All Due Respect" (episode 3.2), 185
"Alliances" (episode 4.5), 259
"All Prologue" (episode 2.6), 13, 20, 60–61, 90–91, 98, 113, 116, 136–37, 139
the American Dream, ix, 148, 202–03, 218
American Gangsta, 166
amor fati, 112
Andre "Old Face" (character), 119, 195
Annapolis, 204
Antigone, 195, 200–02, 205
Apollonian forces, 207–214
Aquinas, Thomas, 260, 298
Aristotle, viii, 289

and ethics 61, 72–75, 81, 140–41, 146, 150
and friendship, 131
and power, 260
and tragedy, 198, 205–07
and wisdom, 64
art, 41, 138, 196, 200, 207, 217, 225, 228
of teaching, 242–45
Artis, Anton "Stinkum" (character), 119, 144
atheism, 108

"Back Burners" (episode 3.7), 22, 92, 158, 261
"Backwash" (episode 2.7), 61, 92, 104
"Bad Dreams" (episode 2.11), 21, 60, 117
Badiou, Alain, 222
Bailey, John (character), 116
Baltimore, 3, 8, 11, 13, 14, 21–23, 25, 26, 28, 35, 41, 50, 55, 57, 66, 88, 90, 111, 113, 115, 121–22, 136–142,

146–48, 165, 167, 193–94,
197–98, 203, 208, 210, 214,
217, 220, 225, 241, 255,
257–260, 262, 264, 266–67,
269–272, 278
drug trade, 25–26, 111, 123,
125, 142, 175, 179, 218, 275
East Side, 47, 63, 98, 102, 116,
242
education system, 17, 27, 36,
76, 80, 222, 242–254, 273
Harbor, 88
police, 8, 15, 16, 27, 51, 74, 76,
90, 124, 130, 153, 161, 209,
243, 270, 287
politics, 41, 204
port, 59, 61–63, 221, 225
Sun (newspaper), ix, 59, 66,
91, 98, 197, 263, 267, 269,
273
West Side/District, 6, 8, 10,
28, 34, 45, 63, 73–74, 89, 97,
98, 99, 104, 123, 125, 175,
195, 198, 239, 242–43,
247–48, 260, 266, 281
B & B Enterprises, 193
Barksdale, Avon (character), 4,
34, 38, 64, 104, 111–12, 118,
133, 139, 146, 176, 179, 201,
208, 256, 261, 265, 270, 273
and Cutty, 92, 179, 189
and D'Angelo, 84–85, 98, 111,
195, 211, 221
and Marlo, 18, 24–25, 34, 89,
258–59
and Omar, 21, 110, 113, 119,
123, 125, 127–28, 134, 139,
142–144, 168, 199, 212
and Stringer, 24, 84, 125, 200,
202–03, 210, 212, 217, 222
Barksdale, Brianna (character),
56, 92, 111, 168, 265
Barksdale, D'Angelo (character),
25, 33, 49, 56, 84, 87, 89,
104, 176, 194, 202, 252, 258,
265, 275, 285–86
and Avon, 84–85, 98, 111, 195,
211, 221
and chess, 15, 240, 256
and desire to escape the
Game, 23, 27, 49, 92, 221
and McNuggets, 86
and Stringer, 87, 211
and Wallace, 24, 195, 256
death of, 24, 168
Bell, Derrick, 171, 289, 298–99
Bell, Roland, 218
Bell, Russell "Stringer"
(character), 4, 7, 18–19, 24,
176, 199–203, 208, 218,
256–58, 261, 265–66, 273,
293
and Avon, 24, 84, 125, 200,
202–03, 210, 212, 217, 222
and D'Angelo, 87, 211
and McNulty, 81, 133, 261
and Omar, 21, 98, 110, 116,
127, 143–44, 168
as businessman, 4, 101–04,
112, 201, 212, 258
death of, 144, 168, 193, 213,
222
Bentham, Jeremy, 50
Berkman, Alexander, 21, 289
Bethlehem Steel, 3, 241
Betts, Omar Isaiah (character).
See Snot Boogie
The Big Lebowski, 205,
208–09
Big Walter (character), 158
Black Panther Party, 155, 163,
174, 290
Blanchard, Pooh (character),
104, 285
Blocker, William "Orlando"
(character), 84, 176
Blum, Lawrence, 242
Bodie (character). *See* Broadus,
Preston "Bodie"
"Boys of Summer" (episode 4.1),
157, 243
Boyz in the Hood, 166

Bratton, Savino (character), 117, 144

Brazil, 220

Brecht, Bertolt, 223

Brewster's Millions, 205

Brice, De'Londa (character), 49, 53, 56–58, 241

Brice, Namond (character), 7, 27–28, 35–37, 45–46, 49, 53, 57–58, 189–190, 200, 241, 250–52, 259, 265, 271, 279

Brice, Roland "Wee-Bey" (character), 45–46, 49, 57–58, 84, 104, 119, 126, 139, 176, 179, 189, 250, 298

Broadus, Preston "Bodie" (character), 15–16, 19, 24, 35, 39, 51, 86, 89, 98, 110, 130, 153, 185, 194, 199, 202, 239–240, 271, 302

Brown, Elaine, 155, 158, 290

Brown, Nino, 166

Brown v. Board of Education, 171

Bubbles (character). *See* Cousins, Reginald "Bubbles"

Bunk (character). *See* Moreland, William "Bunk"

Bunny (character). *See* Colvin, Howard "Bunny"

bureaucracy, 83–86, 94–95, 208, 220

Burn after Reading, 205

Burns, Ed, 198, 206, 225

Burrell, Ervin (character), 66, 74–75, 79, 85–89, 93, 208, 256, 260, 267, 271, 273, 284

Butchie (character), 22, 55, 92, 110, 114, 117, 140, 142, 271

Butler, Judith, 130, 290

"The Buys" (episode 1.3), 15, 24, 86, 128–29, 135, 160, 256

Camden Yards, 66

Campbell, Nerese (character), 25, 67, 204, 265, 270

Camus, Albert, 10–11, 28–29, 290

capitalism, 4, 6, 29, 61, 172, 202, 220, 225–26, 235, 241

Capra, Frank, 223

Carcetti, Tommy (character), viii, 19, 25, 41, 56, 204, 256, 260, 269, 275

Carr, Malik "Poot" (character), 24, 86, 89, 158, 183

Carver, Ellis (character), 8–9, 15, 25, 27, 46, 52–53, 78, 92–94, 98, 125–28, 135, 153, 250, 279–283, 287

Chaplin, Charlie, 227

character, moral, 10, 59–61, 69, 81, 140–41, 150, 180, 189, 224, 230

Charles, Slim (character), 25, 200

Charm City, 3

Cheerios, Honey Nut, 33, 113

Cheryl (character), 131–34

chess, 15–16, 23–25, 86, 125, 240, 302

Chesterton, G.K., 223, 226–27, 290

Christian morality, 108–09, 118, 122

Cinderella, 154

Civil Rights Movement, 171, 174

"Clarifications" (episode 5.8), 60, 65, 67–68, 115, 160

Clark, Kenneth, 166

"Cleaning Up" (episode 1.12), 286

Cleaver, Kathleen, 155, 290

Cole, Ray (character), 98

Colicchio, Anthony (character), 52–53, 93, 125, 279, 283

"Collateral Damage" (episode 2.2), 62, 77, 88

colonialism, 171–73

Columbus Blue Jackets, 205
Colvin, Howard "Bunny"
  (character), 27, 73–76,
  80–82, 125, 202, 248–53,
  268, 273, 283–85, 299, 301
  and corner kids class, 27, 36,
  73–76, 250–53, 271
  and Hamsterdam, 19, 27, 80,
  221–22, 248, 268
  and Namond, 7, 27, 37, 45–46,
  189
comedy, 205–06, 215
consequentialist moral
  philosophy, 109, 115, 181–84
consistency (and morality), 39,
  61–62
"Corner Boys" (episode 4.8), 76,
  78, 245, 250–52, 265
corruption, 17, 165–66
"The Cost" (episode 1.10), 113
Cottingham, John, 53, 290
Cousins, Reginald "Bubbles"
  (character), ix, 7, 10, 26, 28,
  34–37, 89, 101–02, 109, 126,
  135, 146, 149, 176, 182, 195,
  205, 257, 261–66, 277–78, 301
Crutchfield, Michael
  (character), 78, 94
Cuba, 233
Cutty (character). *See* Wise,
  Dennis "Cutty"
cynicism, 10, 13, 26, 88–90

Dangerous Minds, 249, 254
Daniels, Cedric (character), 19,
  23, 25, 35, 47, 52, 53, 56,
  73–83, 87, 92–94, 98, 110,
  115, 124–26, 199, 204, 222,
  257, 267, 270, 283
Daniels, Marla (character), 22,
  92–93
Davis, Angela, 280–83, 290, 292
Davis, Clay (character), ix, 18,
  24, 35, 125, 149, 188, 198,
  257, 265, 270, 273, 302

Dark Ghetto, 166
The Dark Knight, 208
Dawson, Zenobia (character),
  251–52, 265
Deacon (character), viii, 80,
  248–49, 268
"Dead Soldiers" (episode 3.3),
  74, 143, 208, 264
deception, 24, 63–64, 67–68, 99,
  102, 104, 299
De Niro, Robert, 220
"The Detail" (episode 1.2), 23,
  86, 124, 135, 279, 282, 285
determinism, 38, 89, 120, 167,
  226
Dewey, John, 243–48, 251–53,
  290
Dexter, 223–24
Dickens, Charles, 223, 225
"The Dickensian Aspect"
  (episode 5.6), 63, 287
dignity, ix, x, 6–8, 10, 22, 27–29,
  229, 231, 241, 254
Dionysian forces, 207–214
discrimination, 47–48, 143, 181
dogmatism, 108, 111, 114,
  116–17, 121–22
Dohrn, Bernardine, 155–59,
  290, 291
Donat, Yoav, 228
Donette (character), 168, 203
Donnelly, Assistant Principal
  Marcia (character), 271, 286
Donut (character), 282
drug addiction. *See* addiction
drug war, 4, 15, 27, 74, 124,
  165–66, 174–75, 177, 219,
  268, 283–85
Du Bois, W.E.B., 172, 174, 291
"Duck and Cover" (episode 2.8),
  61–62
Dukie (character). *See* Weems,
  Duquan
Dunlop, Fuzzy, 98
Duquette, Miss (character),
  250–51

duty (moral), viii, 60–61, 109,

Easton, Hosea, 172, 291
"Ebb Tide" (episode 2.1), 72, 130
education (*see also* Baltimore,
    Education System), 5, 6, 9,
    17, 27, 32–33, 36, 65, 76, 80,
    84, 155–56, 180, 184, 194,
    202, 221–22, 242–254, 256,
    268, 269, 273–74
Elija (character), 132
Encyclopædia Britannica, 102
ethics, 67, 77, 79, 81–82, 278
    professional, 71–82, 127, 273
eudaimonia, 140
eugenics, 171

"Farmer in the Dell," 13, 107,
    240
fate, viii, 7, 89, 112, 198, 199,
    202, 205, 207–08, 214–15,
    220–21, 224, 234
feminism, 154–56, 163
femininity, 129–131, 134, 154,
    158–59, 162
feminist care ethics, 162
Ferrell, Will, 205
Fields, Barbara, 171, 291
"Final Grades" (episode 4.13),
    16, 46, 58, 185, 251, 253
Fletcher, Mike (character), 26
flourishing, 140–42, 255, 260,
    262
Foerster, Raymond (character),
    75
Foucault, Michel, 5, 6, 9,
    266–275, 291, 298
Franklin, Benjamin, viii
Frazier, Warren (character),
    87–89
Freamon, Lester (character),
    viii, ix, 3, 26, 51, 56, 64–65,
    73, 78, 82, 87, 110, 115, 126,
    128, 133, 161–63, 183, 203,
    210–14, 224, 230–31,
    241–42, 261, 272–75, 299
Fredericks, DeShawn
    (character), 97–98
Freire, Paulo, 243–44, 249–253,
    291
Freud, Sigmund, 130, 291
Friendly, Judge Henry, 187
friendship, 48, 50, 81, 131, 163,
    222, 262
"Fruit" (character), 150, 240
Funny or Die, 154

"Game Day" (episode 1.9), 23
Game of Thrones, 100
Gandhi, 287–88
Gant, William (character), 20,
    33, 87, 98, 104, 116, 221,
    285
Gilliam, Terry, 220
Gilligan, Carol, 162
Godard, Jean-Luc, 234
The Godfather, 202
Goodnight Moon, 161
Google, 217
Gramm, Phil, 186
Gramsci, Antonio, 172
Grant, Oscar, 170
Gray, Tony (character), 275
Greece (ancient), 7, 13, 14, 22,
    48, 83, 136–37, 140, 167,
    193, 195, 200–01, 205, 207,
    208, 218–220, 224, 229
Greek, The (character), 18, 26,
    59, 61–62, 88, 112, 272
*Green v. Board of Elections of
    the City of New York*, 187
Greggs, Shakima "Kima"
    (character), 50, 56, 67, 74,
    81, 93, 101, 104, 115,
    124–138, 153–163, 175, 204,
    259, 301
    and Bubbles, 126, 263, 277–78
    and her partner, Cheryl, 51,
    132, 138, 160

and feminism, 153–163
and homosexuality, 124–138
and McNulty, 50–51, 60, 65,
   81, 110, 115, 128–29, 133,
   135, 159, 161, 163
shooting of, 74–75, 87, 263
Gross, Terry, 207
Guetta, David, 217
Gutierrez, Alma (character), 66

Hamlet, 202
Hamsterdam, viii, 4, 19, 27, 32,
   80, 109, 150, 220, 248, 268
"Hamsterdam" (episode 3.4), 25,
   150, 212, 285
Hanning, Terry (character),
   67–68
"Hard Cases" (episode 2.4), 62, 98
Harlem Nights, 166
Harvard University, 165, 293
Hauk, Thomas "Herc"
   (character), 8, 46, 74, 83, 86,
   93, 98, 125, 130, 134, 153,
   175, 280, 266, 279, 282–83,
   286
Haynes, Augustus "Gus"
   (character), 19, 26, 66–69,
   91–92, 202, 204, 263, 273
Hegel, Georg, 194–96, 199–204,
   214, 217, 225, 234, 239–243,
   290, 292
Hendrix, Ricardo "Fat Face
   Rick" (character), 66
Heraclitus, 13–16, 19, 22–23,
   25–28, 292
Herc (character). *See* Hauk,
   Thomas "Herc"
Hill, Jonah, 205
Hilton, Marquis "Bird"
   (character), 77, 90, 98, 116,
   128, 136–37, 139
Hitchcock, Alfred, 230
Hitler, Adolf, 227
Hobbes, Thomas, 33–36,
   256–260, 292

Hoffman, Dustin, 205
Holland, Agnieszka, 217
Holley, Vernon (character), 78
Holocaust, 230
"Homecoming" (episode 3.6), 18,
   55, 77, 90, 92, 214
"Home Rooms" (episode 4.3), 74,
   113, 119, 127, 242, 249
honor, 125, 147, 214, 253,
   255–260
   in Hobbes, 257–260
Hornby, Nick, 193
hubris, 202, 207, 212
Hughes, Albert, 166
human nature, 16, 28, 29, 109
"The Hunt" (episode 1.11), 75,
   87, 101

impartiality, puzzle of, 47–57
Innes, Shardene (character),
   56
integration, 171, 299
intentions (and morality), 60,
   63, 69, 104, 199, 226
Iverson, Allen, 242

Jackall, Robert, 85–86, 292
Jameson, Frederic, 219, 221–25,
   292
Jameson Whiskey, 64, 209, 261,
   297
Jeffries, Anna (character), 53
Jersey Shore, 198
Jessup Prison, 179, 181
Jim Crow south, 167, 174, 281,
   283
Johns Hopkins University, 3,
   268
Johnson, Jack, 156
The Joker, 208
juking the stats, 17, 25, 59, 75,
   78, 80, 298
Junebug (character), 87,
   156–57, 160, 259

justice/injustice, 15–16, 18, 34, 40, 50, 53, 64, 68, 83, 87, 90, 92, 95, 127, 142, 145, 147, 150, 153, 155–56, 161–63, 175–76, 198, 202, 261–63
justice system, 281–88

Kant, Immanuel, ii, 60–62, 99–104, 292, 301
Kenard (character), 22, 26, 199
Kima (character). *See* Greggs, Shakima "Kima"
Klebanow, Thomas (character), 67–68, 91, 204, 260, 273
"Know Your Place" (episode 4.9), 17, 75–76, 251, 269, 271
Krawczyk, Andy (character), 24, 63
La Berge, Leigh C., 167, 292
labor, 5, 6, 11, 17, 173–74, 196, 219, 240–41
Lacan, Jacques, 225, 226, 302
Landsman, Jay (character), 13, 63, 72, 77–78, 97, 264, 270
"Late Editions" (episode 5.9), 115, 158, 203
Lebanon, 227
Ledger, Heath, 208
Lee, Bug (character), 49, 160
Lee, Michael (character), 6, 26, 36–39, 49, 89, 146–47, 156–160, 168, 189, 200, 243, 259, 269, 281
Lee, Raylene (character), 49, 56
"Lessons" (episode 1.8), 16, 119, 144
Levy, Maurice (character), 18–21, 35, 90, 98, 116, 137, 139, 195, 257
Lewis, David, 99, 103, 292
Lex (character), 240, 286
Life Is Beautiful, 234
The Lion King, 233, 302
Little Kevin (character), 286

Little, Omar (character), vii, ix, 6, 13, 16, 20–26, 32–33, 37, 49, 54–55, 64, 77–78, 87–92, 98, 101, 107–150, 168–69, 189, 194–95, 199, 202–04, 212–13, 223–24, 229–231, 258–59, 269, 271, 298, 301
and Barksdale Crew, 21, 24, 98, 110, 113, 119, 123, 125, 127–28, 134, 139, 142–44, 168, 199, 202–03, 212–13
and Bunk, 20, 54–55, 77–78, 90, 116, 128, 130, 140, 146, 195
and Brother Mouzone, 22, 98, 116–17, 203, 213
and Butchie, 22, 55, 92, 110, 114, 142, 271
and homosexuality, 87, 114, 123–138
and Levy, 20–21, 90, 116, 137, 139, 195
and Marlo, 20, 78, 116–17, 125, 127–28, 139, 144, 149, 258–59
and Michael, 6, 26, 37, 89, 146–47
and Stringer, 21, 98, 110, 116, 127, 143–44, 168
as Nietzschean Overman, 107–122
as virtuous, 139–150
code of, 16, 20–22, 49, 54–55, 64, 90, 109, 128, 143, 189, 223–24
death of, 22, 26, 55, 89, 114, 148, 168–69
popularity of, ix, 127
Locke, John, 34–41, 187, 292
Louis, Joe, 156
Lucas, Professor (character), 101–02
Lukács, Georg, 166, 292
lying, ix, 24, 59, 68, 99–104, 116, 299

Lyles, Nakeesha (character), 33, 286

MacArthur genius award, 165
Mahon, Patrick (character), 153, 279
Malatov, Sergei (character), 139
Maoz, Samuel, 227–28
"Margin of Error" (episode 4.6), 185, 264, 286
Marimow, Charles (character), 74, 241
Martin, Trayvon, 170
Marx, Karl H., 172, 220, 225–27, 235, 241, 243–44, 293
masculinity, 123, 129–131, 134, 154–57, 161–62
McNuggets, 86, 240–41, 297
McNulty, Elena (character), 261
McNulty, Jimmy (character), 3, 10, 26, 56, 59–69, 72, 81–95, 98, 118, 133, 135, 161–63, 167–69, 186, 189, 196, 201, 206, 208–09, 213–14, 218, 220, 222, 225, 229–230, 240–41, 258–260, 266–271, 279, 285, 298, 302
    and Bunk, 63, 64, 81, 88, 91, 94, 126, 218
    and fabrication of serial killer, 59–69, 94–95, 98, 109–110, 162–63, 220, 223, 267
    and Kima Greggs, 50–51, 60, 65, 81, 93, 110, 115, 128–29, 133, 135, 159, 161, 163
    and Lester Freamon, 51, 115, 133, 162, 203, 210, 212, 230–31, 260
    and Omar, 113, 140–41
    and port assignment, 87, 91, 241
Mello, Dennis (character), 74
Menace II Society, 166
"Middle Ground" (episode 3.11), 144, 168, 213

Mill, John Stuart, 50, 60–61, 69, 293
"Misgivings" (episode 4.10), 80, 93, 252
"Mission Accomplished" (episode 3.12), 200, 261
Mitchell, Tosha (character), 114, 143
"Moral Midgetry" (episode 3.8), 24, 80, 169
Morehouse College, 168
Moreland, William "Bunk" (character), 3, 4, 6, 11, 14, 20, 54–59, 63–65, 73, 77, 78, 81, 88, 90–98, 104, 116, 126, 128, 130, 140, 142, 146, 168, 195, 203, 218, 287–88, 300, 302
    and McNulty, 63, 64, 81, 88, 91, 94, 126, 218
    and Omar, 20, 54–55, 77–78, 90, 116, 128, 130, 140, 146, 195
"More With Less" (episode 5.1), 66, 97–98
motives (and morality), 59–63, 69, 199, 201
Mouzone, Brother (character), 21–22, 98, 114, 116–17, 139, 142, 168, 200, 203, 213
Mozart, Wolfgang Amadeus, 217
Murphy, Eddie, 166

natural police, 63, 78, 124, 126
Nazis, 110, 228, 234
"A New Day" (episode 4.11), 143, 279, 281, 283
New Day Co–Op, 100, 122, 128, 203, 212, 258, 269
New Jack City, 165
The Newsroom, 11
Nietzsche, Friedrich, 98, 107–122, 206–214, 293, 298
nihilism, 26–29, 108–09, 280–81, 284–86

No Child Left Behind, 17, 76, 269
Noddings, Nel, 162
Norris, Edward (character), 97
North by Northwest, 230
"Not for Attribution" (episode 5.3), 63–67
NPR, 207

Obama, Barack, 127, 171
Oedipus, 7, 205, 234
"Old Cases" (episode 1.4), 83, 207, 218, 258, 266
Omar (character). *See* Little, Omar
"One Arrest" (episode 1.7), 20, 55, 77, 262
oppression, 40, 167, 169–171, 249

"The Pager" (episode 1.5), 116, 153, 211
Parenti, David (character), 76, 248–253, 271
Parfit, Derek, 101, 293
Parks, Rosa, 143
Partlow, Chris (character), 22, 114, 139, 153, 157, 160, 208, 259–261, 281
Patapsco River, 193
Patapsco Terminal, 62
Pearlman, Rhonda (character), 25, 56, 257
Pearson, Felicia "Snoop" (character), 35, 99, 100, 114, 138–39, 153–161, 168, 203, 259, 301
Percy Jackson, 221
Petty, Tom, 215
Phelan, Judge Daniel (character), 26, 85, 118
philosophy, 4, 124, 137, 148, 150, 194, 196, 244
    Gandhi's, 287–88

legal, 180
Locke's, 41
moral, 59, 69, 107, 180
The Pit, 51, 89, 107
Plato, 50, 54, 61, 72, 73, 76, 79, 123, 137–38, 280, 293
polis, 167, 207, 218
Polk, Augustus (character), 279
Polyneices, 200–01
"Port in a Storm" (episode 2.12), 112
Port of Baltimore. *See* Baltimore, Port of
poverty, 32, 37–41, 48, 147, 155, 165, 169, 173, 177, 198, 268
power, x, 33, 39, 40, 74, 108–121, 125, 134, 137, 144, 149–150, 154, 203, 214, 255–264, 266–275, 280–87
    in Aquinas and Aristotle, 260–64
    in Foucault, 266–275
    in Hobbes, 256–260
    in Nietzsche, 108, 112–13, 118–121
Public Enemy, 7, 36
Puerto Rico, 113, 122
Pulitzer Prize, 17, 19, 67, 68, 91, 92, 273
professional ethics. *See* ethics, professional
Proposition Joe (character). *See* Stewart, Joseph "Proposition Joe"
prosopopoeia, 220, 227
Pryor, Richard, 166
Pryzbylewski, Roland "Prez" (character), 17, 36, 46–48, 52–53, 75–76, 80, 109, 126, 187–88, 193, 201, 222, 242–253, 269, 271, 279–283
Puritans, viii, 32

Quixote, Don, 11

racial profiling, 166, 293
racism, 47, 60, 147, 155, 165, 170–71, 174
Rand, Ayn, 206, 231–33
Rawls, William (character), 18, 65, 71, 73, 76–77, 85, 88, 95, 138, 149, 167–69, 204, 208, 210, 241, 270–71
"React Quotes" (episode 5.5), 23, 259, 265
realism, 166–173, 197–98, 218–19, 226–29
Reed, Ishmael, 165, 293
Reed, Stringer, 218
"Reformation" (episode 3.10), 24, 208, 283
"Refugees" (episode 4.4), 31, 39, 76, 144, 201, 208
religion, 5, 111
Renaldo (character), 113–14, 119
resentment, 64, 120–21
Rico (character), 158
Robert's Rules of Order, 84
Rockefeller drug laws, 282
Rogen, Seth, 205
Rotterdam, 61
Royce, Clarence (character), viii, 41, 87, 185, 198, 241, 256, 267–68, 273, 284
rule-utilitarianism, 115
Russell, Beatrice "Beadie" (character), 56, 60, 65, 91, 132–33, 214, 261

Sampson, Grace (character), 17, 244
Scar (character), 119
Season Four, 6, 36, 45, 54, 78, 128, 130, 133, 221, 222, 239–243, 248, 250, 253, 271, 279
Season Five, 27, 50, 52, 59, 126, 128, 133, 168, 203–04, 221, 267, 273

Season One, 4, 21, 51, 124, 125, 128, 130–31, 187, 209, 211, 218, 221, 230, 240, 252
Season Three, 8, 65, 77, 133, 138, 143, 168, 200, 221–22, 268, 278, 283, 301
Season Two, 13, 59, 103, 130, 132, 221, 241, 268, 272
segregation, 167, 169, 171
"Sentencing" (episode 1.13), 24, 79, 92–93, 104, 258
Sexton, Jared, 176, 293
Shakespeare, William, 207
Sherrod (character), 28, 263
Simmons, Darius, 170
Simon, David, viii, 4–11, 13, 25, 27–28, 46, 100, 127, 149, 165–67, 171, 173–75, 193–98, 201–07, 201, 207, 210, 212, 214, 217, 219, 222, 224, 229, 235–36, 268, 292–94, 299
Singer, Peter, 48, 54, 294
Singleton, John, 166
Sisyphus, 11
"Slapstick" (episode 3.9), 65, 138, 213
Smell-O-Vision, 196
snitching, 37, 87, 162, 167, 176, 277–288
Snoop (character). *See* Pearson, Felicia "Snoop"
Snot Boogie (character), 100, 206, 229–30
Sobotka, Chester "Ziggy" (character), 60, 62, 198, 257
Sobotka, Frank (character), 56, 59–63, 68–69, 73, 193, 196, 257, 260, 270, 272
Sobotka, Lou (character), 62
Sobotka, Nick (character), 62–63, 265, 270, 272
social contract, 187
Socrates, vii–x, 50, 124, 136–37
Socratic method, 137
"Soft Eyes" (episode 4.2), 281

Sophocles, 13
The Sopranos, 197
Sorkin, Aaron, 11
soul, 108, 111, 282
Spears, Britney, 208
Spry, Jay (character), 66
Stanfield, Marlo (character), 3,
    18–20, 22, 25–26, 31–40, 51,
    55, 64–65, 78, 81, 87, 89, 94,
    109–110, 112, 115–17, 125–28,
    139, 142, 144–49, 153,
    156–58, 161–63, 168, 195,
    198, 200–01, 204, 223, 239,
    241, 257–260, 266–67, 270,
    273, 286
state of nature, 33–35
statistics, 6, 14, 71, 77, 222, 267
Stern, Susan, 155, 160, 294
stet, 112
Stewart, Joseph "Proposition
    Joe" (character), 18, 103,
    110, 143–45, 194, 198, 204,
    208, 256–58, 265, 270
Stocker, Michael, 60–61, 294
Stokes, Albert (character), 250,
    252
"Straight and True" (episode
    3.5), 258, 266, 278
Stranger than Fiction, 205
"Stray Rounds" (episode 2.9),
    133
Stuff White People Like, 166
Sun, Baltimore. *See* Baltimore,
    Sun
Sunday truce, 24, 64, 110
Sverdlick, Steven, 60
Sydnor, Leander (character), 26

"The Target" (episode 1.1), 15,
    71, 77, 84–87, 94, 131, 167,
    175–76, 206, 285
Tater Man (character), 45
Templeton, Scott (character), 18,
    59, 61, 66–69, 91–94, 98,
    204, 267, 273

"That's Got His Own" (episode
    4.12), 78, 287
Thebes, 195, 200
"–30–" (episode 5.10), 63, 65–68,
    91–95, 115, 263, 267, 274
Thor, 221
Thrasymachus, 280
"Time after Time" (episode 3.1),
    179, 258
Tiresias, 22
Tommy Boy, 205
"Took" (episode 5.7), 68, 94, 117,
    144, 161
The Towers, 46, 52, 187,
    279–282, 285
Trading Places, 205
tragedy ix, 62–63, 88, 166, 168,
    193–204, 205–215
    ancient Greek, 7, 89, 167, 193,
        198, 200–01, 206–08
    definition of, 198–99, 205
    Hegelian, 194, 199, 200–04, 214
    Nietzschean, 206–09, 214–15
"Transitions" (episode 5.4), 110,
    283
tu quoque, 62
Twigg, Roger (character), 66–67
Tyson, Darnell (character), 252

"Unconfirmed Reports" (episode
    5.2), 3, 25, 69, 153, 157, 259
"Undertow" (episode 2.5), 62, 98,
    102–03
"Unto Others" (episode 4.7), 79,
    109, 116, 134, 244
utilitarianism, 50–52, 60, 115

Valchek, Stan (character), 18,
    25, 46–48, 61, 89
Van Peebles, Mario, 165
Vinson (character), 18, 26
virtue, 48, 63–65, 69, 131,
    141–43, 47, 207, 255,
    263–64

virtue ethics, 50, 61, 140–43
Vondopolous, Spiros (character),
    62, 265

Wagstaff, Melvin "Cheese"
    (character), 149, 265
Wagstaff, Randy (character), 7,
    19, 35–38, 53, 89, 200, 202,
    246, 281, 286–88
Waiting for Superman, 245, 249,
    254
Walker, Eddie (character),
    279–282
Wallace (character), 15, 23–24,
    27, 39, 49, 86, 89, 195, 202,
    240, 256, 266
Walon (character), 261–64
war, 7, 8, 16, 34–36, 38, 48, 123,
    135, 155, 159, 200, 202,
    227–28, 233
Waters, John, 196
weakness of will, 62, 187
Weather Underground,
    155–160, 290, 291, 294, 301
Weber, Max, 83, 294
Wee-Bey (character). *See* Brice,
    Roland "Wee-Bey"
Weeks, Johnny (character), 101,
    103, 202, 205, 266, 277–79
Weems, Duquan "Dukie"
    (character), 7, 23, 26, 36–38,
    89, 160, 193, 200, 202, 241,
    250, 301

West, Cornel, 280, 284, 295
Western District Way, 73–74,
    198, 281
Whitehead, Alfred North,
    244–46, 295
Whiting, James (character),
    66–68, 204, 260, 273
Wilderson, Frank, 172, 177,
    295
Williams, Karim (character),
    243
will to power, 118–19, 206
"The Wire" (episode 1.6), 98
The Wire: The Musical, 154
The Wire: Show Bible, 13, 25,
    294
wisdom, 64, 213, 234–35,
    261
Wise, Dennis "Cutty"
    (character), ix, 23, 25, 28, 35,
    92, 109, 146–47, 179–190,
    261–64, 268, 288
Wright, Brandon (character),
    21, 23–34, 87, 98, 114–17,
    128, 134, 142, 212–13,
    258

YouTube, 179, 294

Ziggy (character). *See* Sobotka,
    Chester "Ziggy"
Žižek, Slavoj, 167, 295, 302